Psychotherapy and Society

THE UNIVERSITY COLLEGE OF RIPON AND YORK ST. JOHN
YORK CAMPUS

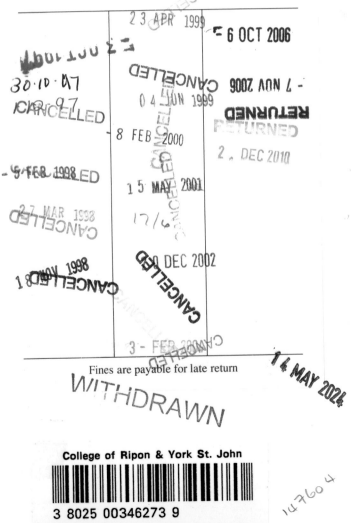

Perspectives on Psychotherapy

editor: Colin Feltham
Sheffield Hallam University

Each book in this challenging and incisive series takes a particular perspective on psychotherapy to place it in its intellectual and cultural context. Disciplines which will be brought to bear in this series will include sociology, anthropology, philosophy, psychology, science and feminism.

Books in the series:

Philosophy and Psychotherapy
Edward Erwin

Psychotherapy and Society
David Pilgrim

Psychotherapy and Society

DAVID PILGRIM

SAGE Publications
London • Thousand Oaks • New Delhi

First published 1997

 SAGE Publications Ltd
6 Bonhill Street
London EC2A 4PU

SAGE Publications Inc
2455 Teller Road
Thousand Oaks, California 91320

SAGE Publications India Pvt Ltd
32, M-Block Market
Greater Kailash − I
New Delhi 110 048

British Library Cataloguing in Publication data

A catalogue record for this book is available
from the British Library.

ISBN 0 8039 7504 X
ISBN 0 8039 7505 8 (pbk)

Library of Congress catalog card number 96-071787

Typeset by Mayhew Typesetting, Rhayader, Powys
Printed in Great Britain by The Cromwell Press Ltd,
Broughton Gifford, Melksham, Wiltshire

Contents

List of Figures and Tables

FIGURES

TABLES

Preface

This book is written with a particular audience in mind. Over the past 10 years I have found that trainee mental health workers have generally been receptive to lectures I have given on psychotherapy in its social context. Despite many therapeutic approaches marginalising or ignoring questions about the latter, students appreciate their relevance. It seemed logical to write a textbook which organised my lecture topics for a wider consumption on counselling and psychotherapy courses or for these within the training of core mental health workers. Thus, what its chapters provide is both a summary of relevant social research on mental health *for* psychotherapists and a critical appraisal *of* psychotherapy in its social context.

It is customary to expect authors to declare their assumptions, interests and values at the outset (although this expectation is frequently not met). Here I will set out mine, at least the ones which are conscious and I judge relevant. An initial conceptual point I would make is that for the purpose of this book no useful distinction is warranted between counselling and psychotherapy. The title of the book could just as easily have replaced one word with the other. The attempts I have witnessed in print and in conferences to make a definitive distinction between the two have never been persuasive. Throughout the book I use the term 'psychotherapy' as a generic shorthand for the two notions, or for what are sometimes still called the 'talking treatments'. What I have in mind is a wide range of professional interventions which are conversations carried out with the intention of facilitating psychological change.

Psychotherapy remains contested for a number of reasons including debates about its scientific status and effectiveness. Culturally, it may be that psychotherapy entails the desire to join or seek the ministrations of a secular priesthood and this breeds the inevitable controversies that attend differences between belief systems. Because human beings are difficult to fathom and are vulnerable to recurring distress it is tempting, for those offering to help them, to believe that they have discovered a mode of understanding and intervention which is pre-eminent in the field. This is the secular equivalent of finding the true light. With such high stakes, hopes of omnipotence and omniscience are always lurking.

The overwhelming complexity of people's lives (they are part of open, not closed systems – see Chapter 2) can push experts into ways of thinking which are sometimes simplistic and reductionist, always partial, and generally associated with bids for legitimacy to exclude others competing in the market place for the same client group (see Chapter 8). Just as religions have emerged to offer a variety of answers to core recurring questions about the frailties of people, the finitude of their lives and their uncertainties thereafter, so too with psychotherapy. The dramas and emotional impact of life (from what T.S. Eliot (1936) described as 'birth, and copulation, and death') are the bread and butter of psychotherapy, just as much as for religion. It is fair to say that humanity manifests recurring problems of fear, sadness and madness, which in 'pre-scientific' times came under the jurisdiction of religious opinion and are now the target of mental health experts. My view (parting company with the arch-conservative poet) is that these trans-historical and trans-cultural constants should not deflect us from attending to the *specific* vulnerabilities and forms of distress experienced by particular social groups in particular contexts.

This is only one way in which the analogy between therapeutic and religious ideologies breaks down. Those in the secular battles between different positions in psychotherapy have, with varying amounts of enthusiasm, required something more than blind faith from their adherents and recipients. In different guises 'science' has been invoked as part of the ensuing rhetorical exchanges. Rationality, systematic investigation and cumulative evidence now, quite properly, are part of the debate about psychotherapy. This reflects a different recent historical 'moment' (of three hundred years!) compared to the major religions, which all originated over a thousand years ago.

However, notions of science are also variable. An obvious example, for our purposes, is that the Institute of Psycho-Analysis in London holds 'scientific meetings' but objectivist critics dismiss psychoanalysis as being pre-scientific. If, in our secularised culture, science has now replaced God or blind faith as the adjudicator on the side lines then a paradox has emerged. The method designed to generate public evidence to resolve disputes is itself not open to a publicly available consensual definition. As I have pointed out elsewhere (Pilgrim and Treacher, 1992) in relation to the scientific credentials of my own profession, clinical psychology, which version of science within its rhetoric of justification are we supposed to take seriously given that more than one are evident? My own view is that the scientism (the dogmatic veneration of one type of investigation) associated with most of the twentieth century's psychology has constituted an error by confusing its persuasive, if variable, methods with a political mandate and by not recognising the differences between natural and social science (see Chapter 1).

Just because science is systematic in producing knowledge (which within its own discourse is called 'evidence', connoting a superior version of knowledge) does not mean that it has any value-free or privileged authority to guide others. Scientists are not disinterested parties. Neither are practitioners such as mental health experts, who deploy, or justify their actions by, the outcome of science. Also, much academic psychology retains a deluded pretension towards a predictive capability associated with natural science. Because people are in open systems, their actions cannot be predicted with certainty.

Applied psychologists have much more in common with historians and journalists than they have with experimental scientists. Psychotherapists, like other types of psychological expert, are very clever at being wise after the event. They can construct elegant and persuasive accounts about the lives of others in the process. Valid claims of incremental progress about this cleverness, compared to common sense, should not mislead us into believing in the ultimate possibility of a predictive science. This is as true of Freud as of Skinner. The latter pushed the predictive capability of psychological science to its limits by constraining action – he imposed the closed system of his box. Try predicting the behaviour of a rat or a pigeon (let alone a human being) outside the boundaries of a contrived experiment.

This question of open systems leads me to a core point about my stance towards psychotherapy. The latter is constituted by a variegated set of social practices. Within the latter, the close attention that is paid to personal and interpersonal change processes has produced a recurring occupational hazard for therapists of different persuasions. There has been a tendency to reify the significance of events in particular isolated contexts (say the patient's unconscious, the transference, or shifts in the group dynamics or the family's functioning) and ignore, or even actively reject, the salience of the wider social context of these events. The territorial control which therapists avidly seek over the boundaries of their work with clients confirms this tendency to construct contexts which are isolated and artificial. As Barham (1986) noted in relation to the study of group dynamics by Bion and his followers, this can lead to an over-valuation of the applicability of psychology to society. By getting carried away with their focus of interest, psychotherapists in general are vulnerable to the occupational hazard of psychological reductionism (see Chapters 1 and 2).

Before misunderstandings creep in at this point, I am not arguing that the descriptions given by therapists cannot be helpful some of the time to people in distress, nor that they are false or wrong-headed. What I am arguing is that a torch held in a boat in the dark can shine on an eddy and yet fail to illuminate a river's source and banks. This unintended or wilful ignorance about the social context of the lives of distressed individuals and the therapeutic relationship itself could provoke an exasperated rejection of the legitimacy of psychotherapy as being blinkered, futile, indulgent and individualistic. This is not my position but I can empathise with the impulse.

Much of this book is about toying with this point about the precarious legitimacy of psychotherapy. To do this I will provide two types of material. First, chapters will contain points from social science about the topic under consideration. Second, in order to press home the problems which have emerged in relation to psychological reductionism, I will offer a series of critical essays of varying lengths. I have set the latter for myself at the end of each chapter in the book for the reader to consider, endorse or contest in order to illuminate the strengths and weaknesses of that part of the mental health industry constituted by psychotherapeutic practice. This structure of each chapter allows me to separate out a first part which concentrates on providing a digest of the existing literature about the topic in hand, from debating points I personally believe arise from that topic.

Since qualifying as a clinical psychologist 20 years ago, I have shifted from believing that verbal psychotherapy is a radical alternative to the dehumanising practices of organic psychiatry and behavioural psychology to a more cautious and ambivalent line. This ambivalence has come from a number of sources. As a well-paid professional, seeing clients in the National Health Service who were poor, I felt increasingly uncomfortable with models of intervention which trivialised or excluded the material reality of their lives and which over-emphasised personal responsibility.

For a while I also worked in a Special Hospital, which taught me that mental health services can be far more anti-rational and corrosive of the human spirit than any amount of psychopathology that can be documented within individuals. It also taught me that in some organisational contexts, psychotherapy is simply untenable if ordinary everyday decency is subordinated to a culture of brutality. The possibility of psychotherapy itself relies on a sustaining *real* context. Without that sustaining context, trying to provide psychotherapy is like trying to fight a blaze with a water pistol.

My experience as a researcher of the views of psychiatric patients about the services they received led me to put into perspective the limited role of professional interventions in mitigating the poor quality of life of people with mental health problems. I also discovered in this process that psychotherapists, despite their humanistic pretensions, have been just as dismissive of the experience of people as any other mental health workers, when their professional interests or therapeutic authority are threatened (Chapter 9).

Moreover, the self-doubt expressed about psychotherapy by some of its practitioners in relation to abuse has been persuasive to me. Over the past 10 years the topic of abuse has had a double impact on the credibility of verbal psychotherapy. The pathogenic effect of childhood sexual abuse is, I believe, now well demonstrated (Chapter 6). Traditionally psychotherapists, particularly those following Freud, all too often acted with complicity with this phenomenon, with the patient's purported fantasies justifying a form of victim blaming. To make matters worse, for an industry which places a disproportionate emphasis on the patriarchal merits of its ancestors, Freud has not come out on the side of the angels about the sexual victimisation of children. As Jeffrey Masson has pointed out, there is a certain paradox (if not hypocrisy) in the fact that psycho-dynamic therapists now offer themselves as experts on childhood sexual abuse (see Chapter 8). The problem is compounded when we examine the evidence about abuse at the hands of therapists.

The phenomenon of sexual abuse underscores the importance of real events in the lives of people with mental health problems. There is a danger of compounding the distress of people who have been victims of circumstance by focusing on their role and responsibility (a general custom and practice in most forms of psychotherapy). This is an example of the social context of distress being evaded by focusing only on the agency of victims. For example, sexual victimisation is a function *inter alia* of the power discrepancy which exists between adults (particularly men) and children. To frame it broadly as psychopathology when talking of 'diagnosing' sexual abuse and when offering 'therapy' to abusers as well as victims, is really to miss the point about the everyday vulnerabilities of children in society.

Sexual abuse reveals power relationships between social groups, not just untoward events within aberrant families or in isolated public spaces. Moreover, the inertia and reluctance of therapists to acknowledge abuse of patients by parents *and* potentially by themselves, or colleagues, demonstrates a reticence to address the objective power differential which exists between professionals and their clients. Given the humanistic mandate associated with psychotherapy and a genuine central concern of its practitioners to pay heed to the experience of clients, it is easy to forget the question of power. Intimacy and empathy can be preconditions of oppression and abuse as well as of helpful interventions. The torturer and the therapist have much in common.

A final set of points to make about my need to shift the frame of reference from the clients of psychotherapy to events which contextualise their current and past lives, as well as their therapy, relate to lessons from sociology. During a period in which I left the NHS to teach in higher education (the late 1980s), I completed a part-time MSc in sociology. This was an enjoyable if occasionally disorientating experience, as I dis-covered the scorn of many sociologists for the individualism of psy-chology, along with their occasionally naive adoration of psychoanalysis as a sort of liberating micro-sociology. The most important lesson I drew was that psychotherapy is no more or less immune from sociological analysis than any other form of social practice.

If the relationship between psychotherapy and society is to be explored it is clear that its existing reflexivity is limited. The limits of reflexivity in therapy are about the extent to which practitioners expose themselves to the activity of their own trade — how much analysis for the analyst, how much work on their family of origin for the family therapist? But any amount of this activity will never situate psychotherapy, as a *collective* practice, within its social context. For this we need other forms of enquiry which examine the wider social system and which can trace the fracture lines of power in society. Class, gender, race and age are a good start. These will be dealt with in Chapters 3, 4 and 5. Before that, the first two chapters will examine the gaps and overlaps between bodies of knowledge informing both psychotherapy and social science.

Acknowledgements

A version of this book was nearly written over 10 years ago. At that time I was involved in discussions with a psychiatrist, Nassos Constantopoulos, and a sociologist, Ray Holland. Although our interesting meetings provided a framework for progress, we failed to put theory into practice. In the interim period I have become more hostile to a reliance on psychoanalysis as a bridge between the individual and society, as will be obvious in the following pages – I guess to the disappointment of my near co-authors. Over the past five years most of my academic work on mental health topics has been done with Anne Rogers. I am particularly grateful to Anne for the support she has given me in all my research and writing.

Having criss-crossed the boundaries of sociology, psychology and social policy, I have drawn eclectically upon the ideas and interests of many colleagues and friends from all three disciplines. Though too many to name, I would like to register my gratitude to them for overwhelming me with more than enough material to select and distil for this book.

1

Psychotherapy and Social Science

Behind every definite question and answer is implicitly or explicitly to be found a model of how fruitful thinking can be carried on.

Karl Mannheim, *Essays on Sociology and Social Psychology*

This chapter has three main aims. First, I will offer some clarifications about social science. Second, I will examine the relationship between psychotherapy and a variety of academic disciplines with reference to psychoanalysis, phenomenology and existentialism. The strengths and weaknesses of these approaches will be summarised. By strengths I mean their persuasiveness or utility for those readers interested in both psychotherapy and society. By weaknesses I refer to the opposite.

DIVERSE FORMS OF SCIENCE AND DIFFERING WORLD VIEWS

D'Andrade (1986) distinguishes between physical, natural and semiotic forms of science. The latter describes the study of 'systems of meaning'. These distinctions are useful because they highlight the point that some but not all of the same academic disciplines cross the boundaries of the three types of science described, viz:

1 *Physical science* physics, chemistry, astronomy and related engineering sciences;
2 *Natural science* biology, geology, oceanography, meteorology, economics, psychology, anthropology and sociology;
3 *Semiotic science* anthropology, linguistics, psychology and sociology.

Note the recurrences across 2 and 3. This arises because *within* the disciplines of anthropology, psychology and sociology there are divergent world views about what constitutes legitimate knowledge and the methods to produce such knowledge. What I will use in this book are insights from the theory and practice of *social science* which appear in *both* groups, 2 and 3.

In Group 1, there is an assumption that legitimate knowledge claims arise from the study of lawful relationships which exist in the world. Description, explanation and prediction characterise this way of doing science. It is assumed further that a consensus of empirical descriptions by independent observers, which are potentially repeatable and falsifiable, contribute to the production of *objective knowledge*. Reality is considered to exist non-problematically and independently of its observers. Knowledge claims are assumed to be *generalisable* from one situation to another.

Most of these assumptions underlying the disciplines in Group 1 are repeated in Group 2. There are two differences, though. First, *prediction* is recognised to be more elusive, but is still attempted. This is because naturally occurring phenomena (like the weather, the seas and the life of organisms) are open, not closed systems. That is, they exist in a complex context and are chaotically and/or plurally determined. Second, and because of this, events are assumed to be limited to time and place: they are *context-specific* and so are not readily generalisable. However, this group of disciplines still treat their object of enquiry as being a machine to be understood. Thus Group 2 work entails the production of knowledge claims about *mechanisms*. Within the disciplines in this group studying human beings, such a mechanistic view of the world entails the assumption of *determinism*. That is, Group 2 work attempts to understand causal relationships. As with Group 1 work its methodology is about testing hypotheses and quantifying or measuring differences between experimental groups or naturally occurring phenomena.

Moving now to assumptions underlying Group 3 activity an important shift takes place. Knowledge claims still involve descriptions but explanations are considered to be tentative and predictions are virtually abandoned. Whereas work in Groups 1 and 2 aspires to objectivity, in Group 3 it is recognised that human life is suffused with *meanings* which are imposed or negotiated intersubjectively by language-using organisms. As a consequence, it is assumed that science and its focus of enquiry (human life) entail the negotiation of meaning. This semiotic version of scientific activity involves the production and justification of *interpretations*. As in Group 2 work, these are made about and within specific contexts and so generalisations are made with caution or they are eschewed. Whereas Group 1 and 2 work explore causes, Group 3 work explores *understanding*. The latter endeavour is called *hermeneutics* (the science of interpretations). Its production of knowledge is based not upon hypothesis testing but upon interpretation – an inductive rather than deductive approach.

This conceptual separation of Group 2 activity from that in Group 3 was made in the late nineteenth century by Dilthey who pointed to the differing assumptions underlying the natural sciences (*Naturwissenschaften*) and the cultural or spiritual sciences (*Geisteswissenschaften*) (Dilthey, 1976). According to Dilthey, the phenomena to be investigated in the latter require a different methodology from that in the former. The notion of understanding (*Verstehen*) in interpretive social science was also high-lighted by Max Weber in sociology and within psychiatry by Karl Jaspers.

Inconveniently, in practice, those disciplines which study, or inform us about, human conduct and society do not neatly fall into Group 3 activity alone. For example, psychology contains forms of enquiry which range from physiology to sociology. When Foucault in *The Order of Things: An Archaeology of the Human Sciences* (1973) came to describe the knowledge claims which developed from the beginning of the nineteenth century, he suggested three planes of activity which came to constitute the modern 'episteme'. The three planes were: the *a priori* sciences (like maths and physics); the *a posteriori* sciences (like biology and geology); and philosophical reflection. When discussing this Foucauldian scheme, Smart (1990) makes the point that:

> The human sciences are not considered to be on or within any of the above planes, their place lies in the ambiguous volume of space constituted by the epistemological arrangement . . . The indeterminate character of the epistemo-logical form of the human sciences leaves a number of methodological and analytical questions and options open. It effectively leaves the human sciences free, or relatively so, to pursue a range of methodological and analytical possibilities, but in addition it means that from the beginning these sciences are in difficulty, are necessarily precarious and uncertain as sciences . . . (Smart, 1990: 401)

In Chapter 2, I will say some more about the relevance of Foucault in relation to post-structuralism. Here I only want to emphasise what Smart summarises as the 'range of methodological and analytical possibilities' for human sciences. As I indicated in the preface to the book, such a range has tended to encourage a search for the security of simple answers instead of a tolerance, or celebration, of complexity. Such a search for security can culminate in *reductionism*, a point I will pursue in the next chapter as well when discussing general systems theory. Another scenario is that this search leads to a cultish authoritarian commitment to a follower and his or her belief system. Psychotherapy has had its fair share of this pitfall with its strongest example being Freudianism (see below).

SOCIAL SCIENCE AND PSYCHOTHERAPY

Having outlined diverse forms of scientific work and their underlying assumptions, I now want to spell out their relevance for this book. It was noted that social science (collectively anthropology, linguistics, psychology and sociology) spreads across the boundaries of Groups 2 and 3. Three of these disciplines, therefore, contain differing assumptions about what a social science should be. Thus within social psychology we find both experimental social psychology (Group 2 activity) and discourse analysis (Group 3 activity). It could be that the insights from either of these versions of psychology might inform the work of psychotherapists.

Similarly, in sociology we find both social surveys (Group 2 activity) and ethnography (Group 3 activity). The first of these might reveal causal relationships between mental health and membership of particular social groups (e.g. Brown and Harris, 1978). The second might help us understand how a therapeutic community functions (e.g. McKegany, 1984).

The fundamental tension between an approach to social science based on explanation (and its associated interest in mechanisms) and understanding or interpretation (hermeneutics) is relevant to the relationship between social science and psychotherapy. In order to highlight this interplay, let us examine the methodological overlap between versions of psychotherapy and the practice of social science in relation to dominant theoretical frameworks.

PSYCHOANALYSIS

Psychoanalysis has enjoyed a privileged position in social science. Outside clinical psychoanalysis and dynamic psychotherapy, a wide range of social scientists have claimed an allegiance or debt to some version of Freudianism or its derivatives. Within sociology the conservative functionalism of Talcott Parsons contained links with psychoanalysis but equally the neo-Marxian critical theorists (the so-called 'Frankfurt School') applied the hermeneutic framework to social relationships. A bridge between clinical psychoanalysis and the latter can be found in a range of analysts who took the risk of trying to apply psychoanalysis to societal understandings with quite varying results (e.g. Kardiner, Fromm, Reich, Horney, Fenichel, Bion). Within anthropology, psychoanalysis has at times been used to inform or augment cultural interpretations (e.g. Scheper-Hughes, 1979).

One of the most notable features of psychoanalysis in relation to neo-Marxian social science is its offer of a deep and pure view of the alienated psyche, uncontaminated by ideology (the surface content of the conscious life of citizens). Within this tradition of social criticism, the alternatives offered by versions of a psychology of the conscious (for example of existentialists and phenomenologists and even the cultural psychology strand within the psychoanalysis of Erikson) are disputed or scorned.

The source of this attack is twofold. First, the conscious agent is distrusted as a bourgeois reification. Second, it is assumed that there is only one essential truth about the functioning of individuals; and that truth, which centred on the sexual instincts and the constraints imposed on them by society, was laid out for the world to believe and admire by Sigmund Freud. All revisions of or alternatives to psychoanalysis after Freud are seen as wrongheaded, even though he was not a revolutionary socialist. Freud's *Civilisation and Its Discontents* (1930/1964) held civilisation in a generic sense responsible for neurosis. He did not highlight the particular alienating character of capitalist society. This has not diverted some neo-Marxians from either an idealisation of classical psychoanalytical theory or an intolerance of other approaches to subjectivity. Freud is depicted as being heroic and unswerving in his intellectual project, whilst the also-rans are seen as anodyne in their capitulation to superficial answers and dominant interests. Here I give two examples. The first is from a psychoanalyst and political commentator, Kovel (1988), discussing the limitations of the work of Erikson:

> Whenever [Erikson] deals with sexuality, one has the sense that a faint sense of moralising hangs over the pages but none of *Freud's remorseful vision*. Indeed, Freud had what Erikson, in the last analysis, lacks: a sense of evil – the conviction that there is real destructiveness, that one should neither flinch from this nor succumb to Manichaeanism but rather give it its due, then *defy it with critical truth*. *This truth* saw history as the struggle between sharply opposed forces not the struggle for a 'more inclusive identity'. (Kovel, 1988: 75, my emphasis)

The second example comes from Jacoby's *Social Amnesia* (1975), which is scattered with dismissals of everybody within, and outwith, the tradition of depth psychology who was not devoted unconditionally to Freud's insights about biology and society. Only Reich and some within the Frankfurt School are treated with any trust or sympathy – an inevitability given that they perceptively blew the whistle on the shortcomings of *Civilisation and Its Discontents*. Jacoby's book's subtitle is *A Critique of Contemporary Psychology from Adler to Laing* and I have chosen one of the many examples he gives of his idealisation of Freud and his disdain for alternative constructions on reality:

> If the history of psychology is the history of forgetting, Adler was the first, but by no means the last to forget. His revision of psychoanalysis was a home made remedy to assuage the pain of the unfamiliar: psychoanalysis. The notions that he, and the neo-Freudians, would champion were borrowings from everyday prattle: the self, values, norms, insecurities and the like. They were offered as antidotes to Freud's illiberalism. Yet just this constituted Freud's strength: his refusal to bow to reigning wisdom. (Jacoby, 1975: 44–5)

However, social science has had its critics of psychoanalysis as well as hagiographers and devotees. For example, Gellner, in *The Psychoanalytical Movement* (1985), points out the similarities between Christ and Freud as charismatic leaders who became slavishly adored by followers. He also notes the strong similarities between psychoanalysis and the Mafia and Leninist parties. The point about charismatic leadership in psychoanalysis has also been made recently about analytical psychology by Noll (1996) in *The Jung Cult*. This suggests that the confluence of medical patriarchy and the temptation to 'dabble . . . self-approvingly in the stuff of others' souls' (see Wootton quoting Virginia Woolf, p. 6 below) has led to the formation of groups of mental health professionals which, despite their appeal to natural or hermeneutic science for authority, are indistinguish-able from religious sects (Sulloway, 1980).

Because Freudianism offered a set of certainties for those studying social policy which potentially provided a link between society and the inner lives of individuals, it provoked strong views of adoration or contempt. Here I quote examples of this polarisation of views from within post-war social policy. The first is from Barbara Wootton, in her *Social Science and Social Pathology*. Here she is talking during the 1950s of the dominant influence of psychoanalysis on social work:

> Happily, it can be presumed that the lamentable arrogance of the [psycho-analytical] language in which contemporary social workers describe their activities is not generally matched by the work they actually do, otherwise it is hardly credible that they would not constantly get their faces slapped . . . The pity is that they have to write such nonsense about [their case work] and to present themselves to the world as so deeply tainted with what Virginia Woolf has called 'the peculiar repulsiveness of those who dabble their fingers self-approvingly in the stuff of others' souls'. (Wootton, 1959: 279)

By contrast, Richard Titmuss, the leading British social policy analyst of the 1950s, suggested that:

> the work of Freud and his successors has been of revolutionary importance to medicine; it has changed our attitudes to the mentally ill, it has at least helped towards the alleviation of mental suffering, it has enlarged the possibility of preventative therapy and it has given us new ways of looking at the growth of personality and the origins of illness . . . it has, for doctors and laymen alike, undermined our psychological innocence, sensitised us to an inner world of reality and made us see all sickness, in whatever guise, as part of a psycho-logical continuum. (Titmuss, 1958: 187)

Probably the most attractive feature of psychoanalysis for sociologists and anthropologists has been that it offers a missing link or bridge between the inner lives of individuals and collective social or cultural life. For example, Freud turned to the constraining forces of civilisation to explain both repression, as a mechanism impacting on the instincts within the individual, and its consequent neurosis.

In addition to those idealising or scorning Freud, there have been some writers who have remained within a depth psychology framework but addressed, head on, the reality of the political context which faces ther-apists and their client alike. One example is from the analytical psycho-logist Samuels who, in *The Political Psyche* (1995), attempts to appraise the relationship between insights from psychodynamic traditions and knowl-edge about the material reality which constrains our existence. (I return to an aspect of his work in Chapter 7.) The other is from the work of a clinical psychologist turned sociologist, Richards. In his edited collection of essays from diverse contributors, *Capitalism and Infancy* (Richards, 1984), we have laid out before us a range of possible ways of reading the social (not psycho-) dynamic between the inner world of individuals and the political context which situates therapeutic work and its resulting knowl-edge claims. In his more recent work, *Disciplines of Delight* (Richards, 1994), he explores aspects of popular culture, such as pop music, the motor car, the use of the countryside for leisure, consumerism and soccer, from a psychoanalytical perspective.

Within psychoanalysis we find one of the best examples of the tension between Group 2 and Group 3 activity. On the one hand, Freudianism was noted for a set of knowledge claims about intrapsychic *mechanisms*; on the other, its central reliance on *interpretations* of interpersonal events placed it squarely within a hermeneutic tradition of social science. This contradiction is made even more obvious given that Freud's conceptual framework was and remains associated with a medical discourse, with his followers, such as Abraham and Fenichel, readily constructing typologies of psychopathology which are congruous with bio-medical psychiatric nosologies.

Notions of the 'dynamic unconscious', 'psychodynamics' and 'mental mechanisms' are consistent with a model derived from Newtonian physics. They are also consistent with a medical discourse about the mechanical inner physical workings of the body. Indeed Freud envisaged that eventually mental events would be explicable in terms of neural activity, leading Wolman (1968) to describe Freud justifiably as a 'hoped-for-reductionist'. By contrast to this neurological emphasis, the exploration of symbolism and the interpretation of utterances and declarations within a personal relationship push the depth psychologies into a hermeneutic direction. What Freudianism has never resolved is how to be in two places at once: a mechanistic universe of explanation or an interpretive universe of understanding and exploration.

Matters became even more complex when the mechanistic emphasis of Freud gave way increasingly to object relations theory (Fairbairn, 1941; Guntrip, 1950; Rayner, 1993). This replaced the nineteenth-century hydraulic model of the mind with one based upon the inward and outward mapping of intimate relationships. The implications of this shift were profound. For Freud, in his classical theory, neurotic behaviour was seen as a mechanical failure (the defence mechanisms had broken down to allow partial de-repression and symptom formation). By contrast, a model based upon object relations implied a different interpretive slant towards clinical material. In particular, it permitted, but did not necessarily ensure, the critical examination of power differentials and other real aspects of those relationships in ways which were far removed from the conservative medical patriarchy of Freud's professional culture (e.g. Laing, 1960; Holland, 1978; Eichenbaum and Orbach, 1982).

Despite the mechanistic emphasis of Freudian theory (a form of Group 2 activity), from the outset Freud's clinical work entailed his making sense of what was said to him within a conversation. This conversation was atypical. One party was expected to talk about themselves but the other was not. Silence from one was deemed to be facilitative but from the other evaluated as resistance to the process of analysis. The patient was flat on their back while the analyst had their feet on the ground. The analyst could see the analysand but not vice versa. Nonetheless it was a conversation of sorts and was thus a form of hermeneutic enquiry. The limitations of this enquiry were threefold: its authoritarianism; its silence about the future; and its over-valuation of the notion of transference. I will expand a little on each.

First, it was authoritative, with interpretations playing the role of, say, the surgeon's scalpel. Psychoanalysis is a game of one-upmanship in which the analyst always ultimately wins (Hayley, 1963). A price paid is that the meanings arrived at by the patients are also ultimately limited by the hermeneutic framework of the *analyst*. Consequently, in one sense, psychoanalysis is just another form of doctor-centred discourse. The spillover from this authoritative source to a form of authoritarianism is present in the quotes I cited above from Kovel and Jacoby, which are dripping with aloof intolerance and blind devotion to a father figure long since buried. Any notion of a definitive truth, about anything, raises a question about the compatibility of Freudianism with a non-authoritarian, sceptical and speculative stance towards human experience within social science. (Note Jacoby's celebration of Freud's 'illiberalism'.) Steele (1982) summarises this problem well here:

> Unfortunately, Freud's belief that his work was science, and as such discovered the truth, and his stance that either someone was for or against him created a dogmatic system. He had not developed the critical consciousness necessary to see that psychoanalysis was a method which constructed a causal historical narrative, but that other methods . . . could formulate different and equally plausible scenarios. His insistence on orthodoxy kept his approach to enquiry from being either truly scientific or truly hermeneutic. (Steele, 1982: 360)

Despite the freedom connoted by the term 'free' association within the psychoanalytical method, if the theory behind it claims to hold a truth which excludes other perspectives (as for example 'prattle') then it can be no more liberating than any other form of unswerving certainty, such as versions of religious fundamentalism. It should be noted, though, that the undoubted authoritarian tendency within psychoanalytical training (Masson, 1990) has still allowed practitioners to develop eclectic and diverse forms of practice (Rayner, 1993).

Second, psychoanalysis ignores the future. Its temporal focus is between the experienced present and the remembered or repressed past. This pre-empts the possibility that both individually and collectively, human beings encounter and anticipate the future with a variety of conclusions and feelings which may determine their current mental health. Think of the parent on a poor housing estate fearing for the welfare of their teenage children in a future dominated by unemployment and a locality marred by street trading in opiates. Think of people in work who see their company 'downsizing' and wait for their turn to come. Growing up today may still entail the Oedipal dramas (at least for those in two-parent families), and their attendant neuroses described by Freud, but it is also awash with more pressing concerns. These include: peer acceptance, illicit drugs, ecocide, AIDS, parental separation, violence from strangers in the street, long-term unemployment and the dangers of urban traffic. The emotional well-being of both children and adults is jeopardised by these features of contemporary existence.

Third, psychoanalysis relied predominantly upon the material constructed within the framework of transference. Even today, the glory or vulnerability of clinical psychoanalysis, and its psychotherapeutic spin-offs, depend on one's assessment of the merits of the notion of transference. Is it a momentous and dazzling discovery or a conveniently invented protection for the analyst against the discomfort of real feelings (Szasz, 1963)? When it comes to helping people (as opposed to understanding the unconscious) there is no empirical evidence that transference interpretations have any privileged position in facilitating personal change. After all, research on psychotherapy outcome shows positive change across a whole range of treatment approaches which are outside the psychoanalytical tradition (see Chapter 8).

Group 3 activity described earlier assumes that meaning emerges and is understood intersubjectively. Psychoanalysis certainly provides one framework for this enterprise; it is a version of hermeneutics. But how robust is it as a basis for *social* science? The central role of transference as an interpretive framework has meant that its particular bridge between the inner life of the individual patient and society as a whole affords a particular salience to one set of meanings. The latter refer to those which are attributed to expressed feelings and thoughts which are made about the analyst but are located historically in the patient's childhood and refer back to their parents.

But what of real problems encountered in the present by people in their work relationships or in relation to a particular set of political interests – women in relation to men, or workers and their employers? Are these secondary phenomena – displacements from the core dynamics of neurosis linked to parents and the projections provoked by the paid presence of an analyst for those who can afford the fees? And what, in the past, of siblings, school friends and enemies, teachers and (during the second half of this century with prepackaged Americanised culture being piped into nearly every home) televisualised relationships? Can we already not spot the difference this combination has made to a mass psychology in Britain of the present '30-something-me-generation'?

The latter was shaped tellingly within a culture rendered insecure and atomised by Thatcherism. The last 20 years have seen a breakdown in post-war consensus politics within a mainly secularised society. Together these cultural constraints have encouraged citizens to be materialistic and self-centred. In such a context, is narcissism best understood within the failures of parenting implied by a psychoanalytical model or should a rich social science offer a more multi-factorial model? To give another, more specifically clinical, example can we understand the tendency of teenage girls to starve themselves by referring only to family dynamics or could the fashion and advertising industries, which promote variable idealised images of the female body, be influential?

Freud's consulting room, like Skinner's box, imposed a constraint on the understanding of social relationships. Consequently, it reduced multiple realities experienced within complex social relationships, in the present and past, to one understood within a tightly limited version of hermeneutics. If a person only has a hammer they tend to see everything as a nail. This tendency is visible within the limited form of hermeneutic enquiry generated by Freudianism, with transference interpretations being the hammer. Of course psychoanalysis did not stop with Freud. As well as the development of object relations theory a different set of social scientific as well as clinical challenges emerged with the development of group therapy.

The emergence of group therapy within a psychoanalytical framework itself was a product of a context-specific set of social forces. These involved the attempt during the Second World War to produce a cost-effective way of treating soldier patients traumatised by battle. There were too many to treat individually. Group work emerged even though psychoanalysts were used to operating with individuals on the couch. This is very evident when reading the early pages of Wilfred Bion's *Experiences in Groups* (1959). Bion is clearly in the dark and keeping an open mind. His candid naivety culminated in new insights about group cultures and individual 'valencies' for these (dependency; fight–flight; and pairing). Had psychoanalysis then become a social rather than an individual science by this forced shift of levels from the psyche to the group? One of its founders felt this to be the case:

> Psychoanalysis is a biological theory which only very reluctantly has been pushed into being a social theory by the pressure of psychotherapy. Group therapy is not psychoanalysis. (Foulkes, 1965: 25)

However, the dangers of psychoanalytical reductionism did not then stop because Freud's methodological individualism had been abandoned. I have discussed elsewhere the way, for instance, that Guntrip reduces homosexuality and prostitution to schizoid defences (Pilgrim, 1992). Whichever hermeneutic systems mutated within psychoanalysis after the classical period, their inventors and adherents retained the same capacity for reductionism as Freud himself. All seemed to repeat the common error when studying the human condition of reducing multi-variable uncertainty to single variable explanations. Professional experts in particular are more prone to hammering a preferred idea to death than conceding that their views are only partial and may even be wrong, a point I return to in Chapter 8.

Psychoanalytical reductionism (whatever school within the tradition we consider) is a function of a deeper logical problem for this venerated framework for psychotherapeutic work. This problem refers to the basic assumption of all versions of depth psychology that human beings can in some sense be understood 'in advance'. That is, whilst psychoanalysis has provided a rich range of views within a hermeneutic framework, the latter is always ultimately privileged over the patient's view about themself. This view is merely unanalysed conscious reflections and therefore inadequate, partial or simply wrong. If the view of the analyst were *not* privileged then it would not be psychoanalysis but something else. The analyst, whatever their particular theoretical allegiance, has a set of prepared hermeneutic templates which are imposed on clients.

I am aware that some respected analysts have, since the death of both Freud and Klein, disavowed the very accusation I am making. One of the best examples of this is the work of Patrick Casement, in his influential book *On Learning from the Patient* (Casement, 1985), who talks of 'resisting preconceptions' (ibid.: 36) and cautions against imposing rather than offering interpretations. He reminds his readers of the advice of Bion that each analytical session should be approached 'without desire, memory or understanding' (Casement, 1985: 17). He also commends therapists to follow the advice of Winnicott and allow patients to play. This is the nearest that psychoanalysis gets to having a genuine open mind. It cannot get beyond this point. To go any further would be to abandon the principle that a complex body of knowledge built up about unconscious life and the processes of transference and counter-transference constitutes the basis of a *superior* insight into the human condition. In Chapter 8 I return to the arrogance this assumption of superiority can create in psychoanalytical writers.

This arrogance, informed by the likes of Bion and Winnicott, as well as their elders, is an alternative to a therapeutic stance which only involves being with, credulously listening to, and then engaging with, the unique narratives patients offer about their lives. The elevated body of knowledge, built around transference interpretations and a few conceded interpretive additions, both constitutes psychoanalysis and prevents it from being properly client-centred. To permit each new patient to have a unique self-constructing narrative would entail psychoanalysis collapsing into phenomenology, existentialism or post-structuralism (see Chapter 2). The work of Laing, who was a psychoanalyst, effectively collapsed in this way and others, such as Guntrip, similarly came near to falling off the edge of psychoanalysis. Some, such as Lomas, retain a broad allegiance to psychoanalysis, despite his thoroughgoing attack upon its hermeneutic strictures and his preference for a tentative but direct knowledge of people through their unique narratives (Lomas, 1987).

This discussion of psychoanalysis assumes that it is close to, or constitutes, a version of psychotherapy. Of course this assumption is in itself problematic. The earlier brief quote from Foulkes raises a basic question about the relationship between psychoanalysis, society and psychotherapy. Foulkes talked of psychoanalysis being transformed by the 'pressure of psychotherapy'. Freud was not really very interested in helping people. His main focus was on understanding unconscious mental life. As he made plain, he practised psychoanalysis-as-therapy in order to make a living. The preservation of psychoanalysis in this mode (i.e. daily and fee-paying for several years) has left a legacy of a version of psychotherapy which is pre-emptively expensive. It can only be afforded by those with the time and money to spend on their chosen version of inner travel or by those who are obliged to submit to analysis as part of a lengthy training ritual within an institute of psychoanalysis. Whatever revolutionary insights psychoanalysis provided for Kovel, Jacoby and Titmuss at a theoretical level, at a practical level it has never been and will never be the therapy of the masses.

The Strengths and Weaknesses of Psychoanalysis

In the light of the above discussion, the main strengths of psychoanalysis can be summarised as follows:

1   It offers a conceptual framework which can be a bridge between the individual and society.
2   In its classical form it offers explanations both for the emergence of human neurosis and for the need for healing practices like psychotherapy in society. In its revised form of object relations it accounts for the inward and outward mapping of relationships.
3   It is a reflexive theory which can be applied to anybody, including therapists themselves.
4   It provides us with a rich hermeneutic framework.

Its main weaknesses are as follows:

1   It is a mechanistic, individualistic and psychologistic theory and is tied to its medical roots.
2   It tends towards authoritarianism and an intolerance of opposition from without and dissent from within.
3   By avoiding a consideration of the personal future it closes off a legitimate field of enquiry about human subjectivity and distress in its social context.
4   It was not conceived primarily as a helping practice and so it is a dubious basis for affordable therapy for most ordinary people.

EXISTENTIALISM AND PHENOMENOLOGY

During the twentieth century psychoanalysis has coexisted, and sometimes competed, with a different orientation towards subjectivity and society. Under this heading I have put together two variants of this: existentialism and phenomenology. They are often run together or conflated (see e.g. Laing, 1960). Strictly they are separate. The first is an *epistemological* position (about existence being the defining source and focus of human enquiry). The second is a *methodological* position guiding human enquiry (the study of how people experience their inner and outer worlds).

Nonetheless, the proximity of the two in practice invites an examination of them together for our purposes.

When it was first conceived by Brentano (1874/1973) in 1874, phenomenological psychology was one amongst other *empirical approaches* which were straining away from the main feature of academic philosophy: the study of mind via reason and introspection. More generally, psychology began to differentiate from philosophy because empirical not introspective or speculative investigation was being privileged. However, what constituted legitimate, empirically based knowledge immediately became contested. Those within psychology who wanted to continue with the empirical methodology of physical science (Group 1 activity above) began to study sensory processes (psychophysics). By contrast, Brentano and his school did not follow this path, nor were they introspectionists. What Brentano emphasised instead was that psychologists should study and classify modes of experiencing and types of consciousness. He called this 'inner perception' (1874/1973), to distinguish it from introspection. He advocated the study of three types of phenomena:

- the inner perception of ongoing conscious mental activity
- the subject's descriptions of conscious memories
- the externalisation of psychic life.

The first two of these offended the sensibilities of those who were proceeding scientifically on the basis of consensually defined (objective) knowledge. The third one was less problematic in this regard and referred to the study of verbal behaviour and conscious acts. In anticipation of later students of animal cognition, Brentano even suggested that the behaviour of animals could be interpreted. Together these would build up a body of knowledge about the relationship between mental life and the encountered world of the subject. Consciousness was *about* something and so what phenomenology provided was knowledge not of inner mental life alone, nor of the external world, but of *the relationship between these two*.

Unlike Dilthey (mentioned earlier – see p. 2) who argued for the separation of types of data and methodologies for the natural and cultural sciences, Brentano considered that non-physiological psychology and phenomenology should complement one another. For Brentano, psychology should be partly about understanding experience and partly about neurological explanations. In this sense his stance was close to that of Freud (– see p. 7). Both Brentano and Freud then straddled the world views underlying Groups 1, 2 and 3 scientific activity discussed earlier.

What marks out Brentano's work from that of either psychoanalysis, on the one hand; or objectivist psychology, on the other, was that his emphasis on subjective consciousness was out of sync with both. Because it was about conscious not unconscious life it was at odds with psychoanalysis. Because it was about subjectivity it was at odds with objectivism in psychology. For this reason, phenomenology was later dubbed 'third force' psychology to distinguish it from psychoanalysis and behaviourism. This may give the misleading impression that it was the third in historical sequence, when it actually preceded the emergence of behaviourism within academic psychology.

Brentano, along with later contributors including Husserl, Merleau-Ponty and Sartre in the first half of the twentieth century, constructed a broad basis for doing social science which is summarised here by Roche (1973):

> it is always an assumption of the phenomenological school that there exists a world of people, whose distinguishing characteristics include the 'possession' of individual consciousness. There exists a world of numerous subjective unities of experience, called Selves or Persons. This is the rock-bottom of assertions about being made by the phenomenological school. (Roche, 1973: 6)

The roots of person–centred counselling, personal construct theory and existential psychotherapy are clearly visible in this history and this version of social science. However, as with psychoanalysis, phenomenology did not remain singularly wedded to the study of the individual (a version only of psychology). Additionally it provided the methodological basis for the investigation of society and social relations. This is an important distinction to recognise about phenomenology. It can be a method of understanding individuals (the focus of psychology) but it can also be a way of understanding social groups (the focus of anthropology and micro-sociology).

The utilisation of personal experience as a basis for enquiry was not the monopoly of any of the particular founders of social science in the nineteenth century. As has been mentioned, even though they held differing assumptions at times, Dilthey, Weber and Brentano put forward a rationale for social science which is based squarely upon understanding or *Verstehen*. Also Marx was not antipathetic to interpretive procedures. Although his emphasis was upon structural, particularly economic, factors, he also emphasised the understanding of ideology and of both the determination and the content of consciousness (Smart, 1976). Like Sartre later, both Marx and Engels considered that people were agents who made choices but within a set of particular material constraints (Sartre's (1963: 15) 'field of possibles'). All these writers accepted that science could also generate *explanations* as well as understandings about the human world. However, they veered away from the science of the unconscious, on the one side, and forms of objectivism which excluded the importance of subjectivity, on the other. What was to unravel over a century within social science was a broad picture in which a set of orientations and approaches to society was guided by *Verstehen*. I will now summarise some of the main features of this type of social scientific activity.

Situated and lay accounts   One implication of phenomenology is that those who try to understand human action need to understand it indirectly via the accounts of ordinary people. Thus if we want to ask basic questions like 'Why do people do the things they do?' or 'What is happening in this group of people?', they have to be answered via the personal accounts of social actors. This clearly is at odds with the strong programme within psychology during the 1940s and 1950s to develop variants of a body of expert knowledge called 'learning theory'. In reaction to this, Peters (1958) suggested that to understand motivation one does not (and cannot) construct an all-embracing theory but instead one must understand how people themselves describe motivated acts. In ordinary language, motives are attributed in three main contexts: when things go wrong; to describe a directed form of action of the self or others; and to distinguish why a person acts in this way rather than that way. What this points up is that *Verstehen* can focus on what people say and what they do or some combination of the two. It also suggests that accounts need to be situated. That is, they reveal what is happening in a certain situation but also their content cannot be understood without referring to that context (Mills, 1940). Sociologists of talk (Scott and Lyman, 1968) and social psychologists investigating the types of accounts which people give in different circumstances (Antaki, 1981) argue that social science should be about naturalistic studies of language use in a variety of contexts.

Accounts as microscopes and the dramaturgical perspective Within social psychology, Harré and Secord (1972), like Peters, rejected the possibility of all-embracing psychological theories. Like Goffman (1967) they argued that a human science should take social actors seriously by interpreting their roles and scripts and the rules underlying these:

> If accounts are to social psychology what microscopes are to natural science, we must look into the general conditions under which accounts are generated. (Harré and Secord, 1972: 259)

This approach emerged at a time when behaviourism was hegemonic within academic psychology. Accordingly, in an ironic vein, Harré and Secord described the need to develop an 'anthropomorphic' approach to human beings.

Meaning is socially negotiated Within sociology, the work of G.H. Mead was elaborated as part of the 'Chicago School' in the 1930s, symbolic interactionism. In the latter, three axioms emerged (Schwartz and Jacobs, 1979). First, human conduct is a function of the meanings that the actor holds of the world. Second, these meanings arise from social interactions. Third, these meanings are maintained and modified through a process of interpretation within personal encounters. Symbolic interactionists thus study how social reality is negotiated between individuals and how it is understood from individual perspectives within such negotiations.

Differing glosses on lay accounts Whilst within a broad phenomenological/existential approach to social science there was a consensus that the accounts of ordinary people should be taken seriously, their potential role was given a slightly different gloss depending upon the disciplinary source. For example, in psychology personal construct theory (Kelly, 1955) depicted people as 'scientists'. As with Harré and Secord this was an ironic turn against scientism and objectivism. People can be constrained to act like laboratory animals but they also have an ability to 'talk back', experiment with their world and anticipate events. In sociology, Garfinkel (1967) suggested that human beings all of the time made sense of their worlds and were sociologists. He argued that the methods and procedures used by ordinary people to account for their worlds should be the focus of professional sociological activity. The study of these methods and procedures of ordinary people was consequently dubbed 'ethnomethodology'. Cicourel (1976), extending this ethno-methodological interest, suggested that (after Chomsky's work on the deep structure of language) human beings have an inherent, pre-linguistic capacity to function socially. He also emphasised that accounts are always partial and incomplete or open to reconstruction and so can be revisited (as a detective or psychotherapist can invite a narrative to be replayed and discussed in a fresh way). Within psychology Kelly (ibid.) described a person's 'personal construct system', whereas Schutz (1962), a sociologist who applied the work of Husserl within sociology, describes a person's 'repertoire of meanings'. These meanings are socially situated in time and place so that particular cultures at a moment in time will contain particular constructs or typifications – 'a stock of knowledge' (Berger and Luckmann, 1966).

Dialectical reasoning about accounts   Both Sartre (1963) and Geertz (1975) emphasised that there should be a toing and froing between the individual and their social context. That is, social contexts can be illuminated by personal accounts but personal accounts can only be understood in relation to the context in which they are situated and generated. For Geertz, an anthropologist, merely to collect accounts in a culture would be to produce 'thin' data. By contrast, 'thick' data is built up by con-currently attending to both the account and what is already known about its context. Similarly Sartre's progressive–regressive method encouraged a continuous 'cross reference' between biography and society as it is assumed that each determines and illuminates the other.

What the phenomenological/existential approach within social science has produced is a theoretical resource in favour of psychotherapy. It offers a rationale for treating people as if they are human beings or conscious reflexive agents. What, maybe, this approach relegates in importance is the *affective* side to human experience. This whole tradition is far less concerned with emotions than is psychoanalysis, although it is important to note that psychoanalysis is more a discourse *about* emotions than an emotional methodology. The analyst is cool under fire and is socialised to distrust any show of feelings as a potentially disruptive acting out of counter-transference. Nonetheless, in comparison to psychoanalysis the notions of typification and construct in phenomenology and its linguistic emphasis all generate an approach to the understanding of human beings which is highly *cognitive*. Phenomenology engenders a cerebral rather than a visceral framework for the study of subjectivity.

Phenomenology is, though Group 3 activity, associated centrally with the semiotic version of science described earlier by D'Andrade (1986). It bears no relationship to cognitivism in academic psychology, which emerged after the fall of behaviourism in the late 1970s. Cognitivism (or 'cognitive science') constitutes a regression in the discipline to the experimental study of inner events and mental processes such as reasoning and memory (Group 2 activity). This approach, augmented as it is now with its affinity for computer models and an interest in artificial intelligence, has no connection with social science in the tradition of Brentano, Dilthey, Weber, Mead and Sartre.

To make matters even more complex, cognitive therapy has very little to do with this cognitive science but much to do with a reaction against psychoanalysis and a pragmatic adaptation of behaviour therapy. Neither Beck nor Ellis, the clinical founders of cognitive therapy, drew upon cognitivism when developing their 'cognitive therapy'. Their books contain no references to cognitive science. However, there have been a few attempts to make *post hoc* connections between recent academic psychology and therapeutic practice. Also some cognitivists (e.g. Guidano, 1987) have attempted to integrate social constructivist and systemic approaches to their work (see Chapter 2). One current of cognitive therapy which is highly theoretically informed is cognitive-analytical therapy (Ryle, 1990). However, this too has no relationship with cognitive science but instead is underpinned by selective insights from psychoanalysis and personal construct theory. It is fair to conclude overall, then, that cognitive therapy and cognitivism, as a theoretical current within academic psychology, have little or no relationship with one another.

Apart from a reaction against psychoanalysis, the emergence of cognitive-behaviour therapy during the 1970s represents a pragmatic admission on the part of behaviour therapists that inner events do matter in clinical practice. Whilst cognitive-behaviour therapy did not have its source in cognitivism, it was rooted in the anti-theoretical stance of disillusioned behaviourists (e.g. Lazarus, 1971) and in the convenient recollection in its advocates that learning theory had, since Pavlov, always considered 'intervening variables' inside the organism (see e.g. Hawton et al., 1989, Ch. 1). The concession to the inner lives of patients may have signalled the belated recognition on the part of jittery behaviourists that, in the words of Harré and Secord, people require 'anthropomorphic' models. However, like its immediate predecessor behaviour therapy, cognitive therapy is not biographical and exploratory but scientistic and prescriptive. Inner life remains the target, like behaviour itself, of the didactic interventions of experts.

To return to phenomenology and existentialism, two final points of criticism will be raised to round off this section. First, because the siting of psychotherapeutic encounters is typically and deliberately on the therapist's territory, all personal accounts given are disconnected, at least spatially, from the client's everyday context. The methodological strength of *social* phenomenology was its encouragement of field work — the study of accounts in natural settings, alongside historical knowledge of the culture and participant or non-participant observation. This is not to argue that accounts given in a clinical setting are not legitimate and a source of insight for the participants. It is simply to recognise the limitations of these accounts when the investigator (therapist) is not directly familiar with the everyday settings of their clients and the other social actors they contain.

My second criticism relates to the question of agency. Because, phenomenology and existentialism can be taken as invitations to push the consciously free agent to the limits of its potential, this has led to some absurd expectations of human actors. Hence the emergence of the 'human *potential*' movement. The latter seems to represent a mere repackaging of the US cultural cult of the individual's all-conquering free will — that anyone can become President. This has spawned an inevitable occupational hazard for humanistic psychotherapists and reflects a lop-sided appreciation of existential philosophy. For example, Sartre emphasised human freedom and the inevitability of choice but he did not argue that people could choose to do or be anything. Following Marx and Engels, he was conscious of the material and contingent *external constraints* impinging upon the human agent. Therapists may, in contrast, fall into the trap of their own rhetoric about 'taking responsibility for one's actions' and ignore these constraints. This culminates in victim blaming. As I have argued elsewhere, those US styles of therapy which play strategic games with clients about agency and choice are of most benefit to those whose advantageous material conditions of life *already* to a large degree sustain the person's mental health (Pilgrim, 1992).

The Strengths and Weaknesses of Phenomenology

The strengths of phenomenology can be summarised as follows:

1   It is a tolerant approach to subjectivity which is open to any connotation on experience reported by human beings.
2   It can inform both an understanding of individuals and of the social relations they experience. It is thus a shared resource for both social scientists and psychotherapists.
3   Its insights are contingent not pre-determined and so it is a flexible and cautious approach to human existence.
4   It provides the basis for personal theorising and methodologies which are suited to human beings.

Its weaknesses can be summarised as follows:

1   Its emphasis on individual experience makes it prone to psychological reductionism.

2   Its emphasis on individual agency makes it prone to victim blaming.

3   Its emphasis on conscious mental activity makes it vulnerable to the criticism that it evades the insights of depth psychology.

4   Its emphasis on language allows it to more readily accommodate the cognitive rather than the affective dimension of human existence.

CONCLUSION

This chapter has made a start at exploring the conceptual bridges which exist between social science and psychotherapy. The two case studies used, psychoanalysis and phenomenology/existentialism, both illustrate the tension which exists about the role of biography. Practices such as psychotherapy are *ipso facto* psychological and individualistic in their focus of interest. By contrast social researchers, be they social psychologists, sociologists or anthropologists, are concerned to understand groups, cultures and other forms of collective, aggregate or supra-individual phenomena. Psychotherapy is interested in biography *in its own right*. By contrast social researchers are interested in biography *as a resource* to understand something which lies beyond the individual.

2

Objectivism, Post-Structuralism and General Systems Theory

Mental facts cannot be properly studied apart from the physical environment of which they take cognizance.

William James, *Textbook of Psychology*

INTRODUCTION

In the last chapter, the interplay between two dominant traditions which are a part of both social science and psychotherapeutic practice was considered. In this chapter I want to extend that exploration. The chapter has four aims. First, I will situate psychotherapy in relation to tensions within social science about objectivism and subjectivism and change and regulation. Second, I will discuss psychotherapy in relation to post-structuralism and postmodernism. Third, I will summarise some points about discourses on abnormality. Fourth, I will introduce some relevant aspects of general systems theory (GST). As with my discussion of psycho-analysis and phenomenology in the previous chapter, I will summarise the strengths and weaknesses of objectivism, post-structuralism and GST.

SITUATING PSYCHOTHERAPY IN RELATION TO OBJECTIVISM

Both psychoanalysis and phenomenology can be found within a range of disciplines in social science. They had jostled with and often been con-fronted by a range of competitors which have either explicitly or implicity rejected a subjective emphasis. One way of describing the relationship between this range of viewpoints has been offered diagram-matically by Burrell and Morgan (1979) (Figure 2.1).

Using this diagram we can situate a range of approaches within both psychotherapy and social science. Psychotherapy can be located in the bottom half of the diagram as part of a range of regulatory practices. The two case studies discussed above would both be placed in the bottom lef

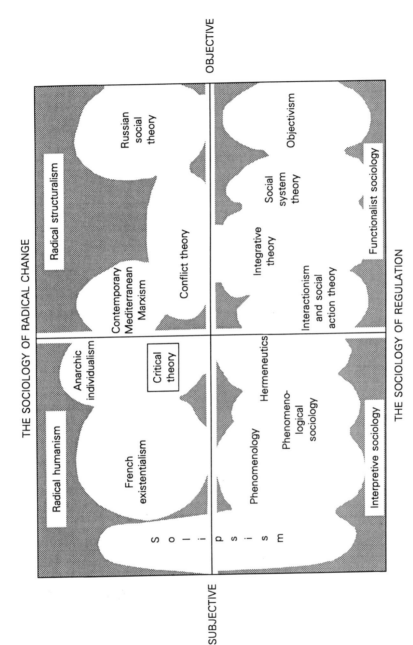

Figure 2.1 *Four paradigms for the analysis of social theory* (from Burrell and Morgan, 1979: 102)

quarter. However, since this overview diagram was constructed by the authors in the 1970s, social science has witnessed a notable change which may prove with time to be a passing fashion or a genuine epistemological shift. I refer to the emerging popularity in social science of post-structuralism and deconstruction, which I shall return to below.

Before that, though, I will raise two important matters arising for psychotherapy which are pointed up by the dimensions on the diagram. The first is the implication that psychotherapy is part of a set of social processes which constitute *regulation*. When this term is alternated with that of 'control' it may make little sense, or can cause offence, to psychotherapists, who see their role as facilitating personal freedom. However, the two notions are not incompatible. The outcome of psychotherapy is undoubtedly, in part at least, about improving a person's capacity to cope and function successfully *in their given context*. In this sense, it is about conformity and adaptation and serves to reinforce the status quo. On the other hand, it is a voluntary negotiation (except under extraordinary conditions such as secure psychiatric provision) designed to elaborate alternatives to the current restriction of psychological distress. The patient submits themself to a relationship in which they will reconstrue their world and they hope, by the end of it, live with themself and their fellows better. In this sense they are exposing themself to a process of *secondary socialisation*, like going through higher education or joining a new religious group (Berger and Luckmann, 1966) (see Chapter 7).

The second implication of the dimensions of Figure 2.1 is about solipsism vs. objectivism. Both of these spectres in the extreme within social science have brought their own versions of nihilism. On one side solipsism is accused of being beyond reason and accountability. On the other side objectivism excludes the use of data derived intersubjectively, even though all enquiry including that within an objectivist framework entails interpretive events (Taylor, 1971).

These tendencies are reflected in disputes between, and the rhetorics surrounding, the quantitative and qualitative methodologies in social science. My own view is that psychotherapy like any other form of situated social practice can only be *understood* within a qualitative framework but equally it can only be *justified* by posing quantitative questions. Put simply, psychotherapy is about intersubjective negotiation and thus the fine grain of its activity must entail methods which are appropriately sensitive to this character. Equally, given that psychotherapy is a paid form of healing practice, on grounds of public accountability it is legitimate to ask such questions as 'Is it cost-effective compared to other mental health interventions?'

Another matter arising from this tension between solipsism and objectivism relates to the tendency of psychotherapists to limit themselves to evidence or knowledge which is within their own framework of pre-ferred intersubjective activity. For example, the scientific meetings of the Institute of Psycho-Analysis in London discuss cases and points of theory without reference to a whole range of other perspectives and studies which are nothing to do with psychoanalysis but have much to do with mental health. More generally, case work, the bread and butter of psychotherapy creates a body of knowledge based on, and limited to, case law.

This poses a number of problems about both accountability and psychological reductionism. How can those not socialised as psychotherapists evaluate the utility of their work? Also suppose that the determinants of mental distress are more plausibly located in a different material realm from that of intrapsychic events or intimate interpersonal relationships. Although psychological models have quite understandably aspired to transcend the dehumanising tendencies of biological determinism, what if the latter still sometimes retains plausible evidence? Brain tumours, temporal lobe epilepsy and toxic states do bring about profound experiential and behavioural changes. Maybe psychotherapists are not only the wrong people to ameliorate these psychological consequences but they may divert attention from other appropriate sources of understanding about these states.

At the same time, the inherent psychologistic nature of psychotherapy may divert attention from the *social* determinants of mental distress. Moreover, as will be made clear in the rest of this book, evidence about these social determinants is derived from versions of social science which are in the objectivist not just the subjectivist halves of Figure 2.1.

For psychotherapists mainly used to individualistic understandings the social has two connotations which need to be encountered and fathomed. On the one hand, intersubjectivity, which is the bread and butter of social phenomenology and post-structuralism, to be discussed below, requires a frame of reference, of social *constructivism*, which is outside the consulting room and the patient. On the other hand, objectivism brings with it assumptions about social *determinism*. In this section I will address the variants of the latter.

The strong case for social determinism is that it appeals to external referents and that it offers persuasive evidence that human beings are shaped by their external context. The first of these qualities, at least in principle, provides the conditions for social (i.e. democratic) accountability. The second makes intuitive sense. Who can seriously argue with the notion that we are all, to some degree, a product of our environment? If this is the case then objectivism provides a position from which such external determination can be studied.

The problem for psychotherapy is that its tradition of privacy and its preoccupation with the quicksilver of inner life has exposed it to the criticism on the first count, about external referents, that it is arcane, solipsistic and unaccountable. On the second count, about social determinism, it is vulnerable to the criticism that explanations are only conceded at the *individual* not social level. Put differently, it is prone to psychological reductionism. For the strong social determinist these two vulnerabilities added together constitute a form of mystification and therefore serve to discredit the case for psychotherapy.

From my viewpoint (which is a critical realist one) the weak case for objectivism is ironically that it is *scientific*. By 'weak' I mean that it is not really persuasive or it is only persuasive if we are asked to believe that physical science (the first of D'Andrade's group of sciences discussed at the beginning of the last chapter) is a sort of gold standard which excludes the legitimacy of other forms of enquiry or derides their importance. In different ways phenomenology, psychoanalysis and post-structuralism (see below) have exposed the futility of objectivism, if the latter is taken to mean a naive commitment to the view that external reality can be studied in a non-problematic way using the hypothetico-deductive method and that such a method generates incontestable 'facts' or, even more ambitiously, 'truth statements'. The latter are proposed by objectivism as simply corresponding to reality rather than representing it.

It is at this point that we have to be cautious about being over-inclusive in our distrust of any position that emphasises the existence of a reality which is independent of its observers (be they professional or lay). A reliance on *empirical* knowledge can be found in both positivism and phenomenology. Naive realism is not the same as critical or sceptical realism. The former is committed to the view that scientific methods are disinterested and can generate a simple 'read out' about the world which is independent of the values or conceptual presuppositions of the investigators. Such a view mistakenly takes it as axiomatic that facts and values are readily separable.

However, whatever weaknesses are inherent to the objectivist rhetoric about disinterest and its lack of acknowledgement of its own practices being saturated in intersubjectivity, the challenges it raises do matter. Social determinism has amassed a persuasive case that supra–individual variables are causal antecedents of individual distress. Indeed, in later chapters (3–6) I will be presenting empirical findings derived from a social determinist form of enquiry. In such circumstances a psychotherapist or anti-objectivist ignores such evidence at their peril. Those studies of the relationship between membership of one or more disadvantaged social groups and mental ill-health manifested (in both objective and subjective indicators) at the individual level simply cannot be dismissed on the grounds that objectivism is offensive to 'tender minded' psychology or post-structuralism (see later).

Before leaving this section I want to return briefly to the question of bio-determinism. Objectivism in medical, as well as social, science has produced a persuasive case about certain phenomena. Above I noted the evidence for this, especially in relation to a neurological substrate associated with conditions which might be construed to be psychogenic. It is not unusual because of their disciplinary location for psychologists and sociologists to be left uncomfortable with this news. Their comfort is then recovered easily by the evidence that the medical profession has made crass bids for legitimacy to medicalise any and every form of personal and social deviance imaginable. The professional preference for medicine to reduce all emotional and behavioural differences to versions of brain disease is a convenient strategy of self-interest. However, this undeniable tendency to medical dominance is not only about the salaries and status of doctors. Anyone who has taken LSD or sat with a child delirious with fever or watched the irritable chaos of a diabetic with low blood sugar knows that whilst biology may not be destiny it can certainly make its presence felt in human conduct.

There is no simple and independent vantage point from which to adjudicate on the merits of subjectivism and objectivism in social science. Those with personal and professional commitments to either camp will develop, rehearse and deliver cogent arguments in their own defence and against their opponent. My concern in this book is to examine how the tension *between* the approaches may enable psychotherapists to think critically about their work. The question of attempting critical readings of knowledge claims brings me to my next topic. Before moving to this I will summarise the strengths and weaknesses of objectivism.

The Strengths and Weaknesses of Objectivism

The strengths of objectivism can be summarised as follows:

1   Its emphasis on the external world provides all of us with the intuitive confidence that our senses report reality.

2   This emphasis on external referents provides a basis for consensual agreement about knowledge – a democratic feature.

3   It may offer us persuasive evidence to justify practices entailing necessary privacy, such as psychotherapy, which rely on the trust of outsiders about their utility.

4   Psychotherapists themselves usually are committed to forms of environmental determinism to explain why people present to them with problems (as opposed to using genetic explanations). Social determinism provides a framework to produce confirmatory evidence of this commitment.

The weaknesses of objectivism can be summarised as follows:

1   Its opposition to, and distrust of, subjectivism and subjectivity produces a lop-sided view of human functioning.

2   It is not a reflexive or recursive position, as it cannot account for its own existence and practices, when it seeks to claim a specious 'disinterestedness' or 'objectivity'.

3   It can lead to objectification and so has a depersonalising or dehumanising potential.

4   It is counter-intuitive. We all know that our inner lives and our intersubjective experiences are necessary components of a full account of human life.

POST-STRUCTURALISM AND POSTMODERNISM

Now I turn to the challenge posed by post-structuralism. This refers to the movement within social science associated with a variety of writers including Foucault, Derrida, Lyotard, Deleuze and Guattari, Cixous, Irigaray and Kristeva. Good practical introductions to the insights of a post-structuralist approach to mental health are provided by Parker et al. (1995) and McNamee and Gergen (1992). One of the best full applications of a post-structuralist account of modern psychological practices is provided by the work of Nikolas Rose in his books *The Psychological Complex* (1985) and *Governing the Soul* (1990). I return to the latter in some detail in Chapter 8.

The term 'post-structuralism' refers to both a shift in emphasis (beyond structuralism) in social science about how society is to be understood, and a pronouncement that the coherence aspired to by individual disciplines, such as psychology and sociology, has failed. Although post-structuralist writers vary in their emphases and targets of interest, the connecting thread in their work is that older attempts to study determinants or structures should be replaced by an examination of what is said and not said within and about social practices. Instead of some aspect of society, or human conduct within it, being studied to produce direct representations of reality, post-structuralism studies the process and content of those representations. In doing so, it explores the relationship between power and knowledge in society.

To summarise the challenge of post-structuralism:

- What post-structuralism has done *inter alia* is highlight that traditional versions of determinism and realism, which have aspired to generate confident knowledge claims about the world, are always problematic. The central reason for this is that knowledge is a set of representations – it is the map not the territory (cf. Gergen, 1985). Post-structuralism for this reason shifts the focus of social scientific activity away from producing knowledge about the *world* to producing knowledge about *knowledge* – discourse analysis or deconstruction. Post-structuralism is constituted by discourses about discourses.

- Discourses are not only the content and silences of texts and conversations (the emphasis of Derrida), they are tied to practices (Foucault's 'discursive practices'). For this reason, to understand discourses is to understand the conjunction of theory and practice, rather than studying one or the other. It is about theory-in-practice. Similarly within a post-structuralist framework power is not conceived as a possession but as a manifestation of action between individuals or social groups.

- Because there are diverse ways of constructing or representing the world, there is no permanent or definitive truth. This challenges the notion of confident knowledge claims within both objectivist and subjectivist social science. Instead of 'facts' we now have the 'undecideability of propositions'. Instead of subjective truth or objective knowledge we have diverse perspectives.

• The diverse ways of representing the world emerge within, and reflect power differentials between, groups in society. Knowledge and reality are not only socially constructed but they reflect differentials of power between people with differing interests. For this reason a distinction is made by some post-structuralists between constructivism and constructionism (Gergen, 1982). The former would include cognitive elements arising from intersubjectivity explored in the phenomenological tradition discussed in the previous chapter. The latter would extend this set of phenomena to a set of external forces and interests which shape constructions independent of the awareness of individuals. Indeed within post-structuralism the emphasis is more on the discourse without a subject, rather than the subject in him- or herself (the shared concern of psychoanalysis and phenomenology). Thus post-structuralism, psycho-analysis and phenomenology all emphasise subjectivity and intersubjectivity but they examine these in differing, if sometimes overlapping, ways. The distinction between constructionism and constructivism is sometimes made as if it is clearcut and self-evident (see e.g. Hoffman, 1992). However, this is more the case in social psychology than in sociology. In the latter, constructivism is used as a generic term to cover a number of approaches which range from recent empirical studies within symbolic interactionism to the deconstruction associated with post-structuralism.

• Post-structuralism has emerged at a time in Western society which both reflects and has created the conditions for such a new form of knowledge. This period and its attendant shifts in social theory are summarised here by Smart:

> A prominent focus of debate within contemporary social theory has been on a series of developments which have been conceptualised as manifestations of a 'postmodern condition' (Lyotard, 1986), a 'postmodern situation' (Arac, 1989), or a 'condition of postmodernity' (Harvey, 1989) . . . In its paradigmatic form the thesis on the postmodern condition of knowledge suggests that it is no longer possible to generate universal solutions or answers to problems and questions concerning contemporary forms of life from within what might be termed a conventional 'modern' problematic. In short, that the analyses, understandings, goals and values, which have been a central feature of Western European civilisation since the Enlightenment, can no longer be assumed to be universally valid or relevant. The project of 'modernity' is finished or incomplete. (Smart, 1992: 80)

The shift in what Smart summarises as 'analyses, understandings, goals and values' has been reflected in the production of postmodern culture (visual art, architecture, film and fiction), which has disrupted both the classical style of representation and realism and the modernist reaction in symbolism and abstraction. Early in his overview of modern art, *The Shock of the New* (1980), Robert Hughes makes the following point, which echoes the summary made by Smart about knowledge and modernity:

Many people think that the modernist laboratory is now empty. It has become less an arena of significant experiment and more like a period room in a museum, a historical space that we can enter, look at but no longer be part of. In art we are at the end of the modernist era. (Hughes, 1980: 9)

• Thus post-structuralism and postmodernism are related but separate notions even though at times they are, I believe unhelpfully, conflated. More generally in the literature, across a range of disciplines, the first term refers to a new way of producing knowledge about society (a theoretical or epistemological project) whereas the second refers to a condition of society itself (a contradictory socio-political state of global organisation alongside cultural diversification and destabilisation). In this state there are rapid transitions occurring about production and consumption. New technologies have created a multiplicity of information inputs to the lives of citizens. The old industrial/factory technologies have become more scarce with a concomitant reduction in a coherent working-class base of society. It has been replaced by a diverse set of oppressed identities based upon features other than class (race, gender, sexuality, age and disability). The cold war has receded but ecological catastrophe looms and religious fundamentalism and petty nationalism put the world on a perpetual war footing. Optimism and pessimism co-exist as a consequence.

A hundred years ago the life of a semi-literate young working-class man might be experienced through the versions of reality produced by the school, the church and the factory within a square mile. Now his equivalent, who has never worked and has no such prospects, sits in his ill-furnished room and flicks his TV channels automatically and produces a cacophony of images which represent diverse forms of global existence. His experience is both 'globalised' by incessant technological improvements and restricted by perpetual poverty. Next door his neighbour, a single mother working on short-term contracts, is cooking instant convenience food in a microwave, while in the next room her 6-year-old daughter is playing interactively not with a person but with a multi-media machine linked to the World Wide Web. In the next 10 years the girl will be both part of an electronic 'global village' and excluded from her immediate physical locality as parental anxieties, degraded public transport systems, 'virtual shopping' and pollution conspire to deny her empirical knowledge of her immediate native environment. Her social life will be conducted mainly by video telephone contact with her peers, if her mother's episodic income can pay.

These points summarised about post-structuralism and postmodernism disturb our traditional ways of thinking about knowledge in social science and there are some more specific destabilisations on offer for psychotherapists. For example, Derrida criticises the reliance within humanism on 'phonocentrism' – the error that authentic accounts can be given by therapists and patients. He also cautions against 'egocentrism' – the idea that there are essentialist human agents or selves with stable *a priori* subjectivities, a cornerstone of traditional phenomenology (note the quote from Roche in the previous chapter, p. 14). Whereas the Freudian would analyse the unconscious or the existentialist would strive for an authentic understanding with the client about their life choices, the post-structuralist would argue that both were *inscribing* versions of subjectivity on their targets. In doing so they would be manifesting disciplinary power. The patient would not so much be understood or analysed by the therapist as created or constructed by them in the relationship.

The stance of post-structuralists towards psychotherapy is decidedly ambivalent. On the one hand some of its founder writers, like Lacan, worked as therapists. On the other hand there remain the criticisms of humanism put forward by Derrida about the search for authenticity and a commitment to the *a priori* self. Also, despite Foucault's respect for psychoanalysis, his inherent irreverence about disciplinary power and surveillance encouraged a resistance to versions of the 'confessional'. The influence of post-structuralism is present today in family therapy more than in individual work which remains under the dominant influence of psychoanalysis or humanistic psychology.

The relationship between societal organisation and forms of knowledge is well illustrated by Freudianism. This emerged at a time of ascendant modernism, which was characterised by a commitment to universal truths generated by versions of rationality. In particular, science offered itself as a pure form of the latter. Freud was a medical practitioner and a scientist (hence my pointing up the traditional notion of 'scientific meetings' in institutes of psychoanalysis). Freud in his classical theory offered a set of universal truths about the mind (the dynamic unconscious and intra-psychic mechanisms) and a universal and systematic methodology (free association and transference interpretations). As such, he was a perfect example of a modernist who constructed a 'grand narrative' about the human condition.

However, the modification and eventual fragmentation of psycho-analysis highlight the shift during the twentieth century away from universal truths and towards diversification. Mechanised and industrialised warfare (1914–18) first produced the death instinct. Post-industrial con-ditions of diversification since 1945 have produced a whole range of constructions on the psyche. As elsewhere in social science, eclecticism has emerged because the possibility of universal truths has proved to be more, not less, elusive over time, defying the incremental logic of modernist scientific rationalism. At one time, particularly in Britain (Hearnshaw, 1964), eclecticism merely represented an empiricist distrust of, or incom-petence at, theory. In a postmodern age, in every country, theory is now distrusted and diverse perspectives celebrated or endured by those most in love with theory. At the same time, the modern is not so much replaced as augmented and churned up.

Thus contemporary psychotherapy, like other forms of social practice exists in a context in which there is both rapid societal transition *and* a breakdown in confidence in theoretical certainties. This is well summarised by an epigraph used at the front of Smart's *Modern Conditions, Postmodern Controversies* (1992) and taken from Eco's *Foucault's Pendulum* – 'I have always thought that doubting was a scientific duty, but now I came to distrust the very masters who had taught me to doubt.' Mirroring this condition of postmodernisn, post-structuralism has brought with it both refreshing critical insights and a danger of nihilism.

Reading too much deconstruction or even being asked to limit social scientific research to this practice can be both demoralising and constraining. The older methodologies it challenges might still offer knowledge claims which help to improve the lives of ordinary people. Moreover, without knowledge claims deconstruction would go out of business. My own view is that the struggle to understand the world directly is still worthwhile (an old modernist and realist assumption) but that such understanding must be tempered by a critical or sceptical attitude towards knowledge production (a postmodernist assumption) (Bhaskar, 1989; Greenwood, 1994; Pilgrim and Rogers, 1994). For this reason, later in the book I will draw liberally on diverse forms of knowledge – subjectivist, objectivist and post-structuralist from within social science – and attempt to discuss these in a critical manner.

If there is even a partial validity in the claim that we now live in an age where certainties are disturbed and that knowledge can be read in different ways, where does this leave us? One option is to retreat from the comforts of knowledge claims into the cynicism, critical distrust and nihilism associated with perpetual deconstruction. This tendency, I think, is implied by those espousing a strong social constructionist viewpoint. For example, Gergen suggests that:

> Social constructionism views discourse about the world not as a reflection or map of the world but as an artifact of communal exchange. (Gergen, 1985: 266)

This seems to be a form of idealism (in the philosophical sense) which deems it futile to work towards better professional map making. Another way forward, which I prefer, is to continue to investigate the world using a mixture of qualitative and quantitative methods but to utilise deconstruction as well. At issue here is whether or not we build up knowledge with humility and scepticism or with arrogance and certainty. The case and conditions for deconstruction have mainly arisen because the scientific project so central to modernism has fallen foul of its own arrogance. In this light, Boyne (1990: 104), discussing the work of Derrida, talks of his attacks upon the 'dishonest certitude that informs the tradition of Western thought'.

However, Western thought has brought with it some advantages despite its 'dishonest certitude'. Rationality, consensual decision making and public accountability are examples of these democratic benefits. Deconstruction, and prior to it the ideological critiques of Marxism, quite properly also expose the oppressive power associated with the veneration of rationality in general, and science in particular. In this light we are not obliged to make a forced choice between knowledge claims and deconstruction – it is possible to value, and be sceptical of, both.

A more systematic philosophical attack upon the strong social constructionist case (of psychologists such as Gergen), which focuses on psychological knowledge, is provided by Greenwood (1994) in his *Realism, Identity and Emotion*. Greenwood carefully elucidates the following main point about naive empiricism and its opposing social constructionism:

> A common error of both empiricist and social constructionist accounts is to assume that linguistic and epistemic objectivity can only be achieved for putative theoretical descriptions of atoms and emotions, if such descriptions are operationally defined in terms of the empirical phenomena they purport to explain. Thus traditional empiricists maintain that linguistic and epistemic objectivity is achieved – and can only be achieved – via the operational definition of theoretical psychological descriptions. Social constructionists deny that psychological descriptions are either linguistically or epistemically objective by denying that they are – and that they can be – operationally defined. According to the realist, this is a fundamental error: theoretical descriptions can be – and regularly are – both linguistically and epistemically objective, even though they are not operationally defined. (Greenwood, 1994: 2–3)

Greenwood focuses on atoms and emotions because they are both hidden from view as internal states (and are thus unobservable). By 'linguistically objective' he means that the statement 'the cat sat on the mat' provides a demonstrable and persuasive case that the statement is accurate, when human observers are faced with a cat which is sitting on a mat. By 'epistemically objective' he refers to a different criterion of objective accuracy or validity, which can be evaluated using agreed rules of deduction (e.g. the statement '2 + 4 = 6' will usually secure agreement from an audience about its accuracy). Greenwood proceeds to argue that inner worlds and subjective accounts can be studied as real phenomena, thereby rejecting the objections of both strong objectivists and strong constructionists. I think that Greenwood is correct in these criticisms.

The Strengths and Weaknesses of Post-Structuralism

The strengths of post-structuralism can be summarised as follows:

1   It challenges the certainties of traditional approaches to knowledge production and potentially exposes the interests which underpin them.
2   It is a non-authoritarian and creative approach to knowledge, encouraging a wide variety of perspectives to be generated.
3   It is suited to our current postmodern times.
4   It encourages diverse forms of practice and perspective and so validates the truism that 'variety is the spice of life'.

Its weaknesses can be summarised as follows:

1   It may encourage a nihilistic attitude towards those who do try to produce knowledge claims about the world – it is easier to find fault from the sidelines than play the game of generating empirical knowledge claims.

2   Accordingly it may throw the baby out with the bath water by rendering material reality unknowable. In problematising representations of reality it rejects reality as a worthy topic of enquiry.

3   It is vulnerable to the accusation that its mandate is dubious. If traditional epistemology appeals to its publicly accountable forms of methodology for its legitimacy, where does the post-structuralist acquire his or her mandate? Why should *their* critical reading be warranted above any other viewpoint about knowledge claims?

4   If post-structuralism favours and celebrates the notion of discourse (and history) without a subject, why has it been associated with the same devotion to individual leadership as any other intellectual movement?

DISCOURSES ON PSYCHOLOGICAL ABNORMALITY

Before leaving the discursive emphasis of post-structuralism, I will address the issue of discourse about psychological abnormality in society. Elsewhere, I have already contributed to a summary of this (Pilgrim and Rogers, 1993, Ch. 1) in relation to mental health and illness. Here I will summarise this summary. Essentially we listed and discussed five perspectives outside sociology and three within:

1   the lay perspective
2   psychiatry
3   psychoanalysis
4   psychology
5   the legal framework
6   social causation
7   societal reaction (labelling theory)
8   social constructivism.

It is immediately obvious from this list that psychotherapy spans 3 and 4. The two case studies given in the last chapter make this location clear. However, a number of ambiguities remain about other points on the list. For example, some psychotherapists use diagnostic criteria and descriptions which are derived from psychiatry. This influence is very clear in the carry-over of psychiatric nosologies within psychoanalysis. The discourse of psychoanalysis remains a medical one. Clients are 'patients'. Inner life is 'psychopathology'. Presenting problems are 'symptoms'. The same is more generally true of 'psychotherapy', indeed by and large in this book I retain this terminology.

Is it possible then to summarise the elements of psychotherapeutic discourses which mark them out as being different from other parts of the above list? The answer to this question is a cautious 'yes'. Let us start with the practical paradigm of individual psychotherapy. Two people sit in a room and have a private conversation. For the purposes of their meeting, one is designated as having a problem, the other is not. The one with the problem is on the territory of the other. The other decides when the meetings take place, how many and for how long. If the room contains a telephone the one with the problem is not supposed to answer it but the other can choose to do so. The one with the problem is expected to talk about themself a lot, the other is not. One may gently interrogate the other but not *vice versa*. One is paid to be there, the other is not. One has many conversations of this type with a variety of people, the other has only limited experience in this regard. This set of rules and assumptions about the conduct of psychotherapy make it different from both ordinary conversations and prescriptive or structured interviews conducted by many psychiatrists and some clinical psychologists.

The therapeutic advantages of the setting for therapy did not escape the notice of some psychoanalysts even before systemic therapy was to appear on the scene (e.g. Winnicott, 1958). However, the latter could only appreciate what he was saying about the setting within a single set of assumptions about the holding environment of infants. But this is only one reading of the complex processes (both enabling and disabling) which might come in to play by setting up such artificial conditions for a conversation between two adults. Like the notion of transference, the expanded version of psychoanalysis offered by revisionists like Winnicott still furnished psychoanalytical therapists with a set of *a priori* constructs to read the significance of the setting. When we think about psychotherapy as a peculiar setting with unexpected rules (compared to everyday life), an alternative construction can be put forward of its being a secular extension of religious rituals, which I discussed in the preface to this book. It is for this reason that Berger and Luckmann (1966) draw parallels between psychotherapy and religious conversion, and Foucault (1981) discusses the similarities between psychoanalysis and the Catholic confessional.

This general point about therapy being a secular mimic of religious activity is reasonably obvious even before we begin to examine the particular theoretical style of the therapist. As with the confessional there is another side to this picture of disciplinary power (or professional dominance). Although the therapist may control the setting, the penitent/patient can resist the process. They may fail to attend, turn up late or drop out. They may agree with the expert and then fail to change between meetings. They may seek to dislodge or unnerve the expert by silence, seduction or hostility. These may be framed as examples of 'resistance' to personal change (the traditional psychoanalytical formulation). They may also represent expressions of defiance and autonomy in which lay people subvert or refuse professional power. On the other hand, the expert retains control of the interpretive framework in the conversation and makes a living independent of the progress of the other party. Because the narrative of the client always operates within a dialogue which the therapist governs or endorses, a power asymmetry remains inevitable (Spence, 1982). The client cannot reverse it during the relationship. This suggests that, provided that the expert keeps their nose clean, or appears to, in one sense their power will remain inviolable. The ultimate threat to this power is when clients no longer take experts seriously and drop out or are provoked into collective oppositional campaigns (like the psychiatric service users' movement).

In what sense, then, are these aspects of therapeutic encounters different from the events or practices implicit in other points on the list of eight above? At first sight the lay perspective might be close to that of a psychotherapist, especially if the latter works within a phenomenological framework. However, these are not ordinary conversations. I referred to Hayley's comment on the processes of power in clinical psychoanalysis. Such one-upmanship does not disappear because, for example, the orientation is Rogerian. As Hayley notes (I guess slightly tongue in cheek) how can you top someone who always agrees with you? To make empathy into a recurring professional habit is to ensure a disjuncture of power. The rhythm and symmetry of ordinary conversations may superficially appear to be like psychotherapeutic encounters, but closer scrutiny reveals a different picture. It is revealing that some family therapists operating now self-consciously within a post-structuralist framework have sought to remove the trappings of expertise in order to create a therapeutic context of ordinariness. But can their designation as paid therapists ever close the gap between the parties and dissolve disciplinary power?

Psychotherapeutic conversations also have some common ground with the professional style of both psychiatry and the less exploratory versions of clinical psychology such as cognitive therapy. Both of these take an interest in what the patient is saying. However, ultimately, if in differing ways, they treat utterances as information to build up an expert formulation. The psychiatrist relies wholly on symptoms (what patients say) in order to make a decision about a diagnosis and to prescribe a treatment. The cognitive therapist builds up a picture of the patient's cognitions and a functional understanding of their role in their life. At a point at which this leads to the person reconstruing some aspect of their life there is clearly a similarity with the process of verbal psychotherapy.

Indeed some have argued (e.g. Bannister, 1983) that even behavioural techniques such as systematic desensitisation are simply one amongst many ways in which people come to a reconstruction. If a distinction can be made at all between these more prescriptive approaches in psychiatry and clinical psychology and exploratory psychotherapy it is that the broader autobiographical content of the latter and the shifting meanings negotiated in the relationship are more complex and open-ended. Bannister is correct to point out, though, that a prescription from an expert-centred process may still lead to subjective reconstructions in its target.

Thus the verbal psychotherapies can be distinguished as forms of social practice from ordinary conversations, on the one side, and more prescriptive versions of mental health work, on the other. However, there are also points of overlap between all of them.

GENERAL SYSTEMS THEORY

Having, in the previous chapter and this one, built up a picture of where psychotherapy is situated in relation to different versions of social science, I now want to note another possible point of contact or connectedness between the two realms. General systems theory (GST) has been influential within both sociology and psychology (Merton, 1949; Lewin, 1951; Parsons, 1951; Allport, 1961). It has also been a specific influence upon some aspects of cognitive psychology, especially in relation to information theory and game theory (Rapoport, 1956, 1959). In psychotherapy its impact is most evident in relation to family therapy.

Before GST was formally set out in a paper by von Bertalanffy (1950b), a biologist, a similar viewpoint about the organismic inter-relationships between diverse features of cultures had been explored by G.H. Mead in his *Mind, Self and Society* (1934). The most ambitious trans-disciplinary potential of GST for social science was generated by the anthropologist Bateson and his colleagues, and is well summarised in Bateson's *Steps To an Ecology of Mind* (1973). As with psychoanalysis, GST has been associated with conservative, functionalist accounts of people in their social context (Parsons, 1951) but has also been a springboard for more radical critiques within social science (e.g. Wilden, 1972, 1987).

The position of GST about human consciousness is different from both psychoanalysis and phenomenology. Essentially it argues that the selective attention of individuals is vital to their functioning but creates a partiality of perception and reasoning. Bateson notes that:

> Our conscious sampling of data will not disclose whole circuits but only arcs of circuits, cut off from their matrix by our selective attention. (Bateson, 1973: 420)

Also, information transfer takes place at the supra-individual level. As a consequence, whilst individuals are conscious reflective beings (the emphasis of phenomenology), they are also ignorant of much that is relevant to them in their external context. This ignorance reframes both the unconscious (the emphasis of psychoanalysis) and consciousness. The former does not reside wholly within the minds of individuals. The latter is a basis for the agency of individuals but its partiality ensures that agents act under conditions of ignorance and uncertainty.

I think that the flexibility of GST offers itself also as ambiguity. As with psychoanalysis it can be moulded for a variety of theoretical and practical purposes. It is celebrated readily by both radical social critics and conservative management consultants. As I note above, GST stems from its roots just after the Second World War in biology rather than in social science (von Bertalanffy, 1950a and b). And yet the advantages as a resource for the latter soon became evident, suggesting that GST might be an acceptable framework to link the three types of scientific assumptions described in the last chapter by D'Andrade (1986). The shift from being a biological and mechanical to a personal and social theoretical framework was made via the work of Bateson and his colleagues. Bateson shifted the focus of attention away from simply the economic and social relationships of human society, the focus of sociology, and towards the relationship between human beings and their ecosystem. In doing so, he provided a theoretical resource for an emerging social movement, from the 1960s onwards, of eco-politics, which was to influence and coexist with more traditional political ideologies.

I turn briefly now to an outline of GST and its implications. Reflecting in later years on the need for a systemic viewpoint across disciplines von Bertalanffy (1987, Ch. 4) noted the following (with my notes in brackets at the end of each point).

1   Classical scientific theory neglected to consider the living organism as part of a set of processes related to continuous change, regulation and teleology. Humans in particular are goal-seeking and purposive. Classical mechanistic biological science is not so much wrong as inadequate for the task of wrestling with these characteristics of human activity. (This is relevant still today, when we consider that current bio-medical explanations in psychiatry retain and replay this inadequacy.)

2   Classical science was concerned with linear causal chains of two variables (one cause, one effect) or with a few variables at the most. Social science, modern physics and engineering entail multi-variable and complex phenomena which are not amenable to understanding or explanation using linear and few variable models. Cause and effect are not merely mechanical events but are also manifestations of information transfer. (This implies new methodologies to respond to complexity, levels of organisation and circular rather than linear relationships. It also implies that behaviour is communication, not merely a response to a stimulus.)

3   The world can be understood as levels of organisation, with a subordinate level being a precondition of the ones above it. However, superordinate levels cannot be reduced to lower levels. (This key insight highlights for us the dangers of reducing personal destiny to biology or social processes to individual characteristics. Moreover, it suggests that with higher levels of organisation of, say, human mind or society, new qualities appear which are not present at lower levels, say, in chemical reactions.)

4   The capacity for prediction diminishes with more complex and open systems. (This introduces the caution against the aspirations of

scientific psychology to become a predictive science, as human beings are part of and constitute open, not closed systems.)

Before leaving this summary from von Bertalanffy, it is worth quoting his anticipation of post-structuralism:

> All scientific constructs are models representing certain aspects or perspectives of reality. This even applies to theoretical physics: far from being a metaphysical presentation of ultimate reality (as the materialism of the past proclaimed and modern positivism implies) it is but one of those models and, as recent developments show, neither exhaustive nor unique. (von Bertalanffy, 1987: 62)

This emphasis on representation is not the only way in which GST prefigured some of the emphases of post-structuralism. For example, Bateson (1973) emphasised that the unit of analysis of human mind is not that of the skin-encapsulated individual. Instead, it relates to both intra- and supra-individual aspects of the person's environment. Unlike post-structuralism, GST is committed unambiguously, though, to a form of realist enquiry. Wilden (1987) provides us here with a clear, if strangely punctuated and programmatic, definition:

> *Reality, real*: What trips you up when you don't pay attention to it – includes matter, energy and the communication of many kinds of information, whether biological like the genetic code or social like the exchange of goods; thus includes nature, society and technology; other people and other minds; food and shelter; race and class and sex; a wealth of wasted human creativity; and the need to change most of it for something better. (Wilden, 1987: 67)

Wilden distinguishes reality from the 'imaginary' (the product of mind alone plus mimicry, fiction, fantasy and camouflage) and the 'symbolic' (information that stands for another kind or level of information – the latter could itself be real, imagined or symbolic).

These principles of GST, which emphasise complexity not simplicity, information and communication not energy or forces, and loops and circles not lines, provide ample opportunity to develop understandings of human beings in interaction. Not surprisingly, therefore, they soon became incorporated into first group and then family therapy. What these practices had access to, which for differing theoretical reasons were absent from the work of individual therapists working within psycho-dymanic or phenomenological frameworks, was a model which emphasised *context*.

However, as Wilden (1972) has pointed out there are ways of using GST to close off a consideration of the socio-political context. For example, psychotherapists may be vulnerable to such an occupational hazard by considering the individual-in-relation-to-therapist system alone (the preoccupation of clinical psychoanalysis with transference) or in relation to a family-system-plus-therapy-team system. Similarly within group therapy or management science it is possible to use a systemic understanding of a small group's function or dysfunction in isolation from its societal context (Barham, 1986). As I noted about the setting earlier, the territorial control that therapists exert is one form of closure. The theoretical constructs applied by therapists can then reinforce this closure.

The human context can be thought of as being constituted by both a sustaining material environment *and* by the type of reality permitted or warranted by language. The sort of radical GST approach used by Wilden encourages a consideration of both of these components rather than placing them in opposition or over-valuing one at the expense of the other. The social determinism associated with much empirical sociology, traceable to both Durkheimian and Marxian social theory, emphasises the first component (the material environment). The linguistic preoccupation of both symbolic interactionism and post-structuralism emphasises the second (language and discourse). GST provides a potential theoretical resource to correct the excessive determinism associated with structuralism in social science, on the one hand, and the distrust or rejection of realist accounts of social constructionists, on the other. Given this flexibility one does not have to choose between objectivism and subjectivism or quantitative or qualitative methods as GST provides legitimacy for both tendencies within social science.

GST does not deny the importance of structure (which is understood as the stable, but not necessarily permanent, elements within a system), nor does it evade the importance of the inputs provided by human agents by their words and deeds. The latter have the potential to destabilise structures and thereby create social change. Consequently, GST can be thought of as an open textured theory which ensures a respect for complexity, offers safeguards against reductionism, recognises the implications of human language use and explains the coexistence of stasis and change. However, as I noted earlier, it offers no guarantees against its proponents introducing forms of analytical closure which obscure rather than expose the socio-political context of human existence.

The Strengths and Weaknesses of GST

GST has the following strengths:

1 The emphasis on goal-seeking and purposive character of living organisms enables us to consider *values* as a legitimate part of systematic human enquiry (positivism seeks the specious separation of values from 'facts').

2 It starts from a position of expecting diversity and the coexistence of both predictability and unpredictability, and stasis and change. The emphasis on levels of organisation within systems ensures accounts of social relationships which are complex, multi-variable and interactive.

3 It incorporates elements of both subjectivity and objectivity and legitimises both quantitative and qualitative methods.

4   Its emphasis on human life as an open system encourages a consideration of both internal inputs from human agents and external inputs from economic and political influences and constraints.

Its weaknesses can be summarised as follows:

1   Its association with mechanical disciplines like engineering may be off-putting to more humanistic social scientists (including some psychotherapists).

2   Despite its potential to produce a form of trans-disciplinary knowledge it still tends to be applied quite separately to the concerns of individual disciplines.

3   In order to produce a manageable focus for enquiry, its principled starting point about levels, complexity and context can be undermined by the artificial introduction of closure.

4   Its more diffuse notion about the relationship between the conscious and unconscious aspects of human functioning may be perplexing and unattractive for psychotherapists in both the psychodynamic and humanistic traditions.

DISCUSSION

This second chapter has extended some of the conceptual explorations started in the first. Across the two chapters I have provided case studies about types of knowledge which are relevant to the focus of this book. I have tried to rehearse, in a short space, some of the complexities surrounding various attempts to provide a stamp of academic authority on the relationship between individuals and their social context. On a couple of occasions, I have reminded the reader that this has been done from a preferred position (of realism). Within this position I consider that empirical studies, even if they are underpinned by a form of *naive empiricism* which I would not sympathise with, provide us with information to consider carefully. Equally, despite my reservations about post-structuralism and the strong version of social constructionism it promotes, I consider that deconstruction provides a useful, irreverent stance to help us think critically. Indeed, I prefer the term 'critical reading' to 'deconstruction'. As a consequence I hope to draw together forms of enquiry which appear to oppose one another, whilst, at the same time, being fully aware of the shortcomings of each.

Before moving on to the next chapter I want to make one further point about the partial adequacy of diverse approaches within social science towards mental health matters. The term 'social' has a different connotation, when we examine the social causation arguments associated with epidemiology, than when we attempt to provide a collective understanding of experiences within social groups. For example, epidemiology provides us with the information that black and Irish people are over-represented in psychiatric statistics (see Chapter 5). This is derived historically from an objectivist paradigm within social medicine. It is essentially about collecting *aggregate* data – it adds up the number of people from particular social backgrounds who do or do not have a mental illness. However, this aggregate approach can tell us nothing about the *collective* identity of black or Irish people or why the white English tend to label them as threatening or odd. Nor can it tell us anything about the construct validity of psychiatric diagnoses or the legitimacy of using racial categories in social research.

These questions can only be addressed using paradigms other than that of epidemiology. However, the limited utility and the lack of reflexivity of epidemiology does not mean that its findings are not useful to consider. Similarly, because social constructionists only provide meta-analyses of empirical claims, rather than offer direct claims of their own, does not mean that deconstruction is not a worthwhile activity. It simply illuminates a topic from a certain direction but not another. I will be happy to selectively draw upon diverse approaches in order to provide both information *and* critical analysis about psychotherapy and society. From this position of unabashed eclecticism, springing from the opportunity created by what Smart, discussing Foucault, called the 'ambiguous volume of space constituted by the epistemological arrangement' (1990: 401) in human science, I will now look at a number of topics of relevance to the title of this book.

3

Class Distinctions

We all rail against class-distinctions, but very few people seriously want to abolish them.

George Orwell, *The Road to Wigan Pier*

INTRODUCTION

This chapter and the subsequent three will examine evidence about the social patterning of mental distress. Whilst it is a truism that anybody, whatever their social background, can experience varieties of fear, sadness or madness, this does not mean that these occur randomly in society. The best predictor of general health is social class and, within this trend, mental health follows a class gradient. Class is also relevant in relation to service responses to particular forms of distress. Basically the rich are more likely to receive psychological treatments, and the poor biological treatments. I will expand on these general points below before unpacking the political arguments surrounding access to psychotherapy. The question I pose at the end of the chapter is not *whether* psychotherapy is an elitist practice but *why*? Thus this chapter is divided into four main sections:

- a conceptual note on social class
- the class gradient of mental health
- social class and psychotherapy
- discussion: on the elitism of psychotherapy

A CONCEPTUAL NOTE ON SOCIAL CLASS

Thirty years ago social stratification, class politics and class consciousness were central concerns for sociologists. More recently these topics have declined, though they have not disappeared, in importance. They have increasingly been superseded by more diverse concerns about intra-class differences and interacting variables, such as race, gender, sexuality and disability. In particular the latter have attracted interest as sources of oppression and dispossession, replacing the singular concern of the Marxian tradition. As the centrality of a Marxian analysis of class has given way in many of its advocates to a post-structuralist perspective (see Chapter 2) there has been little diminution in the long-term non-Marxian interest in social stratification and its link to advantage and disadvantage within society (Runciman, 1990; Evans, 1992; Goldthorpe and Marshall, 1992; Westergaard, 1992; Pahl, 1993; Breen and Rottman, 1995).

In a recent post-structuralist critique of class and psychopathology Parker et al. (1995) make the following points:

> Although by its very nature a 'social' concept, implying a group, increasingly 'class' has been a term applied to individuals. Worse than this, classes are defined in the psychological literature, without any reference to the exploitation of labour, alienation or oppression . . . Indeed class is heard of less and we now hear more of socio-economic status – an individualized variable. Pilgrim and Rogers' (1993) *A Sociology of Mental Health and Illness* includes chapters on gender, race and ethnicity and age but only a section on class . . . (Parker et al., 1995: 46)

Why then has social class become more conceptually problematic than it used to be in social science? The following points could be highlighted.

1   Most of the empirical research on social class in Britain has utilised the Registrar General's classification constructed in 1911. At that time the division of society into a professional elite (social class I), a managerial group beneath (social class II), a skilled artisan class (social class III), a lower unskilled group of employees (social class IV) and then an unemployed group (social class V) was persuasive. The differentials of wealth and correlated educational levels of this gradient were consistent. However, this consistency has now broken down.

2   This scheme defined female class by that of married women's male partners. This definition is now inappropriate on both empirical grounds (as women now dominate the labour market) and political grounds (as feminism has insisted on a new discourse about female identity being defined separately).

3   The size and character of sections of the class structure have changed dramatically during the twentieth century in Western European and North American societies. The skilled working class, associated with factory production, has been eroded. With the growth of new technology and a switch to service industries (a function of a new emphasis on consumption rather than production) a new type of workforce has emerged, incorporating white collar workers with a wide range of salaries and statuses. The breadth of this range is such that a pyramid class structure has been replaced by a more diamond-shaped one. In Chapter 8 when discussing the conceptual problems which Marxism has had with an expanding new middle class, I shall discuss the implications for psychotherapists.

4   The *identity* associated with social class has become highly variegated and contested. This was epitomised by the famous soundbite from Margaret Thatcher in the mid-1980s when she claimed, 'I'm working class – I work jolly hard, I can tell you.' Her lack of embarrassment about

such a self-ascribed status probably reflected an insight that working-class voters were keeping her in power.

5   The politics of oppression have changed in society and this has been reflected in a shift in sociological attention. In particular the changes in the relationship between production and consumption (point 3 above) have defused working-class solidarity. At the same time, new social movements have proved to be enduring alternatives to the old labour movement. New social movements, exemplified by feminism, exist outside the traditional opposition between workers and their bosses and are based on other sources of oppression (such as racism and sexism).

6   The conceptualisation of class has included the following factors: earnings, educational achievement, power and occupation. Unfortunately (for any audience awaiting clarification) sociologists disagree about the relevant permutation and salience of each of these. Put simply, social class remains a highly contested concept.

None of the above points should be taken to mean that class is now an irrelevant social variable. Quite the reverse: once a working definition is provided by empirical researchers, it is still a very good predictor of a number of outcomes, including mental and physical health, longevity, educational achievement and quality of life. These largely sociological debates about the conceptual status of class in modern society may seem to be rather distant from the concerns of psychotherapists. However, class remains important for the latter for the following reasons.

1   As will be clear below, poverty and poor mental health are correlated.

2   Mental health status increases with age in rich people but declines in poor people.

3   Psychotherapists are middle class and so they have an *a priori* congruence with clients from the same background.

4   Because of the norms surrounding private practice in psychotherapy, the cash nexus has taken on a peculiar salience compared to other health and welfare interventions. Those able to pay are privileged compared to those who cannot, as it affects their differential access to therapists.

In the rest of the chapter I shall flesh out these four points.

THE CLASS GRADIENT OF MENTAL HEALTH

That there is a class gradient in mental health is not in dispute. What remains unresolved is *why* there is a correlation between low social class and mental health problems. In this section, the literature about this question will be reviewed. Then I will note some conceptual and methodological problems involved in this literature.

Evidence for the Class Gradient

The relationship between social class and mental health was first studied systematically by a group of Chicago sociologists in the 1930s (Faris and Dunham, 1939). They investigated psychiatric hospital admission diagnosis and locality of origin in the city over a 12-year period. They found that the incidence of schizophrenia was seven times greater in poor, socially disorganised neighbourhoods than it was in stable suburbs. This Chicago study then set a trend for further psychiatric epidemiology for 40 years which tended overall to confirm the class gradient (e.g. Stein, 1957; Hollingshead and Redlich, 1958; Srole et al., 1962; Goldberg and Morrison, 1963; Dunham, 1964; Dohrenwend and Dohrenwend, 1977). However, some studies were at odds with these findings. Most of this was US research but (the fewer) later British studies confirmed the class gradient (Brown and Harris, 1978; Bebbington et al., 1981).

Apart from this general literature on psychiatric epidemiology, there is also that which addresses the impact of unemployment and homelessness. In his book *Down and Out in Paris and London* George Orwell (1933) provides an early ethnographic account of the impact of homelessness on mental health. He comments on those 'who have fallen into solitary half-mad grooves of life and given up trying to be normal or decent. Poverty frees them from ordinary standards of behaviour, just as money frees people from work' (1933: 102). The last point is also a relevant factor in explaining why richer people are buffered from the deleterious effects of unemployment – they can be out of work without being poor or homeless.

The psychiatric literature on homeless populations has focused less on homelessness as a stressor and disinhibitor (Orwell's point) or as a social policy failure, and more on the personal deficits of homeless people. This is a good example of how social problems have been individualised and medicalised. Psychiatric researchers have been keen to emphasise the high prevalence of mental illness in homeless populations at the very time when the profession has been lobbying for more inpatient facilities and seeking a new legitimacy in a post–institutional world. This type of research provides estimates of the prevalence of psychiatric morbidity as high as 90 per cent (Bassuk et al., 1984) and focuses on symptomatology, social functioning and the 'maladaptive behaviour' of homeless people.

Such findings have also been highlighted within a catastrophic discourse about community care during the 1980s and 1990s. Sometimes this is little more than a thinly disguised attempt on the part of some psychiatrists and lobby groups, dominated by the relatives of psychiatric patients, to seek to reverse the demise of large-scale segregation. When madness was warehoused in large institutions patients were accommodated. Thus deinstitutionalisation poses a problem for housing policy. Those lobbies which demand a return to segregation emphasise that patients 'need' to be in hospital. By this demand, a housing policy crisis in part becomes individualised and mystified. Studies which have been less bound up with short-term professional interests claim lower rates of morbidity (15 per cent) and point to the need of other researchers to medicalise social problems (Snow et al., 1986).

Fryer (1995), in his recent summary of the psychological impact of labour market disadvantage, notes that unemployment has systemic effects in families, as well as having a particular mental health toll on the affected adult individual. For example, the school performance of children is significantly adversely affected by parental unemployment, as is their mental health. Other studies reviewed by Fryer also confirmed adverse psychological effects on the spouses of the unemployed person. The shift from employed to unemployed status (and its threat) has a deleterious effect on workers, including putting them at increased risk of depression, alcohol dependence, anxiety states and psychosomatic reactions. Some of these effects may continue even after re-employment.

As well as reviewing the empirical evidence on the effects of labour market disadvantage on mental health, Fryer also outlines causal factors operating. These include: the direct stress of impoverishment; the loss of status after being employed; the disempowering status of being unem-ployed; and a consequent experience of having one's agency thwarted. These points resemble the picture built up by the work of Brown and his colleagues that I discuss in Chapter 6. Their model of the social origins of depression points to a combination of adverse life events, loss and restrictions on personal agency, such that the person is trapped and cannot escape from their life situation.

Apart from the literature from psychiatric epidemiology, the work on 'life events' also informs the debate. Whilst people from all social back-grounds suffer stressful life events such as bereavement, illness and divorce, the ratio between these negative events and buffering positive ones is not distributed equally throughout society. Phillips (1968) found no differ-ences between working-class and middle-class respondents in the reporting of negative life events. However, the latter were twice as likely as the former to report positive feelings about life. These positive feelings may thus act as a buffer to protect self-esteem and ward off distress. This pattern of class and positive buffering experiences was confirmed by Myers (1974, 1975).

If all the literature is put together, although there are some contra-dictory findings and some conceptual and methodological difficulties (see below), a pattern is present of a class gradient in relation to mental health. The most obvious reason for this is in relation to direct social stress and the absence of buffering positive experiences.

To live in poverty means losing control over one's life in a number of ways which are linked to inner vulnerability and outer stress. These include the increased probability of: struggling to provide basic necessities of food and shelter; having a poor diet; resorting to comforts, such as drugs and alcohol, which impact negatively on health and well-being;

aimlessness and powerlessness; cumulative debt; living in an environment which is dirty, traffic-congested and has a high crime rate; and being homeless or living in a cramped, poorly furnished home. All of these lead to a lower sense of self-worth and constricted agency in people living in poor communities. Also the direct deleterious impact on physical health of poverty has an additional indirect impact on mental health. For example, depression is common in people with chronic or multiple disabling conditions. Indeed, when the features of an impoverished context are listed like this, an apposite question could be 'Why aren't *more* poor people sad, frightened or mad?'

Having summarised some of the relevant literature on social class and mental health problems, I now turn to the difficulties of interpretation created by conceptual and methodological uncertainties.

First, some social variables like race intersect with class in such a way that it is not always easy to disaggregate their individual effects. For example, in Britain Afro-Caribbean and Irish people are over-represented in psychiatric statistics. At the same time these groups are over-represented in poor urban areas. To complicate matters further some racial groups, like Asians living in poor areas along with Afro-Caribbeans (and vulnerable, like them, to white racism), are not over-represented in psychiatric statistics (or the evidence is mixed). Even if a straightforward social stress hypothesis is put forward, which stressor predominates to inflict an extra mental health toll on some of these groups (but not others) – poverty or racism? The problem of disaggregating class and race led some early commentators to argue that it was only safe to hold to the view of a class gradient when talking of indigenous whites in a US context. In other cases, such as the relationship between gender and mental health in Britain, a number of studies have established unequivocally that working-class women are more prone to depression than middle-class women although the interaction with child rearing seems to account for this (Brown and Harris, 1978).

Second, the categories used to map the epidemiology of mental health problems are highly contested. For example, much of the work on mental health and class dating back to the epidemiological studies in Chicago uses 'schizophrenia' as the diagnostic category under investigation. However, people with this diagnosis are like apples and oranges. As Bannister (1968) pointed out, schizophrenia is a disjunctive category. That is, two patients with the same diagnosis may share no symptom in common. One may be deluded and excitable. The other may be hallucinating, and be flat in effect. In this light, some psychologists have rejected the schizophrenia concept altogether (Bentall et al., 1988; Boyle, 1990). Even a more obvious notion such as depression is not as simple as it looks. If a person is apathetic and expressionless, are they depressed or are they experiencing a schizoid state of indifference to the world? Why is it that some people who are agitated and irritable are called 'depressed' and so too are those who are still and passive? As with schizophrenia, depression can be a disjunctive category.

Third, there is a danger of extrapolating from the characteristics of a geographical locality (say, a run-down inner city area) to the individuals who reside there. This so-called 'ecological fallacy' is discussed by Cochrane (1983) and was a criticism made of the suggestion put forward by Faris and Dunham (1939) about social causation based upon their study of patients from different parts of the city. It is clear that it is logically possible to live in a socially disorganised and poor neighbourhood and yet have a secure social network and a well-paid job. In a city such as London the social class mix of many localities ensures this prospect. Cochrane also points out a related methodological problem if there is a reliance on inpatient statistics. It could be that people in chaotic circumstances by definition lack the integrative containment of social networks. Consequently they may experience problems which require external help (from services). By contrast people with similar dysfunction in a more stable network may contact services less often. Thus, service utilisation may be a more accurate indication of incidence than prevalence. Incidence refers to first cases recorded. Prevalence refers to the aggregating numbers in a total population – including old and new cases and those outside service contact. For this reason, health surveys done in the community always detect higher levels of morbidity (both physical as well as mental) than studies of diagnosed incidence. This has been called the 'clinical iceberg' (Hannay, 1979).

Fourth, whilst poor mental health is correlated with employment status (both men and women are more likely to suffer problems if they are out of work), more than one causal factor may be operating. For example, becoming unemployed is both disorientating and demoralising but it also leads to loss of income and either relative or absolute poverty ensues. Thus, whilst we know that being unemployed is bad for your mental health it is not always easy to disentangle the intra-individual factors, such as loss of morale and self-esteem, from external stressors such as the direct impact of poverty. This brings us to the next wider question.

Fifth, if poverty and mental ill-health are correlated, is a *causal* relationship inevitable and, if so, in which direction does it operate? That is, does poverty cause mental ill-health or do people become poor because their mental health problems render them less socially competent and employable? The latter possibility became known as the social drift hypothesis, which I now address along with alternatives.

The Social Drift and Other Hypotheses

The question of causality, which is begged by the uncontested and repeated finding, since Faris and Dunham's research in the 1930s, that poverty and mental ill-health are linked, has generated competing answers. The two dominant and opposing hypotheses will be discussed and an alternative which attempts to integrate elements of each will be described.

1   *Social drift/selection*   This accounts for the inverse relationship between socio-economic status and mental ill-health by suggesting that social class is an outcome, not a determinant of disease. The assumption is that those already in a lower-class position will stay there when they become ill, whereas those further up the social scale will become incompetent and dysfunctional in their class position and drift downwards. Such a view is, of course, consistent with a biogenic or genetic view about the determination of mental illness.

2   *Social stress/causation*   This emphasises the contrary view, which is that mental ill-health is caused by social stress. Given that social stress increases with poverty then poor people will have a higher incidence of mental ill-health (Dunham, 1957).

3   *The interactional hypothesis*   This assumes that genetically vulnerable individuals become ill when placed under social stress. Kohn (1973), in putting forward this hypothesis, also argues that lower-class people are not socialised to be able to cope with stress, a view not held by Mechanic (1972).

One of the imponderables about these competing hypotheses is the role of psychiatric diagnosis. Most of the research about the class gradient has been about a patient group with the most conceptually problematic diagnosis ('schizophrenia') – see my second discussion point above. There is little point in psychiatric epidemiologists producing large data sets if the label they count is so flawed. It is also the case that with the diagnosis of what psychiatrists often call 'serious mental illness' there is evidence of class bias in diagnosis. Diagnosticians are middle class, whereas people with a diagnosis of schizophrenia are more likely to be lower class. It is now well established that the greater the gap (of both class and culture) between the labeller and the labelled, the more serious the label that is likely to be given (Wilkinson, 1975; Horwitz, 1983). I shall return to this point about the identity of the labeller and the labelled in relation to both race and gender in subsequent chapters.

The two main hypotheses discussed above are associated with ideologically driven assumptions about the causes of mental distress. The biogenic view has a longstanding association with eugenics and conservative political values. By contrast those with left-wing social values find a social causation hypothesis more acceptable. In addition, particular disciplinary interests are also in play about the two hypotheses. Psychiatry is a medical specialty. The social status and authority of medical practitioners have been associated with their production and control of biological knowledge. This means that during their secondary socialisation of medical training, incipient doctors develop a preference for biological explanations.

By contrast, those disciplines which are competing with medicine for authority about health (such as psychology and sociology) are more likely to hold environmentalist views about causation because of their training. As the 'less serious' psychiatric conditions of anxiety and reactive depression fell to environmentalist explanations, the political significance of the 'more serious' conditions, such as 'schizophrenia', changed. The authority of psychiatry now rests largely with its continuing claim to have a privileged understanding of psychosis. For this reason, it is particularly important that the medical specialty retains its persuasiveness about conditions such as 'schizophrenia'. If the latter too were to fall away to environmentalist explanations then the mandate of psychiatry to retain its dominant position within the mental health industry would be considerably strained.

In the light of these considerations about the relationship between knowledge and professional interests, it may be that the drift versus causation debate will never be resolved by a group of neutral adjudicators, as the latter do not exist.

SOCIAL CLASS AND PSYCHOTHERAPY

This topic has recently been reviewed by Bromley (1983, 1994). Below I will summarise and augment his work. One of the studies mentioned above (Hollingshead and Redlich, 1958) demonstrated that, in the US context of the 1950s, social class was also a predictor of the type of treatment offered to people with mental health problems. Essentially, this showed that biological treatments and coercion increased in probability as the class of patients became lower and, to complement and confirm this, voluntary talking treatments increased in probability with increased social class.

Bromley (1994) has noted that evidence about selection bias has accrued from two types of study. The first are investigations of actual practice and the other are simulation studies in which social class is manipulated as a variable. As with evidence about social class and mental health, the overwhelming number of studies demonstrate class differences in relation to selection for psychotherapy. In relation to simulation studies one study found no class differences in assignment for treatment when asking clinicians to read and judge case studies. By contrast, similar studies found that judges of case studies showed a marked tendency to assign higher-class but not lower-class patients to psychotherapy. The evidence about this bias is much stronger when the practice of assessors of actual cases is investigated. To give a flavour of these findings Marx and Spray in the USA studied the treatment offered to nearly 36,000 private patients and found that only 7.2 per cent were in the lower-class group (cited in Bromley, 1994). Culberg and Steffanson in Sweden found that in a total psychiatric population for one suburb of Stockholm, upper-class patients were twice as likely to be offered psychotherapy as lower-class patients (60 per cent vs. 30 per cent) (cited in Bromley, 1994). Whilst the difference is consistently apparent about social class of patient and probability of assignment to psychotherapy the degree of this seems to be partially a function of the fee. I will return to this question at the end of the chapter.

Most of the studies of selection bias have come from the USA but the fewer investigations elsewhere also confirm the same pattern of selection bias. Given this consistent pattern in the literature, it is obvious that lower-class patients have less access to psychotherapy than those higher up the social order. To my mind this indicates that psychotherapy is an elitist practice. Not only does it exclude patients with similar levels of dysfunction, whilst including their equivalents from better-off circumstances, but it makes those excluded vulnerable to the iatrogenic effects of biological treatments. I am aware that it is possible to construct arguments about selection bias in such a way that elitism is denied. I shall now turn to these and other competing arguments.

DISCUSSION: ON THE ELITISM OF PSYCHOTHERAPY

I noted in the introduction to the chapter that the question is not whether psychotherapy is elitist but why? However, the explanations or rationalisations put forward to account for class bias need to be addressed, especially given that many readers acculturated to the norms and assumptions of private practice will be attracted to such defences. A number of explanations can be traced in the therapeutic discourse about the class bias in the industry. Three of these will be considered below: client expectations; therapist expectations of outcome; and cultural gap.

Client Expectations

The evidence about this is divided. Some studies show that working-class clients limit their expectations to physical treatments, symptom reduction and seem to lack a desire for help within a relationship. Other studies show that working-class clients have strong expectations of help via conversation rather than medication. In reviewing this mixed picture from the literature, Bromley (1994: 8) concludes that 'The evidence is equivocal but clearly there is insufficient evidence to show that the system in offering working class clients less chance of psychotherapy is doing so in response to working class demand.' Those of us (like myself) who have worked in the British NHS will know that their case load includes working-class women and men who, like their middle-class counterparts, eschew drug treatments and make good use of a therapeutic relationship. Thus any conscious explicit rejection of clients on grounds of class would be purely prejudicial. This raises the question of evidence about outcome and therapist expectations.

Therapist Expectations of Outcome

If in both the simulation and actual studies of assignment bias it is clear that therapists have a tendency to reject lower-class patients at assessment, then this must reflect in part their lower expectations of those excluded.

A problem with the studies of this outcome question in relation to social class is that they have mainly used drop-out as a measure of outcome. For example some studies show that working-class patients drop out earlier than others. Other studies have failed to demonstrate length of treatment as being correlated with social class.

Bromley (1994) notes that, as with the literature on client expectation, the literature on therapist expectation is equivocal or inconclusive. However, on balance there appear to be stronger grounds for arguing that lower-class patients do less well in psychotherapy. An important intervening variable here of course is the *interaction* between client and therapist expectations once therapy is under way. This point links with the ones made below on cultural gap. If middle-class therapists start with low expectations then this may be communicated to clients and generate in some cases a self-fulfilling prophecy. In other words early drop-out is a measure of the failure to sustain a relationship between two parties; it is not merely a measure of the expectations of one of these parties.

Cultural Gap

This explanation for assignment bias refers to the notion that in order to develop rapport and a working relationship there needs to be sufficient cultural similarity between therapist and client. As with the point just made about the interaction between client and therapist expectations, this produces a highly ambiguous outcome to interpret. If there *is* a cultural gap between two parties, which of the latter is responsible for its reduction? Surely the onus for this should rest primarily with the professional as they have more power than the client and they have access to information which relates to the problem, whereas clients are unlikely to anticipate the difficulty.

Having explored three aspects of the professional discourse relevant to understanding why psychotherapy is offered less to lower-class patients, I now want to return to the question, flagged in relation to 'cultural gap', of who is responsible for rectifying this bias. I would argue that professionals are only responsible for changing this bias if (a) they recognise that their practice is elitist and (b) they adjudge such bias to be problematic. The very fact that the class differential in the treatment of mental health problems persists so strongly so long after the study by Hollingshead and Redlich shows that there has been substantial inertia within the culture of the mental health industry.

Rather than looking at the cultural deficits of clients in accessing and utilising psychotherapy it may be more fair and useful to address therapist inaction and deficit. Before I go on the offensive about therapists, I recognise that they are hedged around by two constraints outside their control. The first of these is referrer bias. For example, in the NHS in Britain, a salaried therapist may endeavour to work with allcomers but GPs making referrals may introduce pre-assessment bias. A second caveat is that the organisational character of state-funded services may be less supportive of psychotherapeutic practice than of other forms of intervention. An example here would be of a district general psychiatric unit, with a dedicated ECT suite but few quiet rooms for personal therapy.

Bearing these caveats in mind, what then are the accusations that could be made about therapist elitism? My own view is that the social history of psychotherapy has been bound up with class bias in a number of ways and that this history both engenders and legitimises current elitism in individual practitioners. Specifically here I will address Britain as a case study of this claim. Before the First World War the concern about mental abnormality in society was almost wholly limited to the problem of pauper lunacy. A few fee-paying clients were seen outside of the asylum system and in the voluntary sector a precursor of the therapeutic community – moral treatment – was present at the beginning of the nineteenth century. However, once the state asylum system was fully established by the mid-Victorian period there was little evidence of this model being transferred, despite its emphasis within lunacy reform (Donnelly, 1983). Just prior to the outbreak of the First World War, Freudian ideas were rejected by the medical establishment, but this trend reversed during the war years (Stone, 1985).

The 'shellshock' problem altered both the biological bias of psychiatry (to render it more eclectic) and, for a while, service configuration. The latter entailed outpatient treatment centres being added to the legacy of the old asylums during the 1920s. 'Shellshock' (which later became 'battle neurosis' and then 'post-traumatic stress disorder') posed a conceptual challenge to bio-determinism in psychiatry. The latter was linked strongly during the later Victorian years to a tainted gene theory which reflected the wider influence of eugenics in a British colonial context. Essentially, the common psychiatric view was that the lower orders that accumulated in the asylum system (what Marx called the 'Lumpenproletariat') were products of a tainted gene which manifested itself in a wide range of deviance – madness, idleness, idiocy and criminality. This degeneracy view was incompatible with what was becoming evident in 1914 in the trenches. There, both working-class *volunteers* and upper-class officers were becoming psychological casualties in a war of unprecedented carnage and attrition. These were 'England's finest blood', and officers were breaking down at a higher rate than the lower ranks. In such a context, to claim that degeneracy explained mental abnormality was tantamount to treason. This allowed *psychological* explanations a new legitimacy.

In a post-war context of shellshock veterans claiming both compensation and access to help, the British Psycho-Analytical Society was formed in 1919, as was the first section of the British Psychological Society, the Medical Section. These new psychotherapeutic clubs were to set up expectations about the practice of psychotherapy in a number of ways. First, the client group they identified was *special*. It was directed at war veterans and included the officer class. It could be distinguished clearly from the prior group of pauper lunatics. Second, the Freudian domination of this new culture was significant. The medical section of the BPS was constituted by shellshock doctors who were largely psycho-analytical in their bias, and *ipso facto* all from the officer class. This class and Freudian bias was reflected further in the main treatment centres such as the Tavistock Clinic.

Freud had made it clear that his main project in life was studying the unconscious and that therapy was a necessary secondary activity which existed to earn a living. Moreover, the ground rules of what psychotherapy was to become were set by Freud's own private practice. This set a patriarchal precedent in a number of ways, which included (a) an interpretive discourse about the fee, and (b) a preoccupation with personal and territorial boundaries in a bourgeois domestic setting. Private practice was more of a pragmatic necessity than a model therapeutic setting. But once therapists opt to earn their living via private practice, it makes more sense to turn this into a therapeutic virtue than dwell too long on the parallels with prostitution or the charges of exclusivity and elitism it invites.

Freud himself expressed ambivalence about the relevance of the fee. Sometimes he argued that it was an indispensable source for interpretive work in therapy (e.g. Freud, 1913/1968: 132). At other times he was optimistic about a future with free therapy (e.g. Freud, 1918/1968: 167). To this day, therapists express similar mixed views about taking money from their clients (Power and Pilgrim, 1990; Mullan, 1996), which suggests that the ambivalence set up in the early Freudian culture has produced an unresolved legacy about the necessity or otherwise of the fee.

Thus a fee-paying custom and practice preceded and informed the social administrative problem of shellshock and its treatment. When the latter emerged, a set of traditions was already resonating within the shellshock doctors and their post-war followers. Moreover, a gap between neurotic clients (the war veterans) and the old pauper lunatics set the scene for a division of labour between mad-doctors and psychotherapists, which was to be repeated in the Second World War, when a psychoanalyst and director of the Tavistock Clinic, J.R. Rees, headed the Army psychiatric services. I shall return to this topic in Chapter 7. Thus, for most of this century, psychotherapy has had the imprint of a period which stretched between the late Victorian years and the 1920s: psychotherapeutic clients were to be distinguished from a general psychiatric population; the fee became a fetish as both a wage and a symbol in the relationship; the optimal setting advocated was domestic in style; madness was eschewed and neurosis embraced, leading to a separation of two patient populations and two distinct and separate styles of respective psychiatric responses.

It is in this historical context that the selection bias discussed in this chapter needs to be understood. The inertia of individual psychotherapists is part of a wider cultural inertia within psychotherapy about lower-class patients. The latter were rejected from the outset or were treated reluctantly or paternalistically as an addendum to the 'proper' work of engaging with fee-paying middle-class neurotic clients and (later) special soldier patients. Ordinary working-class civilians were rarely of any interest to psychotherapists early this century and the ability to pay shaped this to a large extent. Mad people are usually poor, and significantly they remained outside the interest of psychoanalytical therapists. Even the libertarian maverick Laing, a psychoanalyst interested in madness, eventually returned to earning a living in private practice.

Given this cultural bias of psychotherapy it is significant that the discourse of why lower-class patients do not want or benefit from psychotherapy, discussed earlier, has been framed predominantly in terms of client deficit. This discourse reflects the cultural and class interests of therapists themselves. The question this begs is whether therapists might now want to change the habits of a century. To do so, they would need to accept some political responsibility for class discrimination in mental health services.

4

Women and Men

No one seeking a truly critical perspective would attempt to build a
theory of man-and-womankind primarily on human psychology.

Anthony Wilden, *System and Structure*

INTRODUCTION

Having discussed the relationship between social class, mental health and
service contact, I now turn to the question of gender. The term 'gender'
refers to a social identity (being a girl/woman or being a boy/man). For
most of the time, in both common parlance and social surveys, it is
conflated with 'sex', which is more accurately the biological definition of
people by their genital characteristics. The conceptual tension between
sex and gender is highlighted by such phenomena as the overlap in
distributions between men and women of culturally defined psychological
features of femininity and masculinity, as well as the more obvious play
with social identities, the so-called 'gender bending' of cross-dressing and
trans-sexualism.

Whilst the distinction between sex and gender has been commonplace
in social science over the past 30 years (e.g. Stoller, 1968; Oakley, 1972)
it is also the case that gender, like sex, often denotes a binary division in
empirical investigations (Busfield, 1996). That is, although gender potentially is a more sensitive concept than sex, because it can be used as a
dimension or continuum rather than category, in practice it has still
tended to be used as a binary description of men and women or
masculinity and femininity. Accordingly, this chapter will mainly review
differences between women and men in relation to their mental health
and the way in which services respond to their problems.

WOMEN AND MENTAL HEALTH SERVICES

It is easier to describe the position of women in relation to mental health
services than it is to account for that description. For this reason, I shall
first outline a broad, uncontested picture of women and mental health. I

shall then discuss some of the arguments about why this picture has emerged.

The Broad Uncontested Picture

The following points can be said with relative certainty about women and mental health services:

1 Currently women are over-represented in psychiatric statistics. That is, overall, women are more likely to receive a psychiatric diagnosis than men.
2 Women are more likely to be the recipients of psychotropic medication than are men when in contact with primary care services.
3 The staffing of the mental health industry is gendered. Overall, more women work in the mental health professions than men, although the latter are more likely to hold higher positions in each disciplinary hierarchy.

These main points have been explained in a variety of ways which I shall now examine. Because women as both clients and workers are noted above I shall deal with them below under separate sub-headings.

Reasons for Female Over-Representation in Psychiatric Services

There are a number of explanations for female over-representation which can be summarised as follows. The reader may wish to consider whether these can be read as additive or competing explanations.

1 *Biological vulnerability* The notion that women are biologically vulnerable to mental distress is expressed in different forms in the mental health industry. One example is the post-natal distress of depression and the less common puerperal psychosis. Few people would dispute the added vulnerability women suffer to distress after the birth of a child. Another example is the role of pre-menstrual tension in creating transient distress or amplifying ongoing psychological problems. A third example is the greater prevalence of senile dementia in women. Problems arise, though, in finding a consensus on *why* women are vulnerable in these ways. Is it that their physiology during the menstrual cycle and in the wake of childbirth is a biological substrate for emotional disturbance? In relation to menstruation could it be that women self-attribute their troubles to a ready bodily target, when the source of their distress lies elsewhere? The physiological argument is very tempting in relation to childbirth, given that a woman's body is subjected to dramatic alterations in hormone levels after birth. However, this physiological state is true of all women, but not all women become distressed. What all women are not subjected to, though, are the same social and biographical factors. For this reason, the meaning of childbirth for women is highly variable, even if they are all under a similar cultural pressure to celebrate a birth and feel happy. Being a mother, especially for the first time, entails some degree of

identity loss. Male partners may become more distant or jealous about their loss of intimacy and care. Finally, under this sub-heading, I noted earlier that women live longer, so increasing the chances of dementia. But given that depression is twice as common in older people than dementia, it follows that more female elders equals more elder female depression.

2 *Social causation* Some who do not challenge the validity of psychiatric diagnosis argue that women are simply under greater social stress than men and that this is reflected in over-representation. In other words, because they are under greater stress, they become mentally ill more often. A number of commentators on women's mental health have drawn attention to the social stressors, which are either peculiar to them, or are experienced more than by men. Let us take some examples.

(a) *Domestic violence* Whereas domestic violence may at times entail two-way traffic, women are subjected to violent assaults by male partners more often than vice versa.

(b) *Food is gender-linked* The purchase and preparation of food are bound up with the female role more often than the male role. For this reason food more readily becomes a focus of symptom formation in women, be it compulsive eating, bulimia or anorexia. These problems are present in men but much less frequently.

(c) *The commodification of the body* Women more than men are subjected to a constant barrage of ideal or desired images of the female form than are men (although the latter are more the target of the advertising industry than in the past). It is interesting that much of the psychotherapeutic discourse about eating disorders in women contains more about the gender role–food link than it does about more external factors such as the fashion industry. As one correspondent put it to a newspaper recently – how can women in their variety of shapes and sizes feel good about themselves when regular fashion columns depict chic clothes on 'stick insects'?

(d) *Sexual violence* Girls and women are more prone to be the victims of sexual violence than are boys and men. The one exception to this is stranger assaults on children. I shall return to the interpretation of the evidence about sexual violence later in this chapter and in Chapter 6.

(e) *Dual role stress* Women, particularly in recent years due to changes in the labour market, are more likely than men to juggle and struggle with domestic tasks and paid work. This increases the probability of experienced stress in women compared to men.

(f) *Poverty* Women are more likely to be poor than men and when in work are paid less well. In Chapter 3, I discussed poverty as a source of mental distress.

3   *Over-representation could be a measurement artefact*   Despite the long and persuasive list given to account for why women suffer more stress-related disorders than men, cautions can be introduced about the core evidence base for this – psychiatric epidemiology. Studies of the relationship between mental illness and marital status demonstrate the potential weakness of this approach. For example, Gove (1984) concluded that married women suffer higher levels of psychiatric morbidity than married men and deduced that this was due to the added stress imposed on wives compared to husbands. This added stress was, it was argued, a function of the stress of the nurturant role of wives. The problem with this reasoning is that it assumes a unitary role outcome for married women. But some married women do not have children and some unmarried ones do (for example, a quarter of children in the UK are born out of wedlock). Moreover, as Busfield (1982) points out, single men are admitted to psychiatric facilities more often than married women. Also, Gove limits his interest to diagnoses which have a higher incidence in women (depression and phobic reactions). However, if a wider range of diagnoses is considered, the gap in representation between the sexes virtually disappears, according to some studies (Dohrenwend and Dohrenwend, 1977; Regier et al., 1988). Which diagnoses are included, I think, is telling. Men are more prone to acting out their distress in an anti-social way and so will have service contact more often than women because of drug and alcohol abuse. Consequently, they are also more likely to receive a diagnosis of personality disorder. By contrast, women are more likely to suffer in silence, be self-harming and receive a diagnosis of depression.

4   *Women are pathologised more readily than men*   This factor subsumes three points. First, normality and maleness are conflated in professional discourses. Second, in modern society rationality has been colonised by men and thus is privileged over the non-rational (creativity and our emotional life). Third, women are more likely to disclose problems than men to professionals and are thus more prone to being labelled and recorded as patients.

MEN AND MENTAL HEALTH SERVICES

The case for women being over-represented in recent and current psychiatric statistics is overwhelming. The explanations offered for this picture were rehearsed in the last section. However, in this section I want to address some cautions about focusing singularly on women. This tendency is undoubtedly widespread in the literature on gender and mental health – a tendency to conflate gender with 'female'. Bearing in mind that my need to redress this balance may be reduced to my motivation as a male writer, I will plod on nonetheless. I should also emphasise at this stage that the cautions I make about male mental health in no way imply that men and women *overall* are equally oppressed, either in the sense of experiencing mental distress or of suffering iatrogenic damage for their troubles. Nonetheless, there are three strong arguments for a rebalancing of attention away from women.

1   Some feminist writers on women and mental health have overstated their case and thereby, through poor scholarship, discredited some of their own legitimate arguments.

2   In some ways, some men are more oppressed by the psychiatric system than are some women.

3   An over-emphasis on women may actually contribute to the construction of women as being psychologically weak.

Feminist Overstatement

During the 1980s, a key text emerged which became a rallying point for feminist students of mental health. Elaine Showalter's *The Female Malady* (1987) provided an account of Victorian psychiatry as being a patriarchal attack upon women. She claimed that women were over-represented in asylum life and that the cultural associations of madness of the time were gendered and were focused on women, not men. However, Busfield (1994), herself an established social analyst of women and madness (and thus not dismissable as an anti-feminist male academic), pointed out that Showalter's view had rapidly become:

> part of feminist orthodoxy, yet has little empirical support . . . the picture Showalter constructs of madness in the nineteenth century is one-sided and the one-sidedness generates a distorted reading of history that undermines rather than facilitates our understanding of women in this period . . . rather than being *a* or *the* female malady, madness took many forms, some of which were linked to women and femininity, and others far less so. Indeed . . . some were linked to men and masculinity and it is the complex interrelation of *gender* and madness, not just of women and madness in isolation, that needs to be examined. (Busfield, 1994: 259)

In her paper, Busfield goes on to substantiate two main criticisms of Showalter's book. The first challenge is about her claim that women were over-represented in psychiatric statistics in the nineteenth century. A re-reading by Busfield of the admission rates demonstrates a roughly equal balance between the two. Busfield enables this re-reading by presenting tables of data from the nineteenth century on asylum populations. It is true that there were more women present in asylums (and then only around 55 per cent, which is not a massive over-representation) but the discrepancy can be accounted for by the higher mortality of men than women in the Victorian institutions. Then, as now, women lived longer and so they exceeded men in terms of *prevalence*. First admissions are, however, a measure of *incidence* and they do not suggest that women were over-represented.

The second plank in Showalter's argument, which Busfield removes, is that cultural representations of madness were predominantly female in form. This is simply erroneous. It is true that the suicidal Ophelia, the sentimental Crazy Kate or Crazy Jane and the violent Lucia were to be found in Victorian art. But so too were recurrent associations between masculinity and madness in the creative madman (e.g. Blake and Nietzsche), the criminal lunatic and masturbatory insanity. By counter-posing these male images, but not denying the existence of the three feminised forms of madness highlighted by Showalter, Busfield drives home her point about a 'distorted reading of history'.

The relevance of Showalter's work is that it is so comforting to feminist critics (with the obvious exception of Busfield) that they relay its errors and thereby compound and expand a specious discourse. For example, summary points from *The Female Malady* are repeated uncritically in a number of texts which discuss women and mental health (e.g. Barnes and Maple, 1992; Ussher and Nicolson, 1992; Parker et al., 1995).

The Psychiatric Oppression of Men

In the last section I discussed the over-representation of women in psychiatric statistics. Most of the discrepancy can be accounted for by two diagnostic groups: depression and dementia. The latter is more of a female problem because women, on average, live longer than men. With regard to depression, this is mainly treated on an outpatient basis with a combination of anti-depressant medication and/or talking treatments. As a consequence, if we evaluate the oppressive role of psychiatry as being in large part about incarceration, and the disability and loss of citizenship which follow in its wake, then it becomes clear that men are treated differentially.

Psychiatry functions, in part, as a repressive wing of the state. It removes liberty without trial and exercises *ad hoc* powers to contain dangerous deviance. Men are more violent than women on average and therefore *all* men can attract the attribution of dangerousness from professionals and other parties who refer in to the psychiatric system. For example, men are more likely to be handcuffed than are women when they are apprehended by the police in public places under suspicion of being mentally disordered (Rogers and Faulkner, 1987). Similarly, rates of seclusion of inpatients and forced admission are greater for men than women. Not surprisingly, then, men are greatly over-represented in secure psychiatric facilities. Whether this over-representation is seen as being a product of stereotyping by professionals and/or a reflection of the actual level of dangerousness of men in society is irrelevant to the point here.

For whatever reason it occurs, the outcome is that men are treated more coercively *more often* in the psychiatric system than are women. I emphasise here the issue of frequency of coercion. I am not arguing that when an *individual* woman is treated coercively, she fares better than an individual male patient. In fact, I would then argue the reverse. That is, the relatively small number of women who find themselves in secure psychiatric facilities endure additional forms of oppression, including the greater risk of sexual harassment and assault from male staff and patients. Potier (1993) reports that 34 out of 40 female patients in a maximum secure hospital with a diagnosis of psychopathy had been sexually abused in childhood. This highlights their vulnerability to sexual re-victimisation.

Take another example – the psychiatric 'treatment' of homosexuality. Before it became unpopular in the mid-1970s on empirical grounds about efficacy, and because of cultural pressure from the gay movement, a difference was discernible in the *way* in which gay men were treated compared to lesbians. The former were dealt with by aversion therapy (using electric shocks), whereas lesbians were more likely to be 'treated' using a more benign combination of counselling and desensitisation (Diamont, 1987).

The Construction of Weak Women?

One of the paradoxes of feminist scholarship has been that it may in part have contributed to the construction of weak women. For example, by emphasising the poorer mental health of women this may contribute to the notion that women are less resilient than men. In the literature on iatrogenic addiction to psychotropic medication there is an emphasis on studying women (Waldron, 1977; Cooperstock, 1978; Gabe and Lipshitz-Phillips, 1982; Gabe and Thorogood, 1986). This academic literature is then reinforced by media representations of women addicts:

> Paradoxically, perhaps, in publicising the dangers of addiction, women who have been prescribed such drugs have been subject to what labelling theorists refer to as 'deviance amplification'. The media, in taking up the problem of minor tranquilliser dependency, has tended to reinforce images of women as helpless, dependent and passive victims of addictive behaviour (Bury and Gabe, 1990). Not only did their original behaviour, or primary deviance, expose women more frequently to an addictive prescribed drug but the consequent addiction then became associated with their gender. (Pilgrim and Rogers, 1993: 37)

Similarly, the study by Brown and Harris (1978), *Social Origins of Depression*, produced a study of the relationship between female experience and depression (see Chapter 6). Men do get depressed but we will know much less about their experience if they are excluded from sociological investigation.

It is important to clarify here that I am not arguing that the psychological distress of women is a *mere* construction. There are adequate empirical grounds for arguing that the causes of female problems are real and peculiar. Sexual victimisation, domestic violence and higher poverty in women are clear examples of this point. Also men are socialised to express their emotions in a different way from women – with a greater taboo on distress. Men seem to express their vulnerability in other ways, such as through violence and alcohol and opiate abuse. However, the way that women are represented (as weak and vulnerable) can become a cultural determinant or self-fulfilling prophecy if it becomes attached to a female identity. In the same way, the representation of the male identity as strong can become a determinant of machismo and the development of a taboo on tenderness in young men.

THE GENDERED MENTAL HEALTH WORKFORCE

I noted above that, as a group, professionals as well as clients contain a gender bias. This is a complex question that goes beyond head counting. For example, women predominate numerically in clinical psychology but it is difficult to discern within that profession a stable and influential feminist discourse. Where feminism has emerged it has done so as an oppositional and minority influence (see, for example, Ussher and Nicolson, 1992). The technologies of the self (see Chapter 8) the profession deploys, such as behaviour therapy, cognitive-behaviour therapy and psychodynamic therapy, are rooted firmly in traditions of male innovation. Moreover, the scientific mandate of clinical psychology can be traced in particular to a form of positivist science, which had more to do with classifying than helping people. This differential psychology trend of a century, set by Galton and pursued by Spearman, Burt and Eysenck, notably entailed no major female contribution.

Similarly, the trend of outpatient psychotherapy set after the First World War was dominated by male military doctors. Whilst some female therapists were to make major contributions, it is difficult to discern a female or feminist stamp to this work. As was mentioned above, the work of Klein provided an exaggerated version of some aspects of the patriarch she followed: an obsession with innate aggression and a commitment to the triumph of the analyst's rationality over the patient's irrationality. Given the devoted life of Anna Freud to her father's work it is little surprise that her own work simply provided a loyal continuity. I shall return later to Busfield's critique of this type of legacy for feminist psychodynamic therapists.

As well as the technologies of the self having a set of masculine origins, the structural constitution of the mental health disciplines is also gendered. For example, even though clinical psychology is numerically dominated by women by a ratio of nearly 2:1 (DH, 1994), they are under-represented in the upper echelons of the profession (Pilgrim and Treacher, 1992). The same pattern applies in Britain to mental health nursing (68 per cent female), occupational therapy (95 per cent female) and child psychotherapy (75 per cent female) (DH, ibid.).

The relationship between gender representation and knowledge is also important to consider. For example, if the leadership of the mental health professions is dominated by men *and* the historical roots of a discipline's knowledge base are masculine, this may explain why the customs and practices of the mental health professions may be slow to change, even when women swell a profession's ranks. For example, female psychiatrists may be as biological and traditional in their practice as their male colleagues and female clinical psychologists may be as ready as their male colleagues to promote an applied scientist model to their work.

The patriarchal inertia which creates a conservative drag in the mental health professions at the same time can be identified in its converse – radical challenges in the status quo of mental health work. A scan of the major oppositional currents in mental health work over the past 50 years points to few female innovators. All of the 'anti-psychiatrists' of repute were men (Laing, Cooper, Szasz, Basaglia). Person-centred therapy began with a man (Rogers). Even within Anglo-American sociological work, which has illuminated the oppressed role of women and its link with mental distress, the key research programme leaders have been male (Brown and Gove). The same is even true of innovations about qualitative methods – recently feminist research has pushed strongly for ethnographic and biographical research but the sources of these approaches can be found in one wing of the male-dominated Chicago School of the 1930s.

These points are being raised not to disparage the competence of women, either as clinicians or as mental health researchers, but to highlight the inertia created by male domination, both historically in knowledge production about mental health and, more recently, in terms of clinical innovation. I shall return below to this question of male domination of the mental health industry and Busfield's appraisal of the implications of this legacy for feminist mental health work.

DISCUSSION: WOMEN, MEN AND PSYCHOTHERAPY

Having summarised the literature on gender and mental health, it is clear that men are doubly problematic. First, the development of the masculine identity entails the experience of emotional vulnerability in a different way from women. Men are more prone both to avoid expressing and experimenting with certain sorts of emotion during their early life. This leads to a life-long diffidence in understanding their emotional life via relationships and in sharing their problems. When they do express distress it is more likely than in women to be in terms of aggressive actions which have consequences for others, either directly or indirectly. Examples of these include violence, alcohol and drug misuse and suicide. This is not to argue that men and women are quite distinct groups in this regard. After all, women also engage in these actions as well – but less frequently.

Conversely men may starve and injure themselves, share their distress with others or become depressed but they do so less frequently than women.

A second way in which men are problematic is in terms of their greater propensity as therapists to abuse their clients. Again to be quite clear about this, women may also abuse clients but they do so less frequently. Whether we understand these differences in terms of socially determined expectations of patriarchal power (which tips over into abuse), or in terms of the testosterone levels in men making them more sexually predatory than women, or a combination of the two, the outcome is not in dispute. As with the sexual victimisation of children by adults being dominated by men, so too with abuse in therapy. This leads to a contradictory scenario whereby men are generally more 'emotionally illiterate' and less inter-personally benign than women and yet they have been the trend setters and product champions of psychotherapeutic schools.

In the latter regard the patriarchal character of psychotherapy simply mirrors wider social relations this century. The number of female leaders has been relatively small. Ironically one of these few, Melanie Klein, spawned a form of practice which, as I noted earlier, has the least tenderness of all the therapeutic styles. Overall, men have constructed representations of the world more frequently than women. If their bodies cannot bear children, their minds have created maps and models. For example, Bannister (1983), when summarising core models of practice in psychotherapy, uses a set of metaphors. These models have all been developed by men: 'trainer–trainee' (the behaviourism of Skinner and other male learning theorists); 'friend and friend' (the humanism of Rogers); 'priest–penitent' (Freud's psychoanalytical confessional); and 'supervisor–researcher' (Kelly's personal construct therapy). (I return to Bannister's work in Chapter 7.)

I could offer others to add to this list such as Ellis and Beck, as leaders of cognitive therapy, and the same pattern recurs – men innovate more than women in psychotherapy. However, this role may be the opposite side of the same coin of abusive power in therapy. To lead, innovate and make a mark can be seen *inter alia* as being a manifestation of male domination, imposition and penetration, albeit in a creative form. This contradiction is emphasised because the leadership role of men in psychotherapeutic theory may provide male practitioners with an unwarranted legitimacy. The very rationalism of theory and the bullish desire to proselytise about a new truth system (see my preface to the book) does not necessarily inspire confidence in male practitioner competence.

Given that psychotherapy is of marginal utility, because its overall cost-effectiveness is undermined by deterioration effects, it is important to look carefully at who is letting the side down. The reasons for deterioration effects are complex and implicate a number of client and therapist variables but it is clear that one source of iatrogenic damage in psychological treatments is abuse. If a client makes themself vulnerable in a private situation with a therapist by presenting their distress and sharing their personal life in a way which is not reciprocated by the therapist, then the latter must exercise constant restraint. Generally, men seem to be less successful in this task and professional duty than women.

However, because patients can be sexually abused in therapy by female therapists as well, even if less often, removing male therapists from the mental health industry would constitute an improvement but not a cure. It would penalise competent male therapists who are non-abusers. Other possible strategies are available to protect clients. These include therapist supervision; regular tape recordings of sessions; decisive punitive action against proven abusers; and the separation of clients and therapists according to the sexuality of each. The last of these would entail male–male and female–female therapist/client pairings when both were heterosexual, and male–female or female–male therapist/client pairings when one or both are homosexual, etc. The logic of this is that the sexuality *of the therapist* is predicted to be the main risk factor. It predicts that gay therapists can be trusted not to sexually abuse female clients, heterosexual male therapists can be trusted not to sexually abuse male clients, etc. The erotic emphasis here points up the possibility that potential *emotional* abuse may be present in any relationship and is thus independent of gender or sexuality.

Turning from the question of male dominance in psychotherapy, I now want to briefly address the adequacy of the professional feminist response. In order for feminist therapy and feminist psychologies to emerge, it can be taken for granted that male dominance provoked such an opposition. If this were not the case, then the older patriarchs I noted above would have provided a body of work which was sensitive and fair to women. Feminist objection became possible *because* male professionals had been insensitive and unfair in their depictions of women's emotional lives. The question that is begged, though, is whether or not the feminist objection has successfully diverted male psychology from its original trajectory.

In her recent overview of this field, Busfield (1996, Ch. 9) provides a balance sheet about the success of the feminist psychologies. She argues that the following positive points about feminist work can be listed: it emphasises a sensitivity to the complexities of inner life; it elaborates ways of understanding gender differences in symptom formations and the gendered expression of feelings; and it incorporates the advantages from Freudian psychology of emphasising the importance of childhood. I would sympathise with the second and third of these points, but the first may be less persuasive given that psychodynamic and existentialist male professionals could also boast the first positive point.

What Busfield at the same time persuasively argues is that the feminist psychologies have been inadequate on two main counts. The first of these is that the emphasis upon the psychoanalytical legacy has led to a limited and essentialist conception of female experience. That is, feminist therapists (e.g. Mitchell, 1975; Bordo, 1979; Eichenbaum and Orbach,

1982), in adhering too closely to the logic of psychoanalysis, reproduce its limitations. There is a tendency to generalise about the human condition and this weakness is not lessened by focusing on women rather than the whole of humanity. What it does is produce a body of work which is insensitive to cultural diversity and the variability of experience created by race and class. (In Chapter 8 I will offer a more sustained critique of Orbach's promotion of psychoanalytical ideas, as she has gone out of her way to place herself in the public domain by using journalism.)

A second and related problem for feminist psychologies, which Busfield highlights and I have elaborated elsewhere (Pilgrim, 1992) is that psychodynamic models actively dissuade their audience from considering *external* factors, when understanding mental health problems. The preoccupation of psychoanalysis with inner life is not just a matter of emphasis – there is an active rejection of the role of external reality, with subjectivity, especially the unconscious, being fetishised. In particular Busfield argues we need instead to:

> examine some of the key social and cultural factors that can have a differential impact on men's and women's mental state – either because they impinge unevenly on men and women or because of the socially generated differences in response. (Busfield, 1996: 186–7)

What Busfield draws attention to is a sphere of influence that psychodynamic theories scorn or grudgingly accept as a secondary influence upon psychopathology – a real outer world. In Chapter 9 I will return to this type of critique when discussing the recent work of Smail.

Thus, whilst feminist therapists have made some inroads into the legacy of male-dominated psychology their success has been limited by two main factors: an over-reliance on psychoanalysis and a tendency towards psychological reductionism. Ironically, some objectivist models which account for psychological distress arguably offer a more sensitive, multi-layered and multi-factorial understanding of female experience in its social context than does the substantial input of feminist therapists. For example, the work of Brown and his colleagues, which I pick up in more detail in Chapter 6, can be situated within a Durkheimian positivist framework. However, despite the objectivist pitfalls of this tradition, the work of Brown et al. manages to bring alive both the mental life of women, and the current and past social situations which make them vulnerable to distress or protect them from such a fate. By contrast, the writings of feminist therapists that Busfield critiques are prone to psychological reductionism. The radical (and sincere) subjectivism of feminist therapists may divert necessary attention from the outer material circumstances of women's lives.

To conclude in this chapter, the relationship between women, men and mental health has been unevenly researched and remains a highly contested body of knowledge. A number of unresolved problems remain about women, men and psychotherapy especially in relation to men's trustworthiness to practice. Also, because of the gendered history of mental health work, there remains the contradiction that male researchers have pioneered both qualitative methodologies and the illumination of female distress in its social context. At the same time, to date, this masculine domination of both research and the mental health professions has disabled feminist therapists from developing a body of knowledge which marks a genuine break from its patriarchal past.

The final problem to note about feminist mental health work is that its psychological reductionism may reflect a fault line which goes deeper than gender. The criticism Busfield makes about feminist therapists being flawed in their analysis by an evasion of outer material reality could be made in principle about psychotherapy. The latter, by definition, is psychological not sociological in its focus. As a consequence psychotherapists in general are prone to wear social blinkers and are unreliable commentators about other variables such as race, class and age as well as gender.

5

Races Apart

Take up the White Man's burden –
And reap his old reward:
The blame of those ye better,
The hate of those ye guard

Rudyard Kipling, The White Man's Burden

INTRODUCTION

Just as mental health status is correlated with class and gender, the same is true of race and ethnicity. This chapter will examine the patterning of mental health problems in relation to racial and ethnic background with reference to three social groups: Afro-Caribbean people, Asian people and Irish people. Terminology is contested in relation to this topic. I will note some relevant points but not resolve debates.

The term 'race' is used to denote differences between people according to their external biological features, including, and especially, their skin colour. Some people object to this emphasis on the grounds that it is rooted in the categorisations set up by anthropologists from colonial powers. Moreover, given that outward manifestations of *Homo sapiens* are not strictly or neatly divided but form continua, and given that people from any social group can mate and produce offspring, there are good grounds for not making biological distinctions between people from all over the world. However, because race has also become a focus of identity (i.e. as with 'gender', a social not a biological phenomenon) for the colonised as well as the coloniser, it remains a term used meaningfully by a variety of people for a variety of reasons. In other words it may be logical to ditch racial categorisations, but these retain both a psychological and a sociological salience for both the ex-colonised and the ex-coloniser.

The term 'ethnicity' refers to an identity which emerges from membership of a particular cultural and linguistic group or nationality. Thus, whilst the Dutch and the Irish are, predominantly, both white-skinned, they belong to different ethnic groups. Another example might be the difference between a Bangladeshi and a Sri Lankan. Both might be called 'Asian' within a racial category set up by their ex-coloniser but they have different ethnic backgrounds. The disquiet around notions of race applies also to ethnicity, given that the discourse of ethnicity has been associated with questions of exclusion and inclusion, which, taken to their extreme, become the basis for decisions about genocide. In recent years the practice of 'ethnic cleansing' in the Balkans reminds us of this tendency and, despite the international trauma experienced in the wake of the Nazi Holocaust, of an enduring genocidal impulse across cultures.

However, the terminological controversies about ethnicity are complicated by the tendency for self-proclaimed ethnic identities to emerge from, as well as about, both defensive and offensive groups. For example, the Irish identity is constructed in part by the proud commitment of some Irish people to their cultural traditions, as well as by the derisive stereotypes made about them by some English people. Along with the Scots and the Welsh, who were also colonised by the English, the Irish are concerned with the preservation of Celtic traditions and languages. This struggle has been fought from a reactive or defensive position of exclusion and oppression. By contrast the English coloniser's identity was constructed with an emphasis on an assumed superiority. Thus there is a different political significance if the English self-proclaim their ethnic identity than there is if those on the colonised Celtic fringe do so. A paradox this has set up is that because the Celtic people of Britain have fought to preserve their identity in a post-colonial context, they have produced a clear discourse about themselves. By contrast, the English identity was subsumed within that of being 'British', because the English were the colonial elite. Consequent upon the loss of empire, the English identity has now become fragile and vague. A more elaborate discussion of the contested status of both race and ethnicity in social science can be found in Rex (1986) and Anthias (1992).

The chapter is split into three main sections. The first will outline some general sociological considerations which are relevant to the study of race, ethnicity and health. The second will examine the evidence on the racial and ethnic patterning of mental health problems in relation to three exemplar groups. In the third section I will examine the degree to which psychotherapy has engaged with the material discussed in the first two sections.

SOME GENERAL SOCIOLOGICAL CONSIDERATIONS

The discussion in Chapter 2 about the need to respect objectivist, as well as experiential, methods is particularly relevant in relation to race and ethnicity. For example, take the central question of racism. The micro-process of racism implicates perpetrators and victims, and thus an inter-personal understanding of the phenomenon is clearly important in order to elucidate the motives of the first group and the impact on the second. However, another appropriate question is whether racism has a population level impact. For example, does it lead to systematic differences in, say, morbidity or employment levels? These are essentially quantitative questions addressed appropriately within an objectivist framework. In order to demonstrate the social relevance of racism, *both* qualitative and quantitative methods are relevant and applicable.

As well as the opposition between objectivist and subjectivist methodologies being relevant to debates about the study of race and ethnicity, a related tension exists between structural and cultural accounts. A greater emphasis on the structural determinants of racial differences will expose the role of a racist society but it will lose the fine grain differences which exist between and within cultures. On the other hand, an over-emphasis on cultural differences may capture the experience of being in an ethnic minority but this may give undue salience to 'lifestyle differences', at the expense of considering structural factors such as the impact of institutional racism. This can culminate in 'victim blaming'.

Smaje (1996) has noted that an approach to race, ethnicity and health which avoids these false oppositions should entail the following research agenda: genetics; migration; material factors; cultural factors; and racism. This is a useful framework because the list ensures that every major debate about race, ethnicity and health is raised. I will summarise some points here about each of the items on Smaje's agenda.

• *Genetics* This has been a central part of the discourse of eugenics and so it must be addressed. It has also led to the tendency to reject the relevance of genetic differences in order to avoid the accusation of inevitable racism. However, whilst most (75 per cent) of the genetic material of human beings is identical in all of us, and most (85 per cent) of the genetic variation which does exist occurs between individuals not races, the latter do show some demonstrable differences (about 7 per cent of variation) (Jones, 1981; Rose et al., 1984). The upshot of this is that whilst races cannot be clearly differentiated between one another on genetic grounds there may be some differences in genetic *susceptibility* to levels of disease between one racial group and another. For example, sickle cell anaemia and phenylketonuria both occur in Northern European and African people. However, the incidence of sickle cell disease is greater for Africans than it is for North Europeans. By contrast, the reverse balance of incidence occurs for phenylketonuria.

• *Migration* This can have multiple implications for health. Immigrants may encounter new health threats in their host country. Individual emigrants may represent 'strong' or 'weak' examples from their country of origin. The psychosocial implications of migration in terms of hopes and expectations, dashed or achieved in the host country, can affect health. These effects are also influenced by whether or not the migration is achieved voluntarily, in a spirit of optimism, or coerced under conditions of distress, as in slavery and the refugees of warfare. Finally, the economic reasons for migration may lead to labour patterns which are racialised in a host country. For example, the families of Caribbean men working in low-paid jobs in London and Birmingham, or those of Asian men in Pennine mill work, have left in place racial groups living in circumscribed localities at certain income levels. These specific factors may all be implicated in health outcomes.

- *Material factors* These would include the health impact of low pay, unemployment and housing disadvantage on immigrants. At least some but not all of this impact is as a result of poverty.
- *Cultural factors* As with genetics, considering cultural differences to have a causal influence on health invites charges of racism and victim blaming (Andrews and Jewson, 1993). There is certainly a danger of accounting for the ill-health of ethnic minorities in terms of their peculiar 'lifestyles'. Nonetheless, a series of studies have identified the influence of a number of cultural (and within this familial) factors on health. These include levels of conflict within families (Sweeting and West, 1995); kinship and social networks (Dressler, 1988); and religious belief (Levin, 1994). As Smaje (ibid.) notes, cultural differences may account for health *gains* as well as losses.
- *Racism* This has two potential impacts on health, one direct, the other indirect. The first effect relates to the immediate detrimental impact on the well-being of victims of racism. Examples would include the psychological distress and or physical injury which follow racial abuse or attacks. The second effect entails structural racism mediating socio-economic disadvantage which feeds back into material factors above.

RACE, ETHNICITY AND MENTAL HEALTH

Having considered some general points about race, ethnicity and health I will now move more specifically to the topic of mental health. In this section I will examine the relationship between race, ethnicity and mental health by the use of three case studies in Britain of Afro-Caribbean, Asian and Irish people. The pertinence of these groups is that they are all: derived from ex-British colonies; present in Great Britain (the largest of the British Isles); and have data accumulated about their psychiatric profile. Moreover, whilst they all have separate ethnic identities (from one another and from the white English), the Irish are white and so are indistinguishable, superficially or 'phenotypically', from their ex-coloniser. This sets up an interesting triangular comparison with both race and ethnicity being considerations in part.

Afro-Caribbean Mental Health in Great Britain

Afro-Caribbean people are subject to peculiar scrutiny by the mental health industry in a number of ways.

1   There is consistent evidence that they are over-represented in admissions to psychiatric beds (Carpenter and Brockington, 1980; Dean et al., 1981). Whereas, in Britain, 8 per cent of all psychiatric patients are detained compulsorily, up to 30 per cent of Afro-Caribbean patients are being held in inpatient settings at any point in time against their will.

2   Young black men in Britain are referred to secure psychiatric settings via the courts 29 times more frequently than their white counterparts (Cope, 1989). They are less likely to be given bail and more likely to be subject to court orders requiring compulsory psychiatric treatment than whites (Browne, 1990). They are more likely than whites to be apprehended by the police in public settings and referred by them for psychiatric assessments (Bean et al., 1991).

3   Afro-Caribbeans are *less* likely to be referred by GPs to psychiatrists and are under-represented in outpatient (i.e. voluntary) service contact (Hitch and Clegg, 1980; Littlewood and Cross, 1980).

4   They are more likely to be diagnosed as schizophrenic but less likely to be diagnosed as depressed than white Britons.

5   Afro-Caribbean patients are more likely to receive physical treatment than whites, with major tranquillisers and ECT being used with a greater frequency (Littlewood and Cross, 1980; Chen et al., 1991).

The overall picture is one of black people being labelled as schizophrenic more often than whites and receiving higher levels of ECT and major tranquillisers. Conversely they are under-represented in outpatient and other voluntary settings and are less likely to receive psychological treatments than whites.

Some psychiatrists account for this picture in terms of the higher incidence of schizophrenia in black people. Once this argument is made then the other findings such as greater use of coercion and the use of major tranquillisers falls into place (e.g. Cope, 1989). Others argue that black people have more psychological distress than whites but culturally insensitive professionals misdiagnose this as schizophrenia because they cannot understand their symptoms (Littlewood and Lipsedge, 1982; Fernando, 1988). The argument of those, like Cope, about the greater incidence of 'schizophrenia' in Afro-Caribbeans may or may not be racist. If it implies, eugenic fashion, that black people are genetically vulnerable to madness then racism is suggested. On the other hand, the stress of living as a black person in a racist, white–dominated world might be seen as a precipitating factor. In other words black people (it might be argued) are driven crazy more often than white people.

Asian Mental Health in Great Britain

Studies of psychiatric epidemiology point to a mixed picture about the representation of Asian people. Some indicate over-representation (e.g. Carpenter and Brockington, 1980); others point to over-representation for Pakistani immigrants and under-representation for Indian immigrants

(Hitch, 1981). This highlights a conundrum about this group compared to the others I discuss in this chapter where over-representation is unambiguous. Whilst all three groups discussed in this chapter are subjected to pejorative stereotyping, discrimination and racist attacks, this does not translate into an equal recorded distribution of mental ill-health across the groups within an unwelcoming ex-colonial host country. Arguably Asian people have been subjected to more direct racist vitriol in Great Britain than the other two groups. Fascist groups like the National Front and the British National Party are renowned as a recurring source of racist violence which has been targeted predominantly upon Asians, both in their homes and on the streets. If the direct stress of overt racist violence was the main source of distress then the Asian group should have higher, if not the highest, incidence of recorded mental ill-health of all the black or ethnic groups.

Compared to the work on Afro-Caribbean patients, there has been relatively little research produced on Asian mental health. Moreover, the work which has been produced has focused on Asian women (Currer, 1986; Krause, 1989; Fenton and Sadiq, 1993). Some of these studies emphasise that Asian women 'somatise' their mental distress (Currer, 1986). However, such an assertion is based upon the assumption within Western medical positivism that there are simple, universal distinctions to be made between physical and mental illness. Fenton and Sadiq-Sangster (1996: 69) react against the notion that Asian women simply somatise depression by noting that:

> It could mean several different things: (a) a non-recognition of mental illness, so that ailments are always presented as somatic, (b) a non-recognition of the link between physical ailments and emotional states, (c) a presentation of ailments as somatic despite some recognition of mental distress, and (d) simply a non-presentation of mental symptoms to bio-medical doctors.

Thus two styles of study about mental distress in Asian women can be identified: those based upon the assumption that mental illness is 'disguised' or expressed by physical symptoms; and those which keep an open mind about all four possibilities noted above. In the first group some reviewers assert that Asian culture simply fails to have a notion of psychological causation (Ineichen, 1987). Others argue that family support is a protective factor against mental distress (Cochrane and Stopes-Roe, 1981). Of course tight patriarchal control may mean that distress is not reduced in Asian families but that it is withheld from public domains, including those involving health service contact.

Krause (1989) and Fenton and Sadiq (1993) emphasise the centrality of the heart in South Asian culture so that an elision takes place about 'the heart sinking' (*dil ghirda hai*) and sadness. Experientially one does not stand for the other; they are part of the same subjective state. The separation of bodily and mental distress, though, is itself a product of Western Cartesian dualism. The distinction made by Western medicine between physical and mental illness is just that, a distinction – but one that is reified as a universal, trans-historical truth.

Thus, the arguments about mental health problems in ethnic minorities usefully raise some fundamental problems about psychiatric knowledge. When inside a Western discourse (psychiatric or otherwise) the tendency is to assume that its descriptions of the world are valid and superior to the constructions offered in other parts of the world. For example, the notion of, say, 'depression' is seen as valid and non-problematic. It is further assumed that it is universally encountered and experienced. Any deviation in expression from the Western norm is then described as a distortion of reality. Consequently, because Asian people talk in terms, say, of 'a falling heart', this is construed by Western psychiatric commentators as a disguised or distorted ('somatised') version of another 'true' condition (i.e. 'depression').

All of this may have a bearing on the epidemiological question about why Asian people are not necessarily over-represented in psychiatric statistics, despite their high levels of both poverty and experienced racism. If Asian people themselves do not readily and straightforwardly present with problems that fall neatly into the picture of Western mental illness, and if they have a strong association between mental health problems, stigma and shame, the combined effect might be mental health service 'under-utilisation'. However, substantial caution should be used when speculating about the whole question of mental health service utilisation by Asian people. Watters (1996), in a recent review of the topic of Asian mental health makes the point that despite the contradictory and sparse empirical evidence about the topic, a number of social-psychiatric commentators (e.g. Cochrane and Stopes-Roe, 1981; Littlewood and Lipsedge, 1982) have made rash deductions. Watters points to a number of unsustainable attributions and generalisations in the social-psychiatric literature which include: the uncritical acceptance of the 'somatisation' thesis; the assumption that Islam is a robust protective factor against distress but Hinduism is not; and the assumption that Indians have an easier migration experience than Pakistanis.

Watters goes on to note that as well as these unsustainable claims operating, they are part of a white social-psychiatric research enterprise which is in search of a *consistent pattern applicable to all Asians*. This *a priori* assumption may itself reflect a homogenisation stereotype. Given that 'Asians' are from a vast sub-continent spanning several countries, regions, religions and cultures, why should we expect (simply on logical grounds) to end up with empirical consistency about Asian mental health? Such an expectation of homogeneity can only be explained by the racially biased pre-empirical assumptions of social-psychiatric researchers. Moreover, as well as Asians *not* being a homogenous group, they do not necessarily, encounter the same style or efficiency of services, uniformly, in every locality in their host country. It could be that different rates of psychiatric hospitalisation reported in the literature between Manchester and Bradford are not a result of a patient variable but a service variable. Maybe Bradford has more racially sensitive preventative services than Manchester. Such a consideration is ignored, though, in favour of attempts to speculate about the inconsistent findings being a product of *patient characteristics*.

Irish Mental Health in Great Britain

Unlike Afro-Caribbean people in Britain, the Irish are over-represented in *all* diagnostic categories officially recorded. Moreover, whereas over-representation is a feature in male Afro-Caribbeans, both men and women from an Irish background are over-represented. Table 5.1 shows the elevated rates of diagnosis for schizophrenia and other disorders in different ethnic groups.

Table 5.1 *Ethnicity and psychiatric diagnosis: rates of mental hospital admission per 100,000 population by diagnosis and gender, England 1981*

Diagnosis	Country of birth							
	Eire		N. Ireland		England		Caribbean	
	M	F	M	F	M	F	M	F
Schizophrenia	158	174	103	111	61	58	259	235
Psychoses	36	50	28	52	16	27	28	40
Depression	197	410	143	266	79	166	65	52
Neuroses	62	111	44	80	28	56	6	5
Personality disorder	62	80	50	52	30	35	22	42
Alcohol abuse	332	133	261	90	38	18	13	0
Drug abuse	13	8	17	8	5	3	13	0

Source: from Cochrane and Bal, 1989: 4

The Irish are particularly interesting as a case study for a number of reasons:

1   Their over-representation applies to all diagnostic groups.

2   Both men and women are over-represented, with females showing even more elevated rates of diagnosis than males.

3   Cross-national comparisons demonstrate that this pattern of over-representation applies in host countries other than Great Britain.

4   The Irish have elevated rates for the diagnosis of schizophrenia *in Ireland* compared to the average international incidence.

5   Despite this exaggerated picture of recorded psychopathology, at home and abroad, there has been a relative silence about Irish mental health. For example, in the British psychiatric literature much more has been published on Afro-Caribbean people. Moreover, the latter has come overwhelmingly from white British, not Afro-Caribbean researchers. In the case of the Irish, most of the small literature which has emerged has come from *Irish* researchers (e.g. Clare, 1974; Walsh, 1987) or second generation

Table 5.2   *The relationship*
between the English and the Irish

English	Irish
Dominant	Submissive
Exhibitionism	Spectatorship
Succourance	Dependence

Source: Kenny, 1985: 73

Irish or Anglo-Irish scholars from Great Britain (e.g. Greenslade, 1992; Jones, 1997).

How can we account for the above picture? Given that there are elevated rates of psychiatric diagnosis at home and abroad, it is unlikely that the stress of migration *per se* can explain the picture. Equally, because there is a greater incidence of distress in all diagnostic groups – including those like reactive depression which, *ipso facto*, have exogenous ante-cedents – the picture cannot be accounted for by a crude genetic explanation. Indeed, the work that has been done on Irish mental health seems to have generated more questions than answers.

One influential attempt at explaining the vulnerability of Irish people to psychological distress has centred on the post-colonial identity and the social and existential challenges facing the Irish (Kenny, 1985; Greenslade, 1992). In Greenslade's account (following Fanon, 1970) the Irish faced the historical insults of colonisation, loss of language, forced migration and mass starvation under British rule. They now face an existential uncertainty in the wake of this legacy, which is compounded by continued social dislocation from net emigration and their physical proximity to, and economic reliance on, the ex-colonial power. (At the time of writing, the latter remains in power in the six northern-eastern counties of Ireland.)

Kenny (ibid.) offers another version of this cultural domination hypo-thesis about Irish psychological vulnerability. Kenny applies the ideas of Bateson (1942) on cultural differences in psychological development. He argues that the relationship between England and Ireland can be under-stood in terms of three patterns of relating which are child rearing analogues (see Table 5.2).

According to Kenny these analogues are not accidental – they are derived from the child rearing practices of the English upper middle class. The colonial relationship entailed the English dominating and the Irish submitting. The former exhibited their power and the Irish looked on. The Irish became dependent and the English then offered them succour (e.g. soup kitchens during the great famine). Colonisation entailed the English crushing the autonomy of the Irish and infantilising them. These oppressive processes were internalised by the Irish and so they now are self-oppressing (in their child rearing practices and their inner lives). Such self-oppression increases the probability of mental distress. The idea that Irish child rearing practices may be atypically oppressive was suggested also by Scheper-Hughes (1979) in her ethnographic study of Irish culture and its relationship to mental health.

In a recent comprehensive review of Irish mental health, Jones (1997) suggests that all too often single factor explanations have led investigators into blind alleys. He argues that a more sophisticated and elaborate framework should include a *concomitant* investigation of economic, social, cultural, psychological and biological variables. This more holistic research programme might include the following factors which, to date, have been offered as single (and thus reductionist) explanations for over-representation:

1 class-based factors (low socio-economic status)
2 stress associated with rural living
3 high out-group migration
4 single status
5 maternal age at birth
6 service over-utilisation, including high readmission due to social and cultural factors
7 season of birth
8 viral infection
9 obstetric complication.

This multi-factorial suggestion for a research programme on Irish mental health is made by Jones not only to alert us to the problem of single factor, reductionist, aetiological arguments, but also to draw attention to the need for research which respects notions of meaning as well as cause. That is, psychiatric epidemiology operates in a billiard ball universe of cause and effect. By contrast, the ethnographic approach of anthropology (e.g. Scheper-Hughes, 1979) dwells on the meanings attached to emotions and deviance in their cultural context. Jones argues that *both* causal antecedents and meanings need to be investigated (implicating quantitative and qualitative methods). He provides an example here of this both/and rather than either/or approach:

> For example, when considering a factor such as advanced maternal age, as it relates to the incidence of psychiatric morbidity, we need not only consider the obstetric arguments (preliminary as they may be) but also the psychological influence and sociological implications of having older parents (including an increased risk of parental loss). It is at this level, the level of meaning, that the traditional epidemiological approach has less to offer. (1997: 131)

In other words, personal accounts of ordinary Irish people and ethnographic observations of their culture are a necessary complement in this expanded research programme – epidemiology is not enough.

The plea for a multi-factorial research programme and methodological tolerance from Jones is also a caution against the enthusiastic explanations of cultural researchers, such as Greenslade and Kenny discussed above, who write as if their argument is already won or their case proven. It seems likely that the lessons from Fanon or Bateson about the post-colonial personality may well apply to the Irish, but whether they offer a *definitive* explanation for such a consistent picture of over-representation in psychiatric statistics at home and abroad seems doubtful. Bateson's strictures as a general systems theorist (see Chapter 2) would remind us that multi-factorial models should be the norm not the exception in social scientific explanations.

CRITICAL READING: PSYCHOTHERAPY AND ITS
RELATIVE SILENCE ON RACE

During the time that I have straddled the discourses of clinical psychology and sociology I have come across few examples of a recurring connection being made between psychotherapy, and race and ethnicity. The one major exception to this has been the extensive work on cross-cultural counselling. Draguns (1996) summarises developments in this project in terms of overcoming the challenge of a 'cultural gulf' which can exist when clients do not come from a 'cultural mainstream'. An explicit assumption being made in cross-cultural counselling is that interventions have been conceptualised and practised in such a mainstream. Draguns lists the following response to the challenge this poses when attempting to extend help to racial and ethnic minorities.

1   Culturally sensitive workers from the mainstream start with their dominant understandings of working with clients from their own racial or ethnic group and then tentatively test out how far these work or fail to work with clients from outside their group (Berry, 1969).

2   The second response is to start by developing a full understanding of the values, norms, mores and healing practices of a particular minority with the explicit aim of respecting and even co-opting these practices rather than imposing the models of the 'mainstream' (Nwachuku and Ivey, 1991; Nathan, 1994).

3   Another response has been to identify obstacles to effective and helpful interventions, with a view to overcoming or removing these impediments. For example, there is cultural variability in attitudes towards self-disclosure to strangers and to members of the opposite sex. There are also differences in expectations about levels of directiveness from designated authority figures.

4   Draguns describes the fourth response as the most elaborate, namely 'cultural accommodation' (Higginbotham et al., 1988), which contains and extends all the above three items. It entails planning mental health services by collecting data on a culturally diverse population to be served, negotiating with particular groups about their needs and preferences and then converting this audit into practical steps. The latter would entail

developing culturally sensitive services which were approachable and accessible and which contained personnel and interventions which were acceptable to clients and prospective clients.

These commendable strategies to provide mental health services which are inclusive rather than exclusive are, by definition, pragmatic attempts to respond as widely as is possible to diverse individual expressions of distress. As such, they do not delve too deeply into the racial patterning of distress (as examined above in my three case studies) nor do they debate the possible merits of separatism or collective struggle. Indeed, the central goal of 'cultural gulf' reduction has, as its dominant ideological motif, an optimism about the potential benefits of tolerant multi-culturalism: an interpersonal, not a political, strategy. Its emphasis is on integration and co-operation not the conflict implied by either Marxism or the new social movements which include, for example, the black movement. Cross-cultural counselling has been developed most extensively in the USA where, as a nation receiving voluntary immigrants, refugees and slaves, socio-political stability has depended *inter alia* on the success of multi-culturalism and inter-racial tolerance. As I note below, optimism about the potential of good personal relationships is itself a cultural feature and product of US society.

Despite these cautions about the completeness of cross-cultural coun-selling as a basis for analysing the relationship between race, ethnicity and mental health, it provides substantial advantages compared to the 'colour blind' generalisations of positivistic bio-medical psychiatry. The scientistic assumptions in the latter about both diagnosis and treatment lead tradi-tional Western psychiatric practitioners to be insensitive to the problems created by their ignorance of cross-cultural differences. Therapists working across cultural boundaries cannot hope to develop a positive and empathic alliance with their client group unless they are aware of differences in norms and values (McGoldrick et al., 1982). Indeed, in some cases, they may so fundamentally misconstrue the communications of clients that the professional's incompetence at understanding may be transformed into attributions about client mental illness (Horwitz, 1983; Rosenberg, 1992; Offer and Sabshin, 1984).

Another implication of a failure to understand those from a different background is that talking treatments would not filter in such clients or that such clients would drop out of treatment readily. This is precisely the case according to the US studies which have focused on ethnic minority service use. High drop-out rates from psychotherapy for black patients were noted in an early study by Rosenthal and Franks (1957). This pattern was confirmed by Yamamoto et al. (1968) in relation to black and Hispanic Americans being offered talking treatments less often than whites, and droppping out more frequently at an early stage.

Moving back to my introductory observation in this section, the implications of race in psychotherapy, if the cross-cultural counselling

literature is exempted, are rarely heard. Why is this the case? The
following factors may be relevant in answering the question posed.

1   The two major roots of Western psychotherapy (depth psychology
and humanism) are products of particular cultures. They represented a
break from, but transformation of, Judaistic and Christian cultural values,
over the past hundred years, and a shift towards scientific rationalism,
framed in a clinical context. (An important exception to this was the
insertion by Jung of neo-Paganism into a modern psychotherapeutic
discourse (Noll, 1996).) The fact that these two therapeutic traditions
were subsequently found lacking by later anti-subjectivists (e.g. Eysenck,
1952) does not detract from this point about the epistemological genesis
of psychotherapy. A common feature of psychoanalysis and client-centred
counselling is that they proffer techniques which are *universally and trans-
historically applicable.* They are north hemisphere Western technocentric
rationales, just as much as, say, vaccination or antibiotics.

2   The innovators of these two traditions are, by and large, what some
feminist critics disparagingly dub 'DWEMs' (dead, white European males)
mixed with what could be added as 'DWAMs' (dead, white American
males). In other words, there is a racial and geographical dimension to the
emergence of psychotherapy. This leaves Western mental health workers
with a narrow legacy about healing and an ignorance about other ways of
understanding and responding to distress and difference. As Fernando
(1991) has pointed out, there is a wide range of such alternative approaches
throughout the world but most Western mental health workers remain
ignorant about their existence.

3   The *cultural* aspect of parts of the Western legacy is somewhat
different in each case, even though they share certain assumptions (see
point 5). In the case of depth psychology, a culture of male Jewish medical
practitioners (cf. the note on Jung in Chapter 7) developed a version of
biographical exploration which secularised certain Judaistic themes about
our dark inner nature and individual responsibility. The implications of
childhood sexuality were offensive to bourgeois European society and so
Freud and his followers retained a marginal role for many years. Such
marginality was merely a continuation of the social position of the
European Jewish diaspora. Even today, despite the niche of approval
found for psychoanalysis in Western culture, it is still peripheral to the
mental health industry. As I note in Chapter 6 it has only found mainstream legitimacy around times of warfare. One grim implication of this
association is that Freud revised his theory in the immediate wake of the
carnage of the First World War. In 1920 in *Beyond the Pleasure Principle* he
added the death wish to the libido as part of our putative instinctual
world. This emphasis on aggression was amplified to form the central
building block of Kleinian theory.

4   The American tradition of humanism is more optimistic, being
fostered in a 'new world' of hope and opportunity. Humanistic psychology

is a product of this culture: the folksy optimism of Kelly; the openness to new experience of Rogers; the unending boundaries of the human potential movement. As with psychoanalysis and Judaism, there are secularised resonances of charismatic low church Christianity in humanistic psychology, such as the emphasis on emotional arousal and free expression. The fetish of the individual with his or her rights and responsibilities can be seen readily in home-grown humanism, as well as in its wider national and historical context. American humanism emerged in a land in which slavery occurred, and was then abolished, and in which internal frontiers were expanded before pushing, ever on, to become US imperialism. It takes a steady eye to see that the extermination of native American 'Indians' and the razing of Vietnamese villages were the opposite side of the same coin of a cultural commitment to the freedom of the individual.

5   Both depth psychology and humanism place a faith in rationality and the agency of individuals (both therapists and their clients). They are both preoccupied with methodological individualism. However, secular Jews, living in a context of declining European imperial powers at war with each other, inevitably produced a different style of psychology from that of those in a new imperialist country which, barring Vietnam, has failed in few military adventures abroad. Depth psychology was more circumspect about the therapeutic potential of conscious reflection in relationships. Psychoanalysis emphasised how the power of the irrational, so much of the time, gets the better of our efforts as human agents. Accordingly, in this scheme therapeutic progress for the client is faltering, slow and painful – indeed the need for analysis could be 'interminable'. The patriarchal agency of the analyst was placed centre stage, though. The role of the therapist was elevated via an emphasis on transference and the role of interpretation in effecting psychological change. By contrast, American humanism places more of an emphasis on the *client*'s agency, with the therapist's empathy or cognitive challenges acting as catalysts for potential change stored in their targets.

6   The experiential and individualistic emphasis of both these tradi-tions, combined with a bias towards private practice, may well have deflected attention from the pertinent data being generated by objectivist methodologies. That is, the overwhelming evidence from studies of the social patterning of mental health is that it is related to population level disadvantage, discrimination and oppression. Individualistic methodologies are *ipso facto* insensitive to these insights. Psychological reductionism closes off a consideration of the *social* determination of mental health problems.

7   Whilst the origins of the *professional practice* of psychotherapy may have been a collective product of the careers of DWEMs and DWAMs, the *recipients of the mental health industry* have followed a different social profile. They have been more likely to be female than male, poor than rich etc. Most importantly, in the context of this chapter, they have been drawn disproportionately from people whose racial and ethnic roots were in colonisation or slavery. The industry has then been more likely to

respond to the distressed and distressing legacy of this oppressed history by impersonal means (biological psychiatry) than by talking treatments, leaving black and ethnic minority clients under-represented in the latter.

Drawing these points together, it looks likely that the relative silence within psychotherapeutic theory and practice about race and ethnicity is a result of the following factors: the imperialist national and historical context of its innovators; the restrictive attention of methodological individualism; the under-representation of black and ethnic minorities in the talking treatments; and the relative powerlessness of people from racial and ethnic minorities.

6

The Vagaries of Age

You are born.
It's horrible.
And then you die.

    Graffiti (Anon.)

INTRODUCTION

This chapter has three aims. First, a conceptual note about socialisation will be made. Second, some of the psychosocial vulnerabilities associated with the life span will be explored. Third, the question of ageism in mental health services will be discussed.

A CONCEPTUAL NOTE ON PRIMARY SOCIALISATION

At first glance, the diverse theories which underpin psychotherapy are informed by the common notion that the experience of childhood is a highly important predictor of normal and abnormal functioning in later life. Moreover, despite the occasional objection (e.g. Wrong, 1961) diverse theories in anthropology, psychology and sociology are agreed on one core point – the study of childhood is vital (and some might say all-important) for any understanding of human experience and behaviour for the whole life span. In childhood, in any culture, a person learns their gender identity, the rules and expectations of their parent culture, and how to regulate their body and conduct in line with these expectations. Childhood entails new entrants to a culture and society adopting norms and internalising a sensitivity about mores. A *failure* on either of these counts alerts adult onlookers, like parents and teachers, to the beginnings of abnormal experience and behaviour. Thus, from an early age, what currently in our culture we call 'mental health problems' are constituted by judgements about developmental norms, social conformity (which is 'age appropriate') and rule violation.

Such an overview about a consensus in social science about the nature and importance of primary socialisation takes us so far, but divergences then rapidly appear when we look more closely at competing theories and disciplines. For example, a standard definition of primary socialisation from a psychological viewpoint was provided by English and English (1958):

> The process whereby a person (esp. a child) acquires sensitivity to social stimuli (esp. the pressures and obligations of group life) and learns to get along with, and to behave like, others in his [sic] group or culture. (English and English, 1958: 508)

The authors go on to define the verb to 'socialize':

> 1 To make social 2 To promote socialization 3 To sublimate an impulse 4 To mingle freely 5 (educ) to promote personal interaction (between teacher and pupils) and esp. among pupils as a means of education.

These definitions are quoted not to reify their value and offer them as 'facts' with which I concur, but to highlight the ambiguities which were operating within the discourse of psychology in the mid-1950s. For example, the use of the word 'stimuli' is a nod towards learning theory and behaviourism. The allusion to group life points up the role of social psychology as a sub-discipline. The first two offers about the verb reflect an active notion, which suggests the conscious intentionality of one group (those already socialised) to influence another – those, as yet, unsocialised. By contrast, the third is a nod towards a Freudian viewpoint, which emphasises not intentionality but the importance of unconscious mental mechanisms. The fourth emphasises humans as free agents (an assumption within both humanistic psychology and common sense). The fifth ensures the representation of another sub-discipline (educational psychology) and takes for granted the existence and importance of schools and teachers.

An example of the diversity within a unified emphasis on the concept of primary socialisation is apparent in a popular standard textbook, *Sociology*, by Giddens (1989). Evidence of the close consensus across the disciplines of social science is that its chapter 'Socialisation and the Life-Cycle' begins noticeably (given the book's title) with a review not of sociological work but that of psychologists investigating infant behaviour and experience (beginning with William James). Giddens then unpacks the different and diverging theories of Freud, Piaget and G.H. Mead, before returning to a review of the common elements of their work. He gives no space over, in that chapter, or elsewhere in the book, to Skinner's radical behaviourism. This is arguably the most thoroughgoing of all the psychological theories about organisms over time passing through and reacting to a stimulus environment and, accordingly, having their behaviour 'shaped' by external contingencies. Given the comprehensive scope of Giddens's knowledge about social science, one can only deduce that his silence about behaviourism may stem from ideological distaste.

Only after he has established the importance of the micro-processes of primary socialisation in the inner and outer life of the *individual child* does

Giddens move on to the supra-personal features operating in society. These, which he addresses as 'agencies of socialisation', include the family, the peer group, schools and the mass media. When this list is compared and contrasted with that from the psychologists English and English, the large overlap is clear. The exception is the importance Giddens ascribes to the mass media. Psychodynamic psychotherapists are biased towards a scrutiny of the first on Giddens's list and attend less to the socialising influences of peers and school, which are emphasised by social developmental and educational psychologists. However, as I explore in the discussion of Chapter 8, psychodynamic practitioners are more than aware of the role of the mass media when they seek to persuade the public about their own legitimacy, even if its role is relatively absent in their clinical discourse about clients. Whilst different schools of psychotherapy place varying emphases and constructions on the role of the past in relation to current functioning, all of them implicitly or explicitly deem themselves to be agents of change in the present. Thus, psychotherapy can be considered as a source of resocialisation or secondary socialisation. I return to this point in the next chapter.

PSYCHOSOCIAL VULNERABILITIES IN THE LIFE SPAN

It is a truism that the physical and psychological well-being of people can be jeopardised or aggravated at any point from cradle to grave. However, it remains a matter of dispute, when considering the mental health of adults, whether the insults, privations and deprivations of childhood are causally more salient than the impact of contemporary stressors or influences. Even within a psychoanalytical framework, there is a wide range of positions about this question of contemporary versus historical influences. Moreover, with regard to childhood experience there are diverse hypotheses put forward by psychoanalysts about:

1 the role of biological factors
2 the role of external insults
3 the role of the child's memory and constructions upon 2
4 the role of parental (especially maternal) behaviour.

Take three distinct contributions from prestigious psychoanalysts. The work of the environmentalist Bowlby (1951) on attachment has different implications from the instinctual emphasis of Klein (1960). By contrast, the more eclectic Winnicott (1958) conceptualised three tiers of vulnerability related to: good-enough care in the early months; successful negotiation of separation after the first year; and the Oedipal drama. Other therapeutic orientations, like existential and Gestalt therapy, explore the significance of the person striving *towards* something in life, not just their legacy from the past and their proneness to regression.

These differing approaches are mentioned in order to emphasise that there are diverse methodological preferences about how to best recon- struct, and appraise the salience of, the past with, or about, clients. As a consequence, collectively, psychotherapists can offer no clear agreement on the mental health implications of childhood. This is an irony given that there is a broad consensus between therapists of different orientations that the past is important. However, what they seemingly cannot agree on is precisely in *what way* the past is important.

If therapists themselves cannot offer a consensus, are there clearer conclusions to be drawn from forms of research other than their preferred style of case work accumulation? Here I will summarise three areas of research that go some way to answering this question. The first is about the impact of childhood sexual abuse. The second is about the social origins of depression in young and middle-aged women. The third is the role of social factors in depression in old age.

The Impact of Childhood Sexual Abuse

Whilst there is still an absence of large-scale empirical evidence about those who are sexually victimised as children but do not disclose it to public agencies, we do know that survivors are over-represented in adult mental health services. A complication about disaggregating the specific pathogenic impact of sexual abuse is that, in its intra-familial form, it may be associated with other forms of abuse or neglect (Briere and Runtz, 1987). Although incestuous contact may be an isolated pocket of abuse within a wider benign family system, parents who sexually assault their children are also more likely to be psycho-noxious in other ways. When the abuse *is* experienced in the context of a caring relationship, it might be that survivors are less distressed and then manage to ward off long- term problems. Thus three scenarios are set up:

1　Victims who survive relatively intact psychologically and do not disclose the abuse and/or do not present with problems to professionals.

2　Victims who sporadically become distressed but do not present with problems to professionals.

3　Victims who are sufficiently troubled by the experience that they seek out professional help and sooner or later disclose the abuse.

Sexual assault in childhood can lead to both immediate expressions of distress and acting out and a long-term predisposition to the same in later life (Wyatt and Powell, 1988; Cahill et al., 1991). Victims may start to become aggressive and act out in a sexualised way which is noticeably out of sync with their age group. In addition they may present with a whole range of problems which other distressed children from non- sexually abused backgrounds manifest, including: anxiety, depression, language delay, night terrors, stealing, eating disorders and peer relationship difficulties.

Overall, it seems that girls are more likely to be molested than boys. This is accounted for by the greater number of female victims in intra-familial abuse (Rogers and Terry, 1984). Boys are slightly more likely to be the victims of stranger perpetrators (Abel et al., 1987). Most perpetrators are male. Female assailants are more likely to be co-abusers with their male partner, although on very rare occasions mothers acting alone do sexually assault their children.

A dilemma in interpreting the data on victim gender is that women may be more prone to disclose both the abuse and its consequent distress than men (Finkelhor, 1979). Put differently, whilst it is difficult for men or women to disclose the details of sexual assaults, the masculine avoidance of help-seeking, combined with homophobic anxieties, may amplify such a reluctance in male victims. Also, there has been more research interest shown in female victims than male victims. Together these separate factors (one a victim variable, the other a researcher variable) may raise the profile of one gender group at the expense of the other, within both the academic and clinical discourses about adult survivors (Becker, 1988; Dimock, 1988).

Heterosexual paedophiles have the option of insinuating their way into family life in order to abuse fostered or step-children or they can even directly father their own potential victims. By contrast, predatory homosexual paedophiles *ipso facto* are more likely to be kept out of domestic family contexts, at least in a parental role. Accordingly, they opt instead to prey on children opportunistically, form conspiratorial networks with other perpetrators or seek out child prostitutes at home or abroad. It is also clear that closed residential institutions for children attract both heterosexual and homosexual paedophiles, particularly the latter. In recent years, in England and Wales, there has been a string of police investigations and subsequent prosecutions involving multiple offences by senior residential social work staff, following the testimonies of adult survivors.

In later life problems may continue and a proportion of victims then end up in scenario 3 as listed above. Briere and Runtz (1988) examined the case records of 152 consecutive female patients requesting appointments at a community mental health facility in Canada, and found greater symptomatology in patients who had been sexually abused in childhood compared to those who had not. In a large community survey Stein et al. (1988) found a clear difference in symptom profile between such groups (Table 6.1).

Reviewers of the topic about the prevalence of sexual abuse survivors in mental health services (e.g. Williams et al., 1993) estimate that at least 50 per cent of psychiatric patients have been sexually abused in the past. In one study of the histories of women in a secure hospital with a diagnosis of psychopathy it was found that 34 out of 40 patients were survivors of sexual abuse in childhood or adolescence (Potier, 1993). Once in the mental health services these patients are then vulnerable to revictimisation at the hands of other patients or of staff (HMSO, 1992). A

Table 6.1 *Childhood sexual abuse and adult mental health: lifetime
prevalence of psychiatric problems in those sexually abused (AB) and those not
(NA) in childhood (n = 3132)*

	Men		Women	
	% NA (n = 1249)	% AB (n = 31)	% NA (n = 1307)	% AB (n = 51)
Alcohol abuse	23.2	35.7	4.1	20.8★
Drug abuse	7.8	44.9★	3.1	13.7★
Severe depression	3.9	13.8	5.5	21.9★
Phobic anxiety	7.0	6.5	12.5	34.2★
Any psychiatric diagnosis	34.0	71.2★	24.0	58.6★

★ Significance level of 0.05

Source: summarized from Stein et al., 1988: 54

similar vulnerability is present in child victims of intra-familial abuse who
are taken into care, when staff or older children may revictimise them.

There is some evidence that psychotherapists themselves are part of this
problem of abuse within services, which will at times constitute revictimisation. Concern about the erotic involvement of psychologists with their
therapy clients has been expressed in the professional literature in both
the USA (e.g. Holroyd and Brodsky, 1977; Garrett, 1994) and in Britain
(e.g. Garrett and Davis, 1994). The latter study reported an anonymous
questionnaire sent to British clinical psychologists which sought information on sexual contact with clients. In 20 of the 581 completed returns
analysed, sexual contact was reported (3.4 per cent of the sample).

It is generally assumed that this type of abuse within therapy is over-
whelmingly at the hands of male therapists (see e.g. Aveline, 1996).
However, the British study found that 12 of the 20 abusers were male,
seven female and one respondent did not record their sex. This is still a
male/female ratio of around 2:1 but the total sample did not contain an
equal gender balance, with 61.7 per cent of those reporting themselves as
female. Nonetheless, more female therapists are implicated by this finding
than had been predicted by the earlier US studies reviewed by Garrett
(1994). Most of the US studies suggested that female abusers were in a tiny
minority, with the great majority of scenarios of abuse involving older
male therapists and younger female clients. However, a few studies (e.g.
Stake and Oliver, 1991) suggested that male and female abusers were
equally common. I will return to a discussion about the problem of abuse
and its contribution to deterioration effects in psychotherapy in Chapter 8.

Social Origins of Depression in Young and Middle-Aged Women

One of the most elegant models developed within a social causationist
framework is that provided by George Brown and his colleagues, the

Camberwell (south London) study of depressed women (Brown and Harris, 1978). Over the past 20 years this original study has been extended to include international comparisons. The model they produced in 1978 is summarised in Figure 6.1.

The derivation of depression according to this model is multi-factorial, such that some factors might be present and yet the person may not become depressed. It entails: the notion of protective as well as vulnerability factors; past as well as present social and personal conditions; subjective experience as well as outer events; and the agency as well as the victimhood of people. Current personal relationships are important for two reasons: one related to the role of benign vs. absent or hostile relationships with another adult (such as partner); the other is the stress of child rearing. Past relationships are important because the loss of mother before the age of 11 makes women vulnerable, which may be a function of relatively poor care after the loss (Brown et al., 1986). Material adversity is important in interaction with these personal circumstances. If poverty *per se* were depressogenic, then all poor people would be depressed.

However, the advantage of the Brown and Harris model is that it exposes the role of material adversity, a lack of direct economic power and social class effects. For example, not having access to the labour market is a vulnerability factor. And whilst child rearing is stressful for all parents, its role is put into context here by Brown and Harris:

> Since working class women with children also have a higher rate of severe events and major difficulties, they have a greater chance of experiencing *both* a provoking agent and a vulnerability factor. And this is enough to explain the entire class difference in risk of depression among women with children – at least in statistical terms. (Brown and Harris, 1978: 182)

In their study they found no social class differences between the women studied *except* in relation to the presence of children, i.e. there was no significant difference in depression rates between childless women of different social classes.

The original model offered by Brown and Harris has been modified recently in the light of further data collection and of conceptual influences from other sources. Brown et al. (1995) compared clinical and non-clinical populations in Islington, north London. Drawing upon the work of Gilbert (1992) and Unger (1984), the authors elaborate their position about depression and the *experience* of life events. They deduce that the probability of depression increases not necessarily with loss or threatened loss *per se* but with the coexistence of humiliation and/or entrapment. Gilbert and Unger note that depression is commonly associated with feeling trapped and humiliated such that there is an assault on the person's self-esteem or an indirect undermining of their sense of self-worth and the person has a 'blocked escape'. (Interestingly the latter was the final condition put forward by Bateson et al. (1956) when discussing the

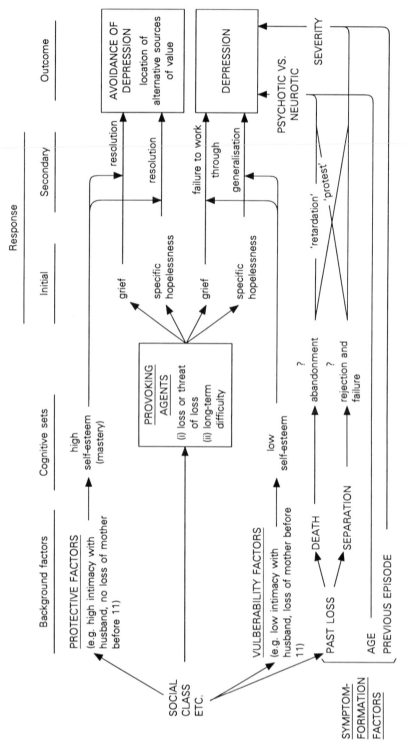

Figure 6.1 *Model for the social origins of depression* (modified from Brown and Harris 1978: 48)

double bind in 'schizophrenia'.) In practical terms Brown et al. (1995) suggest that, for instance, a woman being told that a paralysed husband will not improve might experience entrapment and become depressed but another leaving a feckless husband might feel liberated and recover from a depressive trajectory. Thus, the ability to 'leave the field' might be a protective factor in people who are at risk of depression or even a recovery factor in those already distressed.

The Islington study also highlighted more details about the risk factors associated with adverse childhood experiences. In a third of the depressed women studied there was the presence of neglect or abuse (physical or sexual) in their childhoods. This neglect or abuse doubled the chances of these women becoming depressed as adults in any one year, compared to those without such adverse antecedents (Bifulco et al., 1992). These childhood events also increase the probability of anxiety problems and could account for the common coexistence of depression and anxiety in adult patients (Brown, 1996).

Having reviewed the utility of the work of Brown and his colleagues, the weaknesses of their work can also be noted. Three main ones spring to mind. The first is that the work is positivistic. The broad notion of 'psychiatric disorder' and the specific diagnosis of depression are discussed as if they have a universal and non-problematic status. As I note in Chapter 5 when discussing race and culture there are problems with this line of reasoning. Brown et al. developed a methodology which entailed listening to women's experiences. However, this did not include an inductive approach to distress. Instead psychiatric (i.e. professionally defined) criteria were used to identify the latter. Although Brown and Harris were aware of the arguments which problematised psychiatric knowledge and diagnosis they opted to retain the advantages of 'reducing the variety of psychiatric phenomena to a provisional order' (Brown and Harris, 1978: 19). They conceded the vulnerability of this approach, but argued (as psychiatrists themselves do) that the answer is reform not abolition, in order to increase the validity and reliability of diagnosis.

The second related problem about the commitment of Brown et al. to the legitimacy of psychiatric knowledge is that they emphasise that the psychosocial factors that they uncover, in relation to the aetiology of depression, need to be seen as augmenting a *biological* predisposition to the latter (e.g. Brown et al., 1995: 20). As with bio-deterministic assumptions operating elsewhere in psychiatry, the question is raised about the need for such a leap in faith. In the case of psychiatry itself, the professional interests being served by a form of biological hoped-for-reductionism are pretty clear. It is less clear why Brown (who is a sociologist, not a psychiatrist) holds on so firmly to the preferred speculations of the medical profession.

The third (unintended) problem, which has come in the wake of the original Camberwell study, is that there has been a skewed interest in women. The full title of this original study (Brown and Harris, 1978) was

Social Origins of Depression: A Study of Psychiatric Disorder in Women. This focus on women has led to the Brown et al. work being incorporated into a wider mental health discourse, which characterises depression as a female condition. It is certainly true that depression is diagnosed more often (about twice as much) in women than men. Indeed, this is the main reason why women are over-represented in psychiatric statistics. However, a research focus on women and depression may simply add to this diagnostic bias. Men get depressed too but we will not understand their experience in its social context if it is not researched. The irony about the female bias of the Brown et al. work is that it arose from a methodological convenience. The researchers, for pragmatic reasons, based upon assumptions about the higher base rate of depression in women than men and the greater availability and co-operativeness of the former group, decided only to interview women.

Social Origins of Depression in Old Age

A common stereotype about old age is that the main mental health problem experienced is dementia. In fact depression is diagnosed more often, particularly in the age band 65–80 years. Pilgrim and Rogers (1993) separate out the particular stressors of residential home life for older people and more general factors which might have a depressive toll.

Residential Home Life   In Britain about 2 per cent of people over 65 live in residential or nursing homes. A number of studies conducted in a variety of countries indicate that around a third of this type of population is depressed (e.g. England: Mann et al., 1984; Australia: Snowden and Donnelly, 1986; Italy: Spagnoli et al., 1986).

There are three broad hypotheses for these raised levels of depression in residential settings (which are not mutually exclusive). The first is a selection factor – people referred into such settings may be more likely to be depressed at the outset. Their mental state may be a salient factor prompting referral by service professionals or relatives. The second possibility is that depression is a reaction to the under-stimulation which is common in collective care. With under-stimulation come the time and the mood to ruminate morbidly (what is called 'dysphoria' by some psychiatrists). Indeed this mood state is so common in residential homes for older people that it may be difficult for diagnosticians to make a clear dividing line between 'normal' dysphoria and depression (Murphy, 1988).

The third possibility is that depression may be a function of loss of control, ownership and familiarity in the move from the person's own home to a residential setting. This experience of loss has both objective indicators and subjective consequences. The material environment has actually changed and the person might understandably experience the loss that this entails. The loss factor points to an obvious connection with depression. However, a closely linked variable (as with Brown et al.'s more recent work on women) might be entrapment. If the admission to a residential setting is the only option applied to the plight of the vulnerable older person (one choice is no choice) then this may be a salient trigger for depression.

General Social Factors in Later Life   Whether or not an older person is in a residential setting, they may well experience a number of stressors which singularly or cumulatively might have a depressive toll. Pilgrim and Rogers (1993) list five factors to consider based upon the literature about the social conditions of older people:

1   With age comes a raised probability of physical illness. Moreover, older people are very likely to suffer from *multiple* physical symptoms compared to their younger days. Physical illness, particularly if it is multiple and entails chronic symptoms, is depressing.
2   The longer a person lives, the more people they will outlive. Older people typically contend with the cumulative loss of their peers and the aggregate grief this entails.
3   Poverty produces a depressive toll at any age but material adversity in old age makes people particularly vulnerable to distress. Their physical and psychological resources to survive poverty are depleted compared to younger people.
4   Social isolation increases with age. This lowers the probability of older people having access to ameliorative confiding relationships. The latter relationships are a protective factor against depression.
5   Because older people are physically and psychologically vulnerable, compared to those in young and middle adulthood, they may be abused by the latter. Physical or emotional abuse can precipitate psychological distress in older people as well as in children.

When these factors are listed in this way it is little surprise that recorded depression increases with age.

AGEISM IN MENTAL HEALTH SERVICES

Most of the case law developed in the clinical literature of psycho-therapists is about clients in young and middle adulthood. There is of course a literature about children and older people but it is less prominent or extensive. In a recent review of NHS psychotherapy in England by the Department of Health (NHSE, 1996) it was noted that the evidence base about work with children and adolescents is noticeably small compared to that about adults. The elaborate case law approach to psychotherapy in relation to children, which is evident in the psychoanalytical tradition, emerged as a result of theory building (and disputation). The work of

Anna Freud and Melanie Klein highlights this. The former extended the work of her father in part to confirm his childhood-focused theory. Similarly, Klein was interested in children as a vehicle for theory building about adult psychopathology. The dispute between the two women, which generated much heat and an outpouring of articles, was as much about the 'correct' trajectory for psychoanalysis as a model for adult psychopathology, as it was about providing a form of treatment for distressed or disturbed children.

In the 1920s the direct ('pedagogic') observation of children by his daughter, alongside the explicit psychoanalysis of some of them, combined to provide Freud with a comforting legitimacy for his work, even though he was sceptical about using therapy as a substitute for education. By contrast, Klein considered that psychoanalysis was actually a good prophylaxis against adult neurosis (a sort of psychological vaccination programme). In this sense Klein was more grandiose in her expectations about the role of psychoanalytical work in society than were the Freuds, believing that child analysis would become as commonplace as schooling. She also believed that such treatment could cure psychosis in children (Klein, 1948).

The child and the older person have much in common despite being at opposite ends of the life span. Their economic value is either minimal or negative. Those in young and middle adulthood are economically active (or potentially so), the very young and old are not. Consequently, the latter two groups lack both direct economic power (unless they retain wealth in old age equal to or in excess of wages) and as a result they lack social power. When we look at the other groups in this book which are denied social power (poor people and ethnic minorities) they too are marginalised in psychotherapy services.

Another common feature of older people and children is that they are much more likely to come to the attention of mental health professionals via the actions of third parties than those in the middle years of the life span – very few children self-refer to services. The behavioural deviations, developmental delays and emotional reactions of children tend to be of concern to adults such as parents, teachers or health visitors. The latter, rather than children themselves, then become the source of referral to professionals. Similarly it is the social consequences of loss of functioning in older people that often triggers concern in others, who become referrers to services. Because of the chaos and dangers created by the loss of cognitive functioning in older people, the topic of dementia tends to have a greater salience (leading to a stereotype) as a mental health problem than depression, even though the latter is twice as prevalent as the former. Thus, even though children and older people are seen by mental health services, third parties are in a sense often the client and thus critical parties in the construction of the mental health problems of others. The parent demanding drugs for their 'hyperactive' child, or the nursing home over-using minor and major tranquillisers on their elderly residents, reveal who has the power to define (and control) problematic behaviour and experience.

Psychotherapists themselves have a poor track record in relation to responding to the distress of older people. Few articles about psychotherapy with older people are written and comparatively little research is done involving this age range. Freud went so far as to argue that beyond a certain age people were untreatable (cf. Hildebrand, 1982). By contrast Jung, with a different theoretical emphasis about individuation, argued that people in middle age were ripe for analysis compared to younger adults. The private practice emphasis of both wings of analysis has ensured a common feature, though – analysands should be young enough to be wealthy enough to pay for their treatment. As with the points I raise about social class (Chapter 3), private practice began an elitist trend within psychotherapy which has been associated with the exclusion of those lacking economic power.

Within the psychodynamic tradition, the acknowledged bias of therapists in favour of working with so-called YAVIS (young, attractive, verbal, intelligent, social) clients is understood by Hildebrand (1983) as the aggregate outcome of counter-transference in therapists. However, I think that this is another example of psychological reductionism and it highlights the limitations of a form of reflexivity which is not social but individual. Whilst it may be the case that therapists prefer, for personal reasons, to relate to people in the middle years, it is also the case that therapists themselves collectively are in that age range and, if they work privately, will selectively encourage those with earning power to enter the patient role.

Thus, being of, and preferring to work with, the same age cohort as one's client could be interpreted as an aggregate of counter-transference, but there are other more obvious social explanations. For example, there is a cohort effect of social contact throughout the life span – people share interests, fashions and experiences as they proceed through life together. This is formalised in mild taboos which emerge about social or sexual contact between adults who are deemed by onlookers to be too discrepant in age, as well as the emergence of forms of the 'generation gap'.

Another personal consequence of an age gap in social experience is the psychological constraint this places upon empathy. This is relevant to therapists who work with people older than themselves. (Analogously a childless therapist has a constraint on their empathy for clients struggling to raise children.) My point about raising these interacting variables of economic power and cohort effects, and their impact on empathy, is that they represent *social processes* which are outside, or not peculiar to, the therapeutic relationship. This picture suggests that the limited reflexivity associated with personal therapy for the therapist is insufficient to understand why there is an age bias in psychotherapeutic work. As an indication of the wider social forces at work, we can note that older people also receive poorer *physical* health care, compared to younger people. Again this suggests that their waning economic power and social status affect the quality of care they receive. Part of this ageist effect may also reflect direct impoverishment (not just a relative loss of economic power) as the risk of poverty increases post-retirement.

7

The Contexts of Therapy

We are all in the gutter but some of us are looking at the stars.

Oscar Wilde, *Lady Windermere's Fan*

INTRODUCTION

In Chapter 2, when discussing general systems theory, I drew attention to the notions of context and closure. Closure refers to the capacity and necessity of human beings to deal with a part of a system – one level or a limited number of factors. Bateson's emphasis on selective attention was discussed, along with the partiality and ignorance that necessarily ensue. In this chapter I will outline a variety of levels of the context of therapy: the personal context; the organisational context; the mental health policy context; the macro-political context. Each perspective is partial but important. Together the perspectives build up a picture of the context of therapy which, it is hoped, will be more than the sum of the parts.

THE PERSONAL CONTEXT

Psychotherapy is a type of personal relationship entailing a series of negotiated meetings containing conversations. Therapists are obliged to develop a particular competence at reflecting on its personal context. Because of this competence they introduce a framework of understanding which is separate from the views of particular clients. Clients, as it were, walk into a framed context which has been constructed in advance by therapists. It is true that some versions of psychotherapy, including those informed by phenomenology, existentialism, post-structuralism and even liberal object-relations theory, emphasise the unique contribution which clients make to the construction of the personal relationship with their therapists. However, such freedom is at the latters' discretion. The discretion is a product of the power asymmetry which exists between the parties. (In Chapter 2 I have said something about this already.) The setting and type of conversation warranted or disallowed is under the control of the therapist, although the client can fail to attend, leave the frame temporarily or permanently or episodically resist the expectations of the therapist.

The way in which the above processes are stylised is a function of the theoretical or ideological position of therapists. Bannister (1983) provided a meta-theoretical framework to understand this point, which he offered as a series of metaphors. He starts by making the following general point:

> Clearly the relationship between therapist and client is initially neither reciprocal nor equal. If you are the therapist then you and the client are on either side of *your* desk, in *your* office, on *your* patch. Your presence signifies qualifications, expertise and prestige; the client's presence signifies that he or she has 'given in', 'confessed failure'. You, as therapist, represent (socially if not in fact) the healthy ordered life while the client represents 'sickness' and confusion. You prescribe the pattern of the relationship . . . You may decide to be non-directive but, even so, it will be *you* that decided to be non-directive. You may negotiate all things but you do so from a position of power. (Bannister, 1983: 139)

Bannister then goes on with his checklist of metaphors which I summarise and paraphrase:

1 *Doctor–patient* In this the patient is rendered passive and is involved in a process of attempted cure-while-you-wait. This metaphor applies most strongly in relation to organic psychiatry, in which it is hardly a metaphor.

2 *Trainer–trainee* In this the client is instructed by the therapist. The latter has a bag of tricks – a set of technical fixes which he or she applies to a presenting problem. The client is more active as a participant, though, than in the doctor–patient model. The most obvious examples of this are old-fashioned methodological behaviourism (behaviour therapy) and contemporary forms of cognitive therapy. However, there are also subtle elements of this process in forms of family therapy utilised which have either a supportive or paradoxical intent.

3 *Friend–friend* Here the emotional conditions linked to a good friendship are emphasised by the therapist. This is exemplified by the central therapeutic triad of genuineness, non-possessive warmth and accurate empathy and is celebrated in the work of Carl Rogers. Non-directive therapy assumes that ordinary positive relating will be the basis of personal succour and change.

4 *Priest–penitent* This emphasises the client confessing the dark side of their inner life, a process favoured by both the Catholic Church and depth psychology. The confessional is replaced by the analyst's couch, sin by the unconscious, theology by psychology and absolution by interpretation. In both cases the process is potentially interminable (limited, of course, by the death of the participants) and a clear fixed demarcation exists between those in authority and others.

5 *Supervisor–researcher* This emphasises that each party has a differential expertise. The client is the ultimate and specific expert on themself but the therapist has a general overview of inner life which enables them to enable others. It is an approach which is epitomised by therapy informed by personal construct theory.

This list highlights the point that bodies of knowledge within psychotherapy differentially frame the personal context. It also begs another question: what of the thoughts and feelings imported by the client?

In Chapter 3 when I was discussing the amenability of working-class clients for psychotherapy it was noted that a cultural compatibility between therapist and client may be important. But the matter is more complicated than one of class or race or gender, though all these in each case are important. It is also about cosmology, emotional state, cultural assumptions and motivation for change. Clients are not a blank screen. They already have views about their current problem and assumptions about their genesis (even if this is limited to some vague notion about being ill). These imported client assumptions may not coincide with the model imported by the mental health worker. For example, the history of psychoanalysis is, *inter alia*, a history of the secularisation of Judaeo-Christianity, with an emphasis on the first part of the hyphenated tradition. For this reason a Buddhist, a Muslim or a Hindu may not be readily amenable to psychoanalysis.

This question of client cosmology or ideology and their imported emotional state has been addressed by a number of writers interested in the nature of change in psychotherapy. For example, Pentony (1981), Frank (1973) and Berger and Luckmann (1966) all point out the similarities between religious conversion and psychotherapeutic change. The parallel is that an authoritative figure utilises techniques to alter a pre-existing personal outlook on the part of a target of influence. The skills of the change agent include the ability to identify and utilise the resources present in their target, which might include: the client's belief in authority; group pressure and membership; and an emotional state which creates an amenability to influence and submission to authority.

Political indoctrination represents a third example of secondary socialisation or resocialisation. The difference in this case is that a much larger gap exists at the outset between the views of change agents and their targets. However, a central feature of indoctrination is that the total control that the persuader exerts deliberately engenders an emotional state in the target, which can disorientate them about their existing way of construing their world. Whereas the psychotherapy client imports emotional arousal, the indoctrinator induces this by disorientating their target. This disorientation includes removing them from the daily context which sustains their view of reality, along with the creation of physiological arousal by altering their sense of time and space through meal and sleep disruption.

The overlap between these features of indoctrination and the voluntary submission of paying clients to secular cults emerging in the human potential movement in the 1970s (like EST, Dianetics and Exegesis) is obvious. The similarity between brainwashing and psychotherapy was formally recognised in the early 1970s after the Church of Scientology, which practises and promotes Dianetics, attempted to infiltrate and take over the National Association of Mental Health in Britain (now MIND). The British government set up the Foster Enquiry (Foster, 1971) to examine this event. The enquiry raised the question of the need for State regulation of psychotherapy and other 'mindbending' techniques (to use a term common at the time). In other words, when push comes to shove about State regulation of psychotherapy, it is considered to be on the same broad terrain as brainwashing.

For those practitioners reading this, who have only been socialised in the ways of psychotherapy with little first-hand knowledge of religious conversion or political indoctrination, the parallels being drawn may seem fanciful or even offensive. However, all three processes entail a power asymmetry between the change agent and their target, and an imported or induced existential disorientation and emotional arousal in the latter. Psychotherapy involves a starting point of emotional vulnerability on the part of clients, even if the extent of this varies from client to client. Also, as with religious conversion, the *motivational readiness* of clients is a central feature of personal change. It is a well-known cliche and the butt of recurring jokes about psychotherapy that clients must 'really want to change'.

This readiness has a cognitive as well as an affective dimension. Both the incipient religious convert and the neophyte client in therapy are already looking for answers to their current existential *impasse*. If they lack such an emotional and cognitive set they are 'poor bets'. Those who do have a religious conversion will already have been in a state of mind where the spiritual dimension to their existence has been confused. Similarly, as Bannister notes above, the 'good bet' at the outset of psychotherapy has already conceded their need to change – they have 'given in' or 'confessed failure'. On the cognitive side of readiness there are degrees of *a priori* congruence between the parties. For example, anyone involved in psychotherapy training knows that applicants will *already* hold a theoretical position about stasis and change in human experience and conduct. They will indicate at selection that they will have studied texts relevant to psychotherapy and have participated already in personal work on themselves to varying degrees.

De Swaan (1990) notes that clients entering psychotherapy may well already have developed a degree of theoretical understanding and commitment about the business that he dubs *protoprofessionalisation*. Indeed, this group, alongside those who for emotional reasons are ready for psychotherapeutic help, may together be a particular constituency which is different from the population at large. After all, most people much of

the time struggle on with their problems and eschew disclosing encounters with lay people, let alone seek out the help of experts (Rogers and Pilgrim, 1996b). I will return to this point in Chapter 9.

A final similarity between religious conversion and psychotherapeutic change is that *change maintenance* has to be subjected to surveillance. In religion this is achieved by continued church/temple/mosque/synagogue attendance and submission to regular rituals such as prayer meetings, the mass, communion, confession, holy book reading classes, etc. Analogously, therapy continues to check on progress and follow-up meetings are agreed. After therapy is terminated, any slipping back may trigger the person returning for help. If clients are also professional therapists then their group membership of a secularised priesthood is a source of continued commitment and of forms of surveillance such as supervision.

THE ORGANISATIONAL CONTEXT

Psychotherapists *ipso facto* are interested in scrutinising the personal context of their work. However, they have an occupational vulnerability to closure at this level of analysis. Returning to Bateson's point about partiality and selective attention, being personal can become an all-consuming passion and focus of attention. It can lead to psychological reductionism by psychotherapists – a view that to be relentlessly biographical and personal will produce a pure or pre-eminent version of human science (Young, 1988).

For example, a classic and fascinating paper in the psychoanalytical literature is one produced by Winnicott (1958), with the elaborate title of 'Metapsychological and clinical aspects of regression within the psychoanalytical set-up'. In this article, Winnicott covers a number of points, which still inform many therapists in his tradition, about levels of disturbance of clients and their implications for therapeutic technique. In addition, it addresses the question of setting but it does so in a particular way which misses the point which Bannister grasps in the quote I gave earlier. For Winnicott, the issue is not about power but how the reliability of the setting (including the physical space, time of appointments and mere presence of the analyst) provides a holding environment for those with a schizoid disturbance, and provides evidence of survival for the depressive client. This is a good example of the point I am making about the occupational hazard of psychotherapists. Setting is discussed in personal terms, only because being personal is at the heart of Winnicott's view that to analyse, survive and hold are the alpha and omega of psychotherapy.

The hazard is partially based in psychological reductionism but it has another dimension – the social history of psychotherapy. Winnicott's working assumption is that his setting is one of an 'ordinary house'. This is a reasonable assumption for those working in ordinary houses. However, it is one that could only have arisen because Winnicott worked at home as a private therapist. Moreover, for Winnicott to describe his own particular, middle-class house as 'ordinary' is without reference to whether most people live in such settings. The architecture and typical home contents of one part of north London, where most British psycho-analysts live, are peculiar. They have little in common with, say, a flat in a tower block in Salford or a farmworker's cottage in the Pennines. More importantly, they have little in common with the setting of a hospital in Glasgow, or a health centre in Swansea.

This therapist-centrism about setting probably remains because Freud saw patients privately to make a living. Because clinical psychoanalysis is essentially an authoritarian culture which venerates its founders, it closes off a serious consideration of the socio-political significance of the organisational context of therapy itself. In doing so, it idealises a type of setting which was peculiar to Freud's house. It also accounts, in part, for the anxious pedantry which surrounds question of boundaries in analytical therapy. If therapists see fee-paying clients in their own house and they are to maintain themselves as a neutral blank screen, this understandably creates a daily dilemma of 'impression management', to use Goffman's notion about presentation of self (Goffman, 1967).

Most people with mental health problems either do not have local access to private therapy or they cannot afford what is available. Conse-quently, the therapy that they do access takes place in settings which are different in a number of ways from that described by Winnicott and inherited from Freud. The types of therapeutic activity which have emerged in modern health care, educational and other bureaucracies have been shaped in part by those settings. In other words, *contra* Winnicott, setting is important not because of its therapeutic *role* but because it provides a constraint on, and opportunity for, the *existence* of therapy as a social practice. Consequently, a reliance on the psychotherapeutic dis-course to illuminate the importance of setting will lead to a partial and reductionist account (Barham, 1986).

In Winnicott's classic paper he gives a passing wave to external reality, when indicating that for example the analyst might indicate his or her awareness that the King has died or the country is at war. More recently, one analyst, a Jungian, has gone much further and argued that:

> we need to think about how to engage some of our patients in political, social and cultural discussion and argument. Sometimes, we have to take a frankly educative model for our work (often, assuredly, the patient is educating the analyst). Sometimes, we may even argue with the patient (usually regarded as a *grave* technical error). We should not go on as if all our ideas about the internalisation of the culture, the disunity of the human subject, the meaning-fulness of symptoms, were all a new kind of metaphysics and hence not of immediate practical relevance. (Samuels, 1995: 67–68, emphasis in original)

Elsewhere in this text, Samuels provides a rich source of information and discussion about the attitudes of psychotherapists towards politics when reporting an international survey he carried out with this focus. His questionnaire was sent to psychoanalysts, analytical psychologists and psychodynamic and humanistic psychotherapists in Britain, the USA, Israel, Germany, Russia and Brazil. He received 600 returns out of 2000 dispatched questionnaires. The results were revealing in a number of ways, but I will focus here only on those related to the context of therapy. The first finding of this sort related to national setting. Basically, political material was introduced by clients more often in institutional (i.e. non-fee-paying/state-provided) settings in the USA and in Britain, whereas the Israeli and Brazilian therapists reported that this was more likely in private practice. Samuels speculates, quite reasonably, that this may reflect something about the national political context of different countries. Private practice provides more assured confidentiality for risky material in a country like Brazil with its recent history of political repression and in Israel with its political context of 'nationalistic fervour'.

The second point of interest to me about context from Samuels's survey was that those replying were generally from a self-ascribed left or liberal ideological position. (One of the questions asked for this type of information.) I wondered on reading the findings whether these were representative of the political value positions of the 70 per cent of therapists who did *not* return their questionnaires. In other words, more conservative elements might have treated a survey which explicitly aimed to deal with external political reality with some disdain. Some of the individual negative feedback Samuels invited from respondents pointed to this conclusion.

The third point relates back to the summary given by Bannister earlier about the context of therapy including the power of therapists to 'negotiate all things but . . . from a position of power' (1983: 139). Bearing in mind my caution directly above about the possible self-selection of the respondents, it was noticeable that there was a considerable reported willingness of the therapists who replied to take an interest in political material introduced by clients. Samuels had expected that this would be discussed by therapists predominantly in terms of its symbolic/intrapsychic meaning. A measure of the relative conservative individualism of British and Russian therapists was that they were more likely to concentrate on the symbolic implications of political material than those from other countries. Very few therapists from any country would only concentrate on the 'reality' aspects of the material. However, a large minority (over a third) of the therapists from all backgrounds were interested in exploring the meaning of the material in an open-ended way, rather than ascribing its meaning via interpretations.

My main point here, though, refers to Bannister's insight. What all of Samuels's respondents were in a position to do, because of their social legitimacy and power within some part of the mental health industry, public or private, world-wide, was *decide* what balance to strike in their reponses to clients between interpretation, exploration and credulous conversation. The quote I gave earlier from Samuels itself reveals this point in its first sentence: 'we need to think about how to engage some of our patients . . .'. Note 'some' but not all. And they are 'our' patients. These connotations indicate the discretionary powers which are available to therapists on their territory and denied to their client visitors.

THE MENTAL HEALTH POLICY CONTEXT

The shellshock problem in the First World War created the political conditions under which psychotherapy became possible as a mass form of practice (Stone, 1985). But because of this mass character, therapeutic practice became channelled, shaped and filtered by the organisational context of the clinic. Moreover, this clinical context in later years became stylised by wider health reforms including the formation of the NHS and deinstitutionalisation.

To illustrate the importance of the policy context to psychotherapy I will look at three examples: specialised outpatient psychotherapy in the NHS; the psychiatric hospital; and secure provision.

Specialised Outpatient Psychotherapy

As I note above the shellshock problem of the First World War created the conditions for the spread of psychotherapy outside a narrow band of practitioners and their patients in private practice. In the Victorian period, mental health work had been dominated by the asylum and the control of lunacy. Psychological *models* let alone psychotherapy were marginal to this work. By the turn of the century, the medical profession had legal and administrative control over madness and its management. Within this control the favoured theoretical speculations were about mental abnormality being a function of a yet to be discovered brain disease. This biodeterministic emphasis in psychiatry (which still predominates today) was matched by hostility towards psychological theory. Stone (1985) reports a meeting at the Neurological Section of the British Medical Association before the First World War at which Ernest Jones attempted to present the ideas of Freud, and faced an audience which stood up and walked out. By the end of the war the legitimacy of verbal psychotherapy had altered dramatically.

By 1919 the first section of the British Psychological Society to be formed was the Medical Section, which was dominated by shellshock doctors returning from the war. In the same year the British Psycho-Analytical Society was formed. At the same time the government was facing a massive rehabilitation challenge as psychologically distressed combatants both required help and submitted claims for compensation. When the Tavistock Clinic was set up in 1920 its first Honorary President was Field Marshall Haig, signalling the close connection between civilian outpatient service developments and their roots in the recent war.

This large shift within the mental health industry from a pre-war asylum-based and biologically orientated approach to a post-war out-patient psychotherapy approach rendered psychiatric practice much more eclectic after 1920. Nonetheless it was business as usual in the asylums by the time the 1930s arrived and the shellshock problem was fading in social administrative importance. By 1939, with another war imminent and government fears of a repetition of mass neurosis in the military, psychotherapists were being offered a central role in first preparing for such an eventuality and then responding to it. This work on recruitment, morale management and the treatment of war neurosis was dominated by psychoanalysts (Rees, Bion and Main). Bion and Main were involved in the development first of small group work and then therapeutic community developments at the Northfield Military Hospital. A non-analytical psychiatrist (Jones) and a cardiologist (Wood) experimented with various forms of psychological treatment at the Mill Hill Neurosis Unit. After the war Main and Jones exported versions of the therapeutic community from war to civilian settings in the newly formed NHS, respectively at the Cassel and Southern Hospitals.

Thus warfare has had a double impact on the legitimacy of psychotherapy in mental health work. On the one hand it has installed a modern cultural expectation that outpatient psychotherapy should be available. On the other it played a part in attempting (and failing) to humanise the psychiatric hospital.

The Psychiatric Hospital

The psychiatric hospital was part of a State-funded asylum system which emerged in Britain during the nineteenth century. A fuller account of the rise and fall of this system is provided by Rogers and Pilgrim (1996a, Chs 3 and 4). Here I will only note the historical points which are relevant to the current chapter's emphasis on the mental health policy context of psychotherapy. These can be summarised as follows.

1   The Victorian asylum failed to live up to the aspirations of early lunacy reformers, who were keen on reproducing moral treatment from voluntary institutions, like The Retreat in York, in the State sector. Moral treatment can be understood as a precursor of the therapeutic communities of the second part of the twentieth century.

2   This failure was linked to the decline in the power of lay administration. From the middle of the nineteenth century the asylum system came under the managerial control of medical men.

3   Along with this medical dominance came the ascendency of bio-determinism. The new profession of psychiatry from its inception favoured biological explanations for madness, even though then, as now, no clear empirical evidence existed for this type of aetiological theory.

4   The central function of the asylum was to contain lunacy. The institution existed to remove madness from society, even though medical

superintendents in the late Victorian period made unsustainable claims of 'cure'.

5   Given the emphasis on the management of madness, the mental health industry in its infancy, which had the psychiatric hospital at its core, paid no attention to the types of neurotic difficulties favoured by later psychotherapists in the wake of the shellshock problem (see above).

6   The psychiatric hospital during the twentieth century changed little in its practices and knowledge base. Not only were the same buildings utilised for over a century but medical theory and practice remained the same and the management of madness using physical means continued.

7   The First and Second World Wars created the conditions for an expanded mental health industry to include psychotherapy outpatient work during the 1920s and therapeutic communities inside the old hospitals during the 1950s (see previous sub-section). However, the social problem of madness during peacetime meant that it was business as usual in hospitals between the wars. For example, the therapeutic community movement did not come to dominate inpatient work but was kept on the margins by chemotherapy, psychosurgery and ECT.

8   During the 1960s and 1970s the old hospitals (by now called 'bins') came into crisis for a mixture of fiscal and ideological reasons. These included a series of scandals about neglect and brutality (Martin, 1985); their expense (Scull, 1979; Busfield, 1986); and a consensus about the disabling impact of institutionalisation (Barton, 1959; Brown and Wing, 1962). The rise of 'anti-psychiatry' during this period is sometimes cited as a reason for psychiatric hospitals becoming discredited. However, this movement may have been important in putting a rhetorical gloss on the other factors listed. The proper salience of 'anti-psychiatry' may lie, though, in the confidence it gave to the later rise of the mental health service users' movement (Rogers and Pilgrim, 1991).

9   Despite the older hospitals running out of credibility, there was political and medical support for *reinstitutionalisation* rather than proper deinstitutionalisation (Pilgrim and Rogers, 1994). In particular, investment in mental health services was mainly being switched during the 1970s and 1980s from the old asylums to new hospital facilities, usually in district general hospitals. By the 1990s 85 per cent of NHS spending on mental health services was still on hospitals. Despite this, some lobbies such as the organisation SANE (Schizophrenia A National Emergency) have maintained a campaign to defend institutionalisation right up to the time of writing.

10   The recent, more weakly developed and financed community mental health facilities have contained a greater emphasis on psychosocial interventions including psychotherapy. The latter was being demanded during the 1980s by an increasingly vociferous service users' movement which retained a marked antipathy to physical treatments (Rogers and Pilgrim, 1991).

Secure Provision

Whilst the tension between hospital- and community-centred mental health work was being played out during the twentieth century, there was a core part of the asylum system which remained untouched by wider developments. What started as criminal lunatic asylums in the nineteenth century became maximum security hospitals in the next century. These contained offender patients and some difficult-to-manage patients from other psychiatric hospitals who were not offenders.

Maximum secure psychiatric hospitals and therapeutic units within prisons pose a particular problem for psychotherapists. The latter have been employed in such contexts. Indeed some therapists have even written in positive terms about working with 'offender patients' (e.g. Cox, 1974). By contrast others have argued that voluntarism is axiomatic to proper psychotherapy – the constraints of an imposed relationship negate the possibility of a therapeutic contract or make psychotherapy highly problematic in secure settings (Berman and Segal, 1982; Pilgrim, 1988). The former authors make the following points in this regard.

1   The captive client has little or no choice about their therapist or the orientation utilised. For security reasons, the rules of a secure institution may require that custodial staff escort patients to and from sessions or even be present during them. The right of the patient to resist attendance may exist in principle but in practice such an option may jeopardise the patient's probability of discharge.

2   Therapists cannot offer patients undivided loyalty. Absolute confidentiality is impossible in hospital regimes because of multi-disciplinary team discussions. Also therapists employed by secure institutions are expected to supply information for purposes of risk assessment and management.

3   The non-directive tradition of Rogerian therapy or the therapeutic neutrality of psychoanalysis are challenged or undermined by the employers of therapists expecting goal setting and achievement.

4   Those working in a psychoanalytical way will find it difficult to sustain a neat division between transference or counter-transference material and the reality of daily institutional life. As well as seeing one another in contexts other than therapeutic sessions, each party in therapy is aware of the powers of decision making which the therapist holds about the client's future.

Some of these features appear in contexts other than secure provision. For example, the issue of unachievable undivided loyalty recurs in most therapeutic settings (i.e. only the private fee-paying client may reasonably expect absolute confidentiality). Also, the issue about the therapist holding a sword of Damocles over the client's future applies in the context of psychoanalytical training. In that situation, training analysts are expected to sanction a trainee's progress positively or negatively . However, only secure provision provides a setting in which so many constraints operate simultaneously.

These simultaneous constraints led Berman and Segal (1982: 35) to comment that 'the more authoritarian the hospital the more it sabotages psychotherapy'. It is certainly the case that maximum security hospitals make it difficult, and sometimes impossible, for well-intentioned therapists to carry out their work. As for therapeutic units within prisons, their vulnerability is highlighted by the closure (in 1995) of the special unit at Barlinnie Prison in Scotland, despite highly publicised accounts of its rehabilitative impact on residents (Boyle, 1984).

THE MACRO-POLITICAL CONTEXT

Under this heading there are a number of considerations which include the patterning of mental distress in society and psychotherapists' responses to this pattern, explored in Chapters 3–6. The cognitive and financial interests of therapists themselves permeate this context as do the demands set up by mental health service users, which I will address in the next two chapters.

The macro-political context is one which exerts a constant influence on what does and does not happen in therapy or whether it happens at all. It determines, for example, whether people can pay for therapy and also the extent and quality of psychotherapy services delivered by State bureaucracies. The latter quality would, in part, be about the material setting which local health and social services can provide – rooms, decor, furniture, etc. It would also include the amount of resources made available to train and supervise therapists to work in the State sector. This level of context also influences the knowledge base of the mental health industry, although we have to be cautious about claiming neat correlations. For example, it is generally true that psychosocial models have peaked in popularity shortly after the election of liberal or left governments. An example here was the association between President Kennedy's 1963 Community Mental Health Act in the USA and the expansion and popularity of social psychiatry.

By contrast, biological psychiatry has tended to grow in strength during periods of right-wing government administrations. Under both Reagan and Thatcher in the 1980s, biological models regained substantial legitimacy after their unpopularity in the 1960s and 1970s. However, the balance or tension between types of theorising about mental health is played out between interest groups other than central government. These include financial sponsors of research, opposing factions within and between occupational groups and, latterly, the campaigns of service users. These tensions may amplify, modulate or militate against the direct impact of political administrations.

As well as psychoanalysis' shift in legitimacy as a result of warfare, theoretical controversies were engendered about which version of depth psychology was to be pre-eminent. The one Gentile who stood out in Freud's original inner circle and played a central role in one of these controversies was Carl Jung. Unlike the bulk of his colleagues, he was not Jewish and so he was acceptable to the Nazi government after 1933. Moreover, his own theoretical revisions of psychoanalysis had led him to the claim that Jewish and Aryan psychology differed. (By this he meant that the inner lives and the conduct of Jews and others were different.)

During a period when Jews were fleeing or being exterminated, and Freud's books were being burned, Jung retained a protected position of high status in German society. He was President of the International Medical Society for Psychotherapy and took over as Editor-in-Chief of the *Journal for Psychotherapy and Related Disciplines*. The first volume he edited contained an appeal on the part of Matthias Göring (a cousin of Hermann Göring) to psychotherapists to consult *Mein Kampf* as a guide for their work (Masson, 1988). (A more sympathetic but still damning critique of Jung's collusion with Nazism and his expression of anti-Semitic sentiments can be found in Samuels's *The Political Psyche*, which I cited earlier.)

Despite Jung's later unconvincing denials about his collusion with Nazism, his work has retained substantial legitimacy in psychotherapy. He was by no means the only medical practitioner to throw his lot in with fascism. Moreover, within the medical profession in the first part of this century there had been a widespread interest in eugenics in most Western countries. Accordingly, it is not surprising that the first moves about 'involuntary euthanasia' for 'life devoid of meaning' came not from the German National Socialist Party but from the German Medical Association. Hitler merely endorsed their advice. Thus, Jung's collaboration with the Nazi regime can be seen as part of a wider confluence of interests between the upper echelons of the medical profession and State power. Soviet psychiatry would be another later example of this phenomenon (Bloch and Reddaway, 1977). What makes Jung's case special, in relation to this book, is that it is an example not from psychiatry or medicine in general but from *psychotherapy in particular*.

Moving away from the question of knowledge and back to the issue of the social patterning of mental distress, it is clear that the evidence amassed by social causationists, especially in relation to race, class and gender, points to a circumscribed role for psychotherapy in promoting mental health or preventing mental ill-health. Indeed, its *promotional* role is arguably non-existent in practice, though it can play a part in building developmental models of vulnerability to distress (Kessler and Albee, 1977).

Secondary prevention refers to early interventions in community settings and is aimed at nipping problems in the bud before they amplify or become chronic (an example of this might be counselling in primary care settings). Tertiary prevention refers to interventions designed to limit deterioration or prevent relapse in people who have severe or enduring problems. This is indistinguishable from the bulk of the treatment for mental health problems being offered by counsellors and psychotherapists in a range of educational and medical settings.

The strategies for primary prevention necessitate social and political action, guided by a notion of social justice, which would ensure that all people born into a society would have equal access to benign and life-enhancing experiences in their domestic, school and public environments. Thus, the disadvantages associated with fracture lines in society of race, class, age and gender will entail the differential effects on the well-being of individuals created by racism, relative poverty, child abuse, ageism and sexism. It is impossible to address the primary prevention of mental health problems unless these oppressive processes are addressed and opposed (Joffe and Albee, 1981). The discussions in earlier chapters (3–6) make it clear that psychotherapy has a limited and sometimes, because of its silences, even a reactionary role in this regard.

DISCUSSION: THE STRUGGLE TO KEEP CONTEXT IN MIND

By the end of the section on the personal context I was pointing to an occupational hazard for psychotherapists which I have touched on earlier in the book – psychological reductionism. The central insight of Bateson about human selective attention and its consequences applies as much to psychotherapists as anybody else. The problem of reductionism is endemic to human thought. All of us when asked for explanations will tend to opt not only for one *level* of analysis but often for one preferred *variable* within that level. Multi-levelled, multi-factorial reasoning is extremely difficult to maintain.

Basically contextual reasoning is hard work. However, it is not impossible work. We are rescued by our capacity for reflection and the time to revisit our problems and reconstruct our previous accounts. We can make statements about statements (meta-statements). These include introspective reflections, monologues about our own oral and written statements and feedback from and dialogue with others. Without this capacity, the literary critic, the novelist, the academic writer and psycho-therapists and their clients would not be able to function. Moreover, writing contains an iterative potential – we actually learn something new about a topic in the process of assembling our thoughts and knowledge about it *and then* reading what we have assembled.

The inherent tendency towards partiality and reductionism, mitigated by reflectiveness, is not only a cognitive state we share as individuals but it is also driven by collective interests. In other words, a full account of why we tend to be cut off from a world of multi-layered complexity itself needs to invoke more than one level, and these contain several variables. I am aware, to give an iterative example, when reflecting on the list of levels I laid out above, that I omitted at the outset to attend to the biological level. The physical domain of our existence (the existentialist's *Umwelt*) refers to our external material reality *and* our bodies. Why did I make the error of missing out this final building block of understanding?

On reflection, my first answer to this question would be in terms of my goal in this book to strive towards a social understanding of mental health and psychotherapy. But there is more to this. For example, my own professional and disciplinary background in clinical psychology and then sociology has influenced my level of focus. Within that disciplinary context, my judgements about bio-determinism were formed and consolidated. These judgements were and are oppositional and critical. In my clinical work I have witnessed psychiatry as a dehumanising machine, oiled by drug company money and made possible by the cognitive blinkers which many doctors and nurses put on during their professional training. The machine, in my view, has all too often destroyed the self-esteem of people who had more than their fair share of pre-existing problems, and created iatrogenic disability to add insult to injury.

In Chapter 2 I pointed out that a persuasive case can be made *sometimes* for emotional problems being explained in terms of brain dysfunction (e.g. temporal lobe epilepsy). However, the history of psychiatry is the history *inter alia* of a pervasive and highly financed hoped-for-reductionism, with each research corner being turned about to reveal the mystery of mental illness. Despite this, to date there is not a scrap of evidence that any of the main functional problems in people diagnosed as being schizophrenic, manic-depressive, depressed or anxious (i.e. the panoply of 'major and minor mental illnesses') can be partially, let alone fully, explained by bio-determinism. Given the dominant discourse of biological psychiatry, I have a tendency to minimise, evade or forget the relevance of an already over-valued and over-publicised position in the mental health industry.

My main point about drawing attention here to the inadequacies of bio-determinism, then, is not to introduce a perverse anti-psychiatric red-herring within this chapter. Instead, it is being discussed to provide a reflexive example of how collective disciplinary interests, in this case my own, can contribute to the partiality of an analysis.

To summarise, the problem of keeping context in mind has three main components.

1 *Information overload* Individuals cannot keep everything in mind at the same time.

2 *Occupational hazards* Individuals socialised within particular disciplines will prefer one level of analysis to another. To shift a level is not only difficult because of cognitive inertia and ignorance of other levels, but professional identities require epistemological allegiances. To countenance a level of analysis outside that preferred by one's occupational

group entails a form of disloyalty. Moreover, a commitment to a form of working knowledge is a precondition of confident professional performance. If, say, a psychiatrist or psychologist were asked to abandon or radically question their disciplinary knowledge base their work would prove difficult or impossible.

3   *Structural influences*   For example, the way in which research is financed will shape and maintain what is said and not said, what is sponsored and not sponsored, what is formulated and what is ignored. As I noted in the section on macro-political context, there are some circumstances in which the political ideology of the ruling elite within a society will directly engender a particular outlook in those currying favour with their political masters, or simply seeking to maintain their previous social status. Psychotherapists are no more or less immune from such contextual influences.

Bearing in mind these three general considerations about the struggle to reason in a fully contextual way, psychotherapists are prone to two pressures. The first I touch on recurrently in this book – psychological reductionism. The second I noted when discussing, in Chapters 3–6, the resentment of, and resistance to, an objectivist discourse. It is in the latter that findings about structural influence and population level disadvantage are apparent. Yet it is also in this discourse that most offence is given about the legitimacy of subjectivist methodologies, which inform the major styles of psychotherapy. As a consequence, there has been an absence of a productive dialogue between objectivism and subjectivism. This absence constrains participants in both camps from developing a full contextual understanding of the causes, experience and amelioration of mental distress.

8

Watching the Professionals

We do analysis for two reasons: to understand the unconscious and to make a living.

Sigmund Freud, cited in Franz Alexander (ed.), *Psychoanalytic Pioneers*

INTRODUCTION

This chapter has three aims. First, the professionalisation of psychotherapy will be examined. Second, some relevant theoretical perspectives from the sociology of the professions will be outlined. Third, the self-promotion of psychoanalytical psychotherapy will be discussed.

THE PROFESSIONALISATION OF PSYCHOTHERAPY

An unusual aspect of psychotherapy is that it fails to denote a coherent professional group or discipline. At the same time, it can produce a strong subjective identity on the part of individual practitioners. For example, there is a reasonably good conflation between practices like surgery and dentistry and their implied professional groups – surgeons and dentists. This is not the case with psychotherapy, which is largely embedded in a wide range of mental health disciplines. Despite this, individual practitioners who construe themselves as psychotherapists may have a strong sense of professional identity in that role (Kottler, 1986; Guy, 1987). A tension may then exist between a strong subjective role identity, alongside a weak sense of disciplinary affiliation. For example, Mollon (1989) trained first as a clinical psychologist and then as a psychoanalytical therapist at the Tavistock Clinic, London. He reports a clear view of himself in the latter role but a weak sense of himself as a psychologist, even though he is formally employed in the NHS in this capacity. This apparent paradox is probably accounted for by the broad eclecticism within clinical psychology compared to the tighter coherence of the psychoanalytical therapy associated with the Tavistock Clinic.

There are a couple of historical reasons for the stunted professionalisation of psychotherapy. One is that the dominant professions which
subsume the practice began life with a different occupational rationale.
For example, in the British NHS in adult mental health services people
designated as 'consultant psychotherapists' are psychiatrists. However,
psychiatry emerged in the nineteenth century as the dominant profession
involved in the social control of madness, with a preference for biological
interventions. In other words, its primary professional project was never
about the amelioration of distress using talk.

The nearest there was in the nineteenth century to a version of
psychotherapy was moral treatment, which was championed by lay, not
medical managers of asylums (Scull, 1979; Donnelly, 1983). Even much
later in the twentieth century, when warfare created the conditions for
medical psychotherapy to gain legitimacy, it remained a *sub-specialty*
within psychiatry. It has never constituted the core identity of the
latter. Psychotherapeutic initiatives engendered by warfare were kept
very much on the margins of psychiatry. One of the founders of the
therapeutic community movement, Maxwell Jones, makes this point
clearly:

> For orthodox psychiatry it [the therapeutic community] has provided a name
> to be wheeled out whenever it wants to defend Britain's reputation as the
> country which pioneered social psychiatry and to be conveniently forgotten
> otherwise. (quoted in *The Guardian*, 4 August 1984)

Similarly, clinical psychology, which today contains practitioners who
spend some or all of their time practising some version of verbal psychotherapy, was, during its early professional development, not just hostile to
this practice but to *any* treatment role (Eysenck, 1949). Clinical psychology at first focused on psychometric assessment, in line with its wider
disciplinary aspiration of 'disinterested' scientific research. Only later did it
transform itself into a therapeutic profession, by championing behaviour
therapy in the early 1960s, before capitulating to eclecticism, which
brought verbal psychotherapy in from the cold, during the 1970s
(Richards, 1983; Pilgrim and Treacher, 1992).

The second reason why psychotherapy retains a nebulous occupational
status is the utter failure of professionalisers to develop a consensus on
theory and practice. All professions contain differences of style and
emphasis and they have fads of practice which wax and wane. Nonetheless, at any moment in time, they contain a core consensus of theory
and practice. Psychotherapy has never enjoyed this privilege of occupational certainty. Quite the contrary, it has been, and remains, riven
with splits and disagreements which are not minor and technical but
substantial and fundamental. Despite this divided terrain, or maybe
because of it, psychotherapists can be found making statements *implying*
expert certainty, which are unfounded and can border on the ridiculous. I

will return to this question of self-promotion under conditions of an absent consensus in the discussion at the end of this chapter.

De Swaan (1990), in his set of interconnected and illuminating essays (*The Management of Normality*), talks of 'the incomplete professionalisation of psychotherapy' in the light of the embeddedness of the practice within separate occupational groups. Henry et al. (1971) refer to psychotherapy as a 'fifth profession' which (at the time of their writing in a US context) was implied by the intersecting interests of psychology, psychiatry, social work and psychoanalysis. In other words the pre-existence of these groups could only point to an incipient profession of psychotherapy. The four antecedent groups prevented the practice being defined clearly and, because of battles over its content and control, might even impede the development of a genuinely independent profession. This conflict-ridden character of psychotherapy remains today, given the variety of groups which have an interest in the practice and the theoretical disputes which cut across all of them. In Figure 8.1, de Swaan (1990) suggests eight, not four professions which feed into a potential profession of psychotherapy. De Swaan goes on to make the following observation:

> The question remains how those specialists who are trained in other, adjacent occupations but now practise some kind of psychotherapy will be classified: whether and how they are to gain admission to the inner circle of psycho- therapy. In other words there is an occupational circle of psychotherapy, divided into various schools, which is professional in many respects but has not yet succeeded in closing itself off to the adjacent professions and struggles to guard its borders. The umpires in this conflict are the state's subsidising agencies. That does not make the final outcome of the development any more predictable. (de Swaan, 1990: 105)

De Swaan draws upon a working definition from Wilensky (1964) of what constitutes professionalisation. The following components are typically present:

1 A new profession must be a full-time occupational group not just a secondary task embedded in a pre-existing profession with a different core task.
2 A training institute is founded and teaching is later situated in a university setting.
3 Local and then national organisations representing the profession are established.
4 The State begins to allocate credentials to the profession's prac- titioners (or oversees the process of this allocation).
5 The profession imposes a code of conduct on its membership.

Let us take these points one by one. Currently psychotherapy remains a secondary not primary task within occupational groups. Some psycho- therapy training occurs in institutes and some in universities. However,

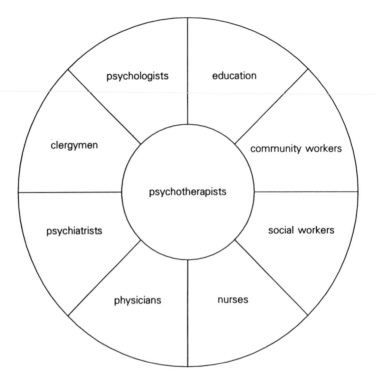

Figure 8.1   *The circle of therapeutic occupations* (from de Swaan 1990: 104)

the curricula of these courses are so variable that marked discrepancies and antagonisms of focus occur between them. Recently in Britain, following 20 years of uncertainty about the state registration of psychotherapy, a credential-awarding umbrella body appeared to be developing (the United Kingdom Council for Psychotherapy). However, from its ranks the self-assigned pre-eminence of psychoanalytical psychotherapy emerged. This splinter group competed first within, and then with, the fragile unitary body and set up its own separate register (the British Confederation of Psychotherapists). One of the problems that these registration bodies have encountered is how to codify good practice, given the wide variations in theory within psychotherapy and the diverse types of practitioner conduct they imply.

Confusion in the area of psychotherapy is heightened by contemporary professionalisation processes being visible in the key feeder professions, of clinical psychology, counselling and counselling psychology. This confusion is a further indication that given a host of pre-existent and nascent professions, and the marked lack of theoretical consensus within them, we cannot speak meaningfully at present of a 'profession of psychotherapy'.

As I note in the discussion later, some writers speak authoritatively, but erroneously, as if such a profession already exists. This may be a reflection of the point I made earlier about psychotherapists having a strong subjective sense of professional identity, even when their external reference group currently does not constitute a profession. By any criterion applied, the professionalisation of psychotherapy is problematic and substantially incomplete.

Before moving on to situate the question of the professionalisation of psychotherapy within three major frameworks from the sociology of the professions, I want to return to a set of insights provided by de Swaan about the micro-processes of therapy and their professional context (de Swaan, 1990, Ch. 6). He deconstructs the initial psychotherapeutic interview to reveal a set of features about a professional's status and peculiar competence. The first interview is a challenge-cum-opportunity for the therapist, via the dialogue, to build and reconstruct their power and credibility with each new encounter. The therapist, not just the client, has a difficult task on their hands.

The situational difficulty for all clients is that this first encounter is inscrutable for three reasons. First there is a discrepancy of knowledge between the two parties about what therapy is as a process, ritual or stylised conversation. Therapists know its character in advance, whereas clients import various degrees of ignorance. It is true that clients vary in how much they already know in general about the nature of therapy, what de Swaan calls 'protoprofessionalisation', but even the most sophisticated neophyte is in the dark compared to the professional.

Second, the presence of the client with *this particular type of professional* rather than another signifies a set of professional processes. The fact that the person has been referred to this professional indicates that the referrer has made an attribution about their special competence, even if the client is not quite sure about the precise nature of this expertise. The client faces a person who has already been conferred with social legitimacy of a particular type.

Third, the ambiguity and vagueness about the nature of the referral protects professionals from revealing hurtful attributions – a diagnosis, a formulation of psychopathology or a reason why the person cannot be helped. The latter dilemma may apply particularly when therapists operate *selection criteria* in which rejected clients are deemed to be 'too damaged', 'borderline' or 'bad bets' for therapy.

The first of these points is elaborated in the quotation I cited from Bannister (1983) in Chapter 7 (see p. 98). The second point contains within it a set of pointers about the social history of the division of labour or jostling for legitimacy associated with the various forms of helping professional. For example, a general practitioner may refer one patient with psychotic symptoms or severe depression to a psychiatrist, another with enduring interpersonal difficulties to a clinical psychologist and a third recovering from a recent bereavement to a counsellor. In turn, each of these therapists may refer on to one another if they feel out of their depth or, conversely, because they do not consider that a client's presenting problem is serious enough to warrant their scarce time and resources.

Some mythologies about these discrepancies of competence may permeate a mental health professional culture. For example, psychiatric staff may believe that, in principle, one should not converse with a patient deemed to be deluded, even though there is no empirical evidence that it will lead to dire consequences. It is likely that the division of labour between psychological therapists and bio-medical therapists has been maintained by this separation of client groups. Some professionalisers have even made such a separation explicit. For example, Eysenck (1975) in his programmatic monograph *The Future of Psychiatry* makes a case for psychologists treating neurosis and leaving madness to the biological jurisdiction of psychiatrists.

All of these considerations about the 'appropriateness' of a referral to this or that therapist are swirling around the unknowing client at their first interview. They are nothing to do with clients, in one sense, and yet highly relevant to their attendance now and possibly in the future. They are within the jurisdiction of the professional web which processes clients and filters some into therapeutic systems and others out.

The third point about inscrutability may appear to be merely a safeguard for the therapist, to avoid the embarrassment of the veiled value judgements which are constituted by psychiatric diagnoses and psychological formulations. There is more to it than this, though. The professional's right to reject as well as accept referrals is vital to their performance, role and status. Early in the relationship the client has to show that they are conversing in a way which is compatible and appropriate for the *therapist*'s needs.

A therapist may look for transference reactions and introduce test interpretations. The client must reveal their biography in a limited time span, in a reasonably coherent manner and with enough effect to suggest appropriate motivation but not too much to suggest that there may be a problem of 'acting out'. Too much hostility early on might make the therapist wary. Too much crazy talk might prevent 'rapport' developing. The biography must be selected by the client in an appropriately negative way – problems must be revealed and strengths submerged, otherwise they may not be considered worthy for treatment. If their presentation is somatic they must show a willingness, or at least a potential, to drop their bodily focus in favour of a discourse about their inner lives or their personal relationships. Of greatest importance, they must all demonstrate 'psychological mindedness' – the more the better. Just as an incorrigible philistine would be out of place even in their first lesson in fine art, a psychotherapy client must on their first encounter *already* show some signs of being psychologically preoccupied.

PERSPECTIVES FROM THE SOCIOLOGY OF THE PROFESSIONS

If it is any comfort to the dispute-ridden world of psychotherapists, sociologists hold varying views about understanding the professions in modern society. (For a fuller review of the sociology of the professions in relation to mental health work see Pilgrim and Rogers, 1993.) Here I will pick out three main perspectives: neo-Weberian; neo-Marxian; and post-structuralist.

The Neo-Weberian Perspective

Two interlinked concepts are at the heart of the neo-Weberian perspective on the professions: social closure and professional dominance (Freidson, 1970; Abel, 1988). The first of these refers to the strategy of occupational groups, to corner the market in a set of practices. This closes these off from other occupational groups working with the same client group. If closure is complete, an occupational group becomes a profession via the phases from Wilensky listed above. A profession defines its own body of knowledge and policies and regulates this knowledge base via training and credentials ('boundary maintenance'). Those on the outside of the profession's boundaries are denied access to its body of knowledge and so cannot appraise its worth. Expert knowledge is thus a source of power to its possessors and of powerlessness to the uninitiated. Rhetorical devices develop with expertise. Experts must communicate enough about their special body of knowledge and practice to convince the public about special and scarce skills. However, too much must not be disclosed or power might leak from the profession's boundaries. Thus, successful social closure provides enough information to persuade but not enough to fully demystify the public.

Professional dominance then flows from social closure. Professionals exercise dominance over others in three senses. First, they hold power over their clients because specialised knowledge renders them ignorant, dependent, vulnerable and insecure. Second, they hold power over their new recruits. The latter are selected, assessed and referenced by their superiors in a dominance hierarchy within professions. Third, professions seek to exercise a dominant relationship over other professions working with the same group.

The disputes about the registration of psychotherapy and the separation of psychoanalytical therapists indicates a jostling for legitimacy about professional dominance in the field of psychotherapy. At this stage it cannot be taken for granted that the registers of practitioners and the codes of practices they imply will improve standards of work or protect the public. The rhetoric of professionals always emphasises these advantages but, as is indicated above, professionalisation *inter alia* is about social advancement of one group in society compared to others. This advancement implies: the struggle for, or maintenance of, dominance; the generation of professional rhetoric; the evasion of public accountability and an emphasis on self-policing; and the disempowerment of those outside professional boundaries. All these features are at their most visible in relation to current attempts by psychoanalytical therapists to define themselves as a pre-eminent group in the field (see later discussion). Whether the professionalisation of psychotherapy, even in its incomplete form, will actually improve the care of people with mental health problems is a moot point.

Another example which is consistent with the neo-Weberian view of modern professions was the battle which took place in the 1950s in the USA and Britain about the control of psychological therapies. In 1954 the American Medical Association declared that psychotherapy was a *medical* procedure. This stance was supported in 1958 by the American Psychiatric Association. Similarly, in Britain clinical psychologists made a bid to control the treatment of neurosis (Eysenck, 1958) and establish a division of labour which would leave madness to medicine. In response psychiatrists set about trying to recapture their monopoly over treatment, re-emphasising, like their US counterparts, that the latter is a medical procedure (Pilgrim and Treacher, 1992).

The Neo-Marxian Perspective

This contains a conflicting mixture of ideas about professions in modern society. The conflict of ideas probably stems from the poor capacity of early Marxian theory to deal with what was then a small social group – the middle class. Only two groups were considered – the ruling class (the bourgeoisie) and the working class (the proletariat), which were associated with the structural opposition between capital and labour. During the twentieth century, with the massive expansion of white-collar work, a middle-class group of managers, scientists, administrators and service workers emerged who did not directly make products for sale and profit by their employers (the production of surplus value). Moreover, some of this new middle class enjoyed very high social status and earnings, even though technically they relied on being employed, and so were wage slaves like their blue-collar equivalents. The mature professions like medicine and law produced practitioners who enjoyed so much status, wealth and autonomy that the notion that all workers were powerless and oppressed became highly stretched.

All these changes in the class formation of Western society posed a problem for Marxism, with its axiomatic vertical opposition between a capitalist and a working class. Three analytical responses were provoked within neo-Marxian work which envisaged:

1 professions as part of the working class (e.g. Oppenheimer, 1975)
2 professions as part of the ruling class (e.g. Navarro, 1979)
3 professions as a contradictory new class (e.g. Carchedi, 1975).

It can be seen on purely logical grounds that positions 1 and 2 from Marxian writers cannot be squared. Position 3 allowed an escape from this conceptual embarrassment. Carchedi argues that the new middle class serves the interest of capital but is constituted by wage slaves with variable economic and social power. The middle class thus contains both reactionary and progressive political interests. Consequently, there is a 'cleavage' of political consciousness in its ranks. This claim is evident in a number of contemporary phenomena. For example, left-of-centre political parties are now led by middle-class people. Also, professionals often have dual affiliations – one straining towards social advancement and the other emphasising worker solidarity. For example, clinical psychologists may typically belong to both a trade union *and* their professional organisation. The profession will contain a mixture of right- and left-wing political opinion. Their work is regulated by the regimes of health service management such as having to record their daily activity. On the other hand (unlike most blue-collar workers) they are not required to clock on and off from their working day.

The examples just given demonstrate that the neo-Marxian perspective has a capacity to explain the role of professionals in modern society in a way which is more sympathetic but with less clarity than the critical stance of the neo-Weberians. For example, psychotherapists can be seen as agents of regulation by gently returning misfits to the conformity of life in capitalist society. At the same time, they can be framed as sources of mitigation, social support and personal comfort – humane palliatives for the victims of alienation in that society.

Within a Marxian framework, mental health work spans two functions in capitalist societies. It is part of an ideological apparatus, which individualises distress and deflects scrutiny from, or closes off, oppressive and alienating social conditions. But it is also part of a repressive state apparatus (Althusser, 1971). Currently in Britain the Mental Health Act and the Prevention of Terrorism Act allow for the lawful incarceration of people without trial. Moreover, mental health law can lead to long-term detention even when no law has been broken by the detainee. The dual ideological and repressive role of mental health workers creates a tension about talking treatments. As I noted in Chapter 7, when discussing treatment in secure provision, psychotherapy fits poorly inside repressive structures. It works at its best in a voluntary and individual contract. Indeed psychotherapy celebrates voluntarism and individualism. Thus by and large its role is ideological, benign and even emancipatory, not repressive. It is for this reason that the leadership of 'anti-psychiatry' both in Britain and the USA was constituted by psychoanalysts (Laing and Szasz) who focused their critical writings on coercive psychiatry. However, psychotherapy may still be framed within a Marxian account as serving the interests of the capitalist state (Keane, 1984).

The Post-Structuralist Perspective

The post-structuralist account of psychological expertise is close to, but not identical to, the ideological emphasis of Marxism but fairly antagon-istic to its repressive concerns. For example, Miller and Rose (1988) make the following point:

> We argue that it is more fruitful to consider the ways that regulatory systems have sought to promote subjectivity than to document the ways in which they have crushed it. (Miller and Rose, 1988: 174)

Miller and Rose develop the work of Foucault, whose early writings on the emergence of psychiatry emphasised the coercive role attacked by 'anti-psychiatry'. This is why Foucault is sometimes classified as an 'anti-psychiatrist' and why he has provoked the ire of defenders of the psy-chiatric faith (e.g. Wing, 1978). Once the twentieth century was reached, the demonstrable repressive role of psychiatry certainly became clouded by psychological interventions offered within voluntary relationships, which were anxiously sought and gratefully received. Miller and Rose are correct to note that, at that juncture, power shifted in form from its repressive to its 'disciplinary' form, even if they overstate the degree of this transition (Pilgrim and Rogers, 1994).

The work I noted by Stone about shellshock and psychotherapy in Chapter 6 highlighted the shifting discourse within mental health work away from the incarceration and institutional treatment of madness and towards outpatient psychotherapy. This development meant that psycho-therapists were part of a range of expertise which increasingly 'sought to promote subjectivity'. As I noted in Chapter 2, the post-structuralist emphasis is on the construction of subjectivity, not upon the older humanistic assumption of *a priori* selves.

Rose (1990) develops this line of reasoning expansively in the last four chapters of his *Governing the Soul*, when discussing psychotherapy. Here I will summarise some of his main points:

1   The discourses of psychotherapy now permeate modern society, influencing groups beyond the narrow confines of the psychologically distressed and the experts who treat them. They can be found, for example, in general medicine, education, advertising, journalism and business management.

2   There has also been a countervailing discourse from critical social analysts and historians about a 'modern obsession with the self' and a 'tyranny of intimacy in which narcissism is mobilised in social relations'.

3   Modern psychotherapeutic discourses mimic, and to some degree displace, the older focus of religion upon spiritual pilgrimages. The growth of Protestantism, with its emphases on individual guilt and responsibility, marked a bridge between medieval religion and the modern culture of

the self and individualism. At the same time, what Elias (1978) calls the 'civilising process' began to define modernity by self (i.e. not State) regulation and by the attention of ordinary people to the minutiae of their everyday conduct (the growth in importance of etiquette and manners). This shifted the focus of social regulation away from the repressive power of the State and towards self-surveillance and self-control. One impact of this shift, according to Foucault (1981), was an emphasis on confession to oneself and others. Another was that spontaneity and impulsiveness were rendered as problematic, and thus in need of careful self-management.

4   Versions of the confession then become a means by which identities are described or subjectivity is inscribed upon the confessor. The confession 'is installed at the heart of contemporary procedures of individualisation' (Rose, 1990: 240). Once inserted as a general principle into modern human relationships, the confession creates the conditions for expertise about subjectivity to develop. This expertise, which is constituted by psychotherapists and counsellors, has been associated with the 'subjectification of work'; 'the psychologisation of the mundane'; 'a therapeutics of finitude'; and 'a neuroticisation of social intercourse'. These four strands that Rose picks out refer to ways in which work, common life transitions, disappointment, death and, more pervasively, our relationships with friends, lovers and colleagues, have become saturated with diverse authoritative constructions from therapists.

5   Rose applies a threefold Foucauldian scheme to psychotherapeutic expertise. First, there are *moral codes* which are spelt out in the language used by, and the ethical principles of, therapy. These counterpose mental health and psychopathology and imply some notion of 'the good life'. Second, there are *ethical scenarios*,

> the apparatuses and contexts in which the moral codes are administered and the means by which they are enjoined – in the school and the courts, in the practices of social work and medicine, in the private consultation, in the radio phone-in, in the solitary act of reading or viewing. (Rose, 1990: 241)

Third, there are *techniques of the self* (Foucault, 1988) which are developed to systematise and codify the exploration, confrontation and development of the self. These do not constitute a unitary body of practices and ideas, although all are concerned to create psychological change in their targets. Instead, heterogeneity characterises the terrain of psychotherapy – narratives of the self are developed in a large variety of forms.

6   These technologies of the self, which are promoted and celebrated by psychotherapists, are not designed to serve the interests of capital, nor are they a form of directed social control from the State (cf. one neo-Marxian view). There is no conspiracy or hidden hand, which affords therapists a role or pulls their strings. Instead, the overarching purpose of the therapies is to align or reconcile the desires and needs of individuals with the social, political or organisational goals which situate their existence – to produce, if possible, a 'win/win' outcome.

Thus, it can be seen that the post-structuralist account of professional psychotherapy enters the analysis from a different angle from the neo-Weberians and the neo-Marxians. The latter start their understanding with a focus on practitioners, as an *a priori* social group to be described, analysed and evaluated. The post-structuralists end up with an understanding of professional work (discursive practices) but do so as part of a wider critical reading of the rise of modernity. As a consequence, whereas the neo-Marxians have mixed sympathies for healing professionals, and the neo-Weberians are sceptical about their antics, the post-structuralists place more of an emphasis on their being trapped (like their clients) in a variety of discourses of subjectivity and individualism.

In one sense this is more damning, even than the scepticism of the neo-Weberians. In another sense, it refuses to attribute blame or make accusations, given that stable and coherent identities are brought into question (including those of therapists themselves). Having said this, Rose, in a rare moment in his text, slips into a language close to the neo-Weberians to a point where therapists are accused of dominating other professions:

> The practitioners of psychotherapy have succeeded in colonising [sic] the professions with their own vocabularies, images, evaluations, and techniques, and in extending and increasing these sites for the operation of therapeutic encounters. (Rose, 1990: 244)

With this ambiguity around, about the 'colonising' power of psychotherapists, let me now turn to my own critical reading of their self-promotion.

DISCUSSION: SHRINK RAP AND SHRINK RESISTANCE

Psychotherapy has suffered from a drip, drip, drip of criticism over time from a number of sources. This, as yet unresolved, problem about its legitimacy has been softened by the countervailing tendency on the part of some key players in mental health debates to idealise talking treatments. Over the past 20 years disaffected psychiatric patients, in rejecting psychiatric drugs, psychosurgery and ECT, have placed their faith instead in counselling and psychotherapy (see Chapter 9). This tendency has been reinforced by the wave of critical clinicians ('anti-psychiatry') which preceded and encouraged the rise of the users' movement (Rogers and Pilgrim, 1991). These mental health workers were psychotherapists as well as social critics.

The unresolved battle for credibility about psychotherapy is manifested currently in the ways in which therapists are given free, or paid, space within newsprint. The representation of psychotherapy *by its own practitioners* in newspapers highlights this question of credibility well. On the one hand, therapists are given free rein to promote their wares and to extend their authority outside the consulting room by becoming pundits on family life and politics. On the other hand, the fact that they feel obliged to ascribe this role of modern-day sage to themselves implies that the legitimacy of their work may be under threat. Therapists taking time away from their clients to defend their trade suggests that they find the need to market their product to a lay audience, which may contain hostile or unconvinced elements. Let me turn to some illustrative example of these points.

In 1996 the main liberal 'quality' newspaper in Britain, *The Guardian*, ran a series of articles by psychoanalysts about psychoanalysis. Tellingly, in marketing terms, the series was kickstarted by an analyst who was widely known, and liked, in a previous career – Mike Brearley, the ex-England cricket captain. In the third in the series, Sally Weintrobe provided a simple, if not simplistic, account in response to her rhetorical query, 'Just what is a psychoanalyst?' In answering, the author made these, amongst other, points:

> The psychoanalyst has become an icon – usually as a man although just as likely these days to be a woman – of popular culture. The public has its own relationship with what the psychoanalyst is, quite separate from how the profession sees and defines itself. One place their relationship shows is in cartoons and jokes. Through humour we can focus and defuse our fear of finding ourselves in the vulnerable position of needing help with emotional problems and putting our trust in another person. In the world of the joke, the doctor is bound to let us die, the lawyer will certainly fleece us and the psychoanalyst along with the psychiatrist will be a head shrinker . . . Jokes about shrinks can be revealing about people's ambivalence about gaining self-knowledge and looking at *the truth* about themselves. People tend to disown thoughts and feelings when they cause too much conflict or distress. 'It's not we who are out of touch! It's the shrink.' We can locate in the psychoanalyst what we don't like to see in ourselves. We send her up and send her on her way. (Weintrobe, 1996: 7, my emphasis)

This is a rather lengthy quote but I kept it rolling because each sentence has an illustrative relevance to points I make episodically in this book. I would suggest the following sub-textual messages of the patronising vignette, sentence by sentence:

S1   Psychoanalysts are very important, quasi-mystical people to the laity. The latter are ignorant of the reality of the former's work, including its gendered nature. The word 'icon' has a religious connotation – a concrete manifestation of God or a product of a religious order. Psychoanalysts have a status near to Godliness.
S2   Being outsiders the public do not (and, maybe, can never) understand the actuality of psychoanalysis.
S3   Lay people, being ignorant, have to substitute facts with jokes.

S4   These jokes are products of the unconscious life of ordinary people who, unlike psychoanalysts, are fearful of dependency, intimacy and 'the truth'.

S5   Lay people have the ridiculous idea that experts cannot be trusted or can do them harm.

S6   Lay people, unlike psychoanalysts, are fearful of the truth (sic) about themselves. 'The truth' has a non-problematic existence but it eludes ordinary, unanalysed, mortals.

S7 and S8   Lay people make faulty critical judgements of mental health professionals to protect themselves and evade responsibility for their inner angry impulses. The author illustrates the notion of projection without naming it. This elision indicates a central tool of ideological pre-eminence held by analysts and analytical therapists. As an explanatory concept, projection affords them unique powers of human understanding and so unique *power*.

S9   In irrationally rejecting psychoanalysis, the silly public do not realise that they are missing out on a close-by source of treasure.

Like all interpretations and paraphrases, mine may be faulty – but they are plausible. Moreover, unlike the insights from the case work of psychoanalysts, which we are asked to take on trust, mine are based on, and are close to, public material – we can all read and re-read the text the therapists have deliberately made into public property. The plausibility of my preferred critical reading increases when the cumulative sub-text is overviewed. This is something like this: 'Psychoanalysts are special trustworthy experts and their prospective clients, as inferior souls, are unaware and evasive about their need for help. This evasiveness itself is a symptom of psychopathology.'

If there was not a hidden agenda, which assumed the need for therapeutic redemption for the pre-analysed reader, why was the series of articles negotiated by psychoanalysts at all? This is the first of a few silences. Potentially image-damaging internal divisions and feuds within psychoanalysis are ignored or papered over. The many substantive arguments against psychoanalysis, as a body of knowledge, including those from other styles of verbal psychotherapy, are not raised or addressed. Empirical evidence is ignored about psychotherapy outcome. Whilst ordinary people are blamed for their ignorance, institutional psycho-analysis is not blamed for its elitist and secretive culture, which seals it off from public scrutiny and accountability.

At the end of Weintrobe's article, in an italicised postscript, is an announcement for readers about the register of practitioners held by the BCP and information on how they might access free therapy from trainees at the Institute of Psycho-Analysis. No point is made in the core text, though, about the Confederation's aloof separation from the UKCP, nor the fact that the pre-emptively expensive nature of psychoanalysis excludes the great majority of the population from its practice.

In another article in *The Guardian* series, Eric Brenman (12 June 1996) tells us how psychoanalysis 'helps us to bear the unbearable and think the unthinkable'. In addition to enabling us in this heroic task, assuming we can afford the fees, psychoanalysis, according to Brenman, has to suffer attacks from hostile critics who are driven by 'cannibalistic impulses'. The latter are:

> inherent primitive forces that motivate human beings. This syndrome [sic] can be observed in wealth seeking, wars, sexual conquests, racism, political beliefs, religious corruption . . . It is the capacity to know about our primitive selves and know of our human and truth[sic]-seeking values which conflict with them which offers hope for humanising our barbarism . . . Whatever part environmental factors may play in helping or impairing the capacity to meet life, which indeed need to be understood, at the end of the day, the most difficult and the most disturbing area is coming to terms with oneself. (Brenman, 1996: 7)

This is psychological reductionism at its most arrogant and offensive. Its arrogance rests conceptually in its imperialistic scope, which reduces complex socio-political phenomena about power, inequality and oppression to a 'syndrome' arising from 'inherent' forces inside individuals. Who needs a wealth of scholarship in history, economics, sociology or political science, when Brenman's version of psychoanalysis, with its focus on cannibalistic impulses, will explain everything at one go? It is offensive because of its casual dismissal of the salience of material reality. Yes, he concedes, environmental factors 'need to be understood' (read this as 'they are only of secondary or marginal importance') but, from the Kleinian psychoanalyst's perspective, self-knowledge must be privileged. It is not made explicit by Brenman that he is a Kleinian. Only if one is privy to the language and logic of Klein (re inherent cannibalistic impulses) can one make this deduction.

It is the latter part of the quote that I cite which is an example of the discourse of psychoanalysis being a muddle of asserted psychological over-determinism and smug middle-class morality. It may be that in the comfortable world of Hampstead, and its immediate surroundings in north London, coming to terms with oneself can or should be privileged. But if you are an unemployed teenage mother on a run-down council estate and fungus is growing on the wall by your baby's cot, social justice could be considered as a more important priority than exhortations about individual self-knowledge. In such circumstances, it might also be that the 'most difficult and the most disturbing area' for such a young mother is not about knowing herself but about learning how to bear the daily grind of poverty. It could also be the case that people who survive poverty might in their own way be more heroic than those who after being many hours on the couch, and several thousand pounds lighter in the pocket, learn how to 'bear the unbearable and think the unthinkable'.

I mentioned in Chapter 1 that psychoanalysis has enjoyed a privileged cultural position. To reinforce this point it is noticeable that *The Guardian* does not run a series on teaching by teachers or engineering by engineers, nor are these professionals given *carte blanche* to demonstrate their moral superiority to the rest of humanity. This suggests that psychoanalysts are afforded a special niche of credibility within the educated classes of contemporary Western democracies. Despite this niche, they are prone to complain about being misunderstood and unappreciated, as Brenman's note about cannibalistic critics indicates. (I explore this point further below.)

One of the less noted contradictions about psychotherapists becoming general experts in living in the pages of newspapers is that they draw their authority from clinical practice, where idiosyncratic biographical meanings are supposed to be explored over a long period of time *in strict confidence*. A few years ago, one prestigious family therapist and psychoanalyst drew the wrath of a client, who understandably complained in a letter to the newspaper hosting a regular column by the practitioner. The latter had provided a too thinly disguised case study of the client and her family. This was a fair cop. My only surprise is that so many therapists still get away with their exploitation of their clients in print so often.

Composite, disguised or possibly invented case material is awash in the regular column of another therapist, Susie Orbach, who writes 'Shrink Rap' for the weekend magazine supplement of *The Guardian*. Just as it was no coincidence that the prior public persona of Mike Brearley was chosen as an opening marketing gambit, Orbach's prior credibility has a relevance. She was already well known, particularly in a social stratum of feminists who had passed through higher education in the 1960s and 1970s, for her popular books on women and mental health. Her founding, with Luise Eichenbaum, of Women's Therapy Centres in London and New York has led to her name being respectfully linked to progressive innovations in contemporary psychotherapy. Recently she has been a co-founder of Antidote, an organisation aiming to improve levels of 'emotional literacy' in society. She is not a formally trained psychoanalyst but she vigorously disseminates psychoanalytical ideas in her 'Shrink Rap'.

When reading her column in the 1990s (which I do regularly with a mixture of admiration and despair) it is never quite clear whence her constructed cases arise. On the one hand, if the material is literally invented, then these are Orbach's fictions, begging the question, 'What is her mandate to draw general lessons about living from her own imagination?' Could any of us simply make up stories and scenarios and turn them into morality tales? Alternatively, if they are *not* invented, then they are about real people she knows. Does she secure their permission for using them as case material? If so, do they get part of her writing fee? If not, and it applies to clients, is there a potential breach of hallowed confidentiality?

Typically, there is a ritualistic *denouement* to Orbach's articles – a moral or technical conclusion deduced from the case material presented. For those who have not read 'Shrink Rap', let me give the gist of its style and content by providing some examples. The first I take from *The Guardian Weekend* (14 October 1995). It is entitled 'Remembrance Day' and is about the nature of remembering and forgetting in everyday family life. I will quote the first and final paragraphs to illustrate the case-material-build-up and the wisdom-clinching-punch-line approach which often typifies 'Shrink Rap':

> She looked down and realised he'd forgotten his physics book. Yesterday it was his trainers. 'Shit', she cursed. 'Testosterone.' Her 17-year-old son was forgetful. She alternated between blaming his Dad, whose forgetfulness drove her crazy, and self-recrimination: 'Maybe it's all that remembering I did for him that stops him remembering for himself.' (Orbach, 1995: 6)

There are then three large paragraphs in which Orbach becomes pedagogic about Freud's notion of repression. She then returns, in the core of the article, to the conduct and inner lives of the family members she introduces. She imputes intrapsychic motives and summarises interpersonal dynamics within this family. We are not told how she knows all this stuff, let alone in this amount of personal detail. Conversely there are also gaps in what is depicted. Is the family poor, rich, urban, rural, living, dead, black, white? Was one or more of them her client? We are not told. The family description is gendered and inter-generational, and that is all we know. Of course the author is inevitably constrained for space, but that is a hazard she chooses actively when seeking to peddle her views in a newspaper column.

Then there are three paragraphs of discussion in which Orbach leaps out of the family scenario and into the type of grandiose and reductionist political extrapolation I noted from Brenman above, such as: 'This seesaw of remembering and forgetting in the family environment echoes less benign conflicts between nations, groups of people or intimates.' The article finishes on a dreamy note of self-assigned profundity:

> But remembering from the psychoanalytical perspective is not so much a moral issue as an inter-personal one and a collective contract. What's easily [sic] observed [sic] is that when more of us take responsibility for remembering what mustn't be forgotten, for acknowledging rather than denying, the less painful becomes the task of the rememberers. The less attractive too becomes the way of forgetfulness. (Orbach, 1995: 6)

The silent majority of therapists are coy compared to Orbach. They pursue their work with clients quietly and with probity. Maybe they are the unassuming corner shop which is happy to let therapist-cum-journalists advertise their wares on billboards to encourage an inflow of customers. There is a demand as well as supply side to this question of a sustained self-promoting discourse from therapists. We live in an age where self-help literature, in general, and popular psychological guides to living, in particular, are consumed with relish by enough people to pay their authors well (Giddens, 1992).

Given the incidence of mental health problems, and demands for talking treatments within this group, there is no overall need, at present, for psychotherapists to generate demand. The latter emerges spontaneously from a mixture of pathogenic social forces discussed in Chapters 3–6. However, what psychotherapists are probably sensitive about is sustaining a mandate for their *particular* orientation, clique or club. I think that this, as well as wage slavery, personal vanity and professional arrogance, explains the self-promotion deployed by journalistic therapists.

The tendency for psychodynamic therapists in particular to set their stall out may suggest that they, more than practitioners with other orientations, are suffering a crisis of confidence about their assumed superiority in the field of psychotherapy. The formation of the BCP Register signals this assumption. But maybe such bravado covers up internal doubt. The latter may have arisen from sensitivities about the recent wide societal concern about the impact of child sexual abuse (see Chapter 6). In such a context, analytical therapists have been trying over the past 10 years to distance themselves from the evidence of Freud's betrayal of the victims of incest (Masson, 1985) whilst, at the same time, preserving an authoritative mandate to respond to the emotional legacy of this and other forms of psychological insult in childhood. But, why should the public trust a tradition whose founding father capitulated so readily to social pressure about his early findings about intra-familial abuse?

To return to the regular column of Orbach. In some examples of 'Shrink Rap' (e.g. 1996a, 1996c) she devotes whole articles to potted lectures about psychoanalysis or draws upon real-life events. In the first of these she is concerned to defend analytical therapy from misconceptions ('parodies' and 'distortions') promoted by the media. She does concede, though (cf. Weintrobe, 1996), that these are fuelled by ambivalence within psychoanalysis and psychotherapy about dissemination. Despite the unacknowledged position of privilege she holds *inside* a respectable journalistic outlet, she claims that these media inspired attributions have led to 'the profession' [sic] becoming a victim of 'scorn, confusion, ridicule and fear' (1996a). This is followed by a brief pedagogical exercise in putting the record straight about the nature of psychoanalytical therapy and culminating in the emphatic statement that the 'psychoanalytical enterprise' is devoted to 'Freud's most eloquent aphorism: psychoanalysis is about transforming hysteria into ordinary human misery' (Orbach, 1996a).

The choice of this particular Freudian point by Orbach is curious given the style of feminist therapy she has championed and nurtured. It is at odds with her own published claim that during her career of 25 years as a therapist she has only seen 'two neurotics' (Orbach, 1996b). Moreover, the aphorism leaves too many loose ends to be a persuasive clinching statement about the utility of psychoanalytical therapy in modern society.

Which Freud, now long dead, are we supposed to venerate? Is it the one of this aphorism? Is it the inventor of classical psychoanalysis or the major revisionist of his own work? Is it the one who believed in the reality of the sexual molestation of daughters by fathers or the one who changed his mind and began blaming the victims of incest? Maybe it is the Freud who considered that the writings of 'emancipated' women were driven by penis envy, the source of the 'hostile embitterment' of women against men. Orbach would certainly fall squarely within this target of misogyny from the founder of psychoanalysis she so admires.

And what of psychoanalysts who are not Freudians – the Kleinians (like Brenman), the object relations theorists, the Independents and the Lacanians? They are part of the tellingly termed 'psychoanalytical enterprise' but would they stand by the aphorism? And where and what is 'hysteria' in 1996 rather than 1896? The final question these loose ends beg is this: is it that the media have mischievously created confusion about psychoanalysis or is it simply that the latter is divided within its own secretive ranks and so is predictably mystifying to its potential clientele?

The factionalism inside psychoanalysis is evident in a recent aborted media stunt of an analyst from a different theoretical stable from Orbach. On 2 May 1996, British TV's Channel 4 announced its withdrawal of a controversial programme it was near to screening. In 'Psychoanalysing Diana' the Lacanian analyst Dylan Evans is placed at the back of a Princess Di look-alike reclining on a couch. He proceeds to construct an analytical dialogue, with a script partially culled from actual public statements of the real royal. If these diverse statements were to be the bricks in the dialogue, the cement was to be the fabricated wizardry of Evans. The scripted interventions from Evans were to include this pointed example of 'product placement':

> 'Princess Di': What is psychoanalysis about?
> Evans: It's about speaking the truth about your desire.

Here we are back to 'the truth' again, which is a high-risk, if grand, product to market. As an indication of Evans's factionalism, he scripts himself the following intervention, in a snipe against Orbach: 'Fat isn't just a feminist issue' (cited in Jeffries, 1996: 8). Orbach has been the Princess's real life therapist, which might account for Jeffries making this point.

Psychotherapy and Society

The programme was also to include a statement of unintended multiple irony. Evans says to 'Di', 'Nothing you say here will go outside these four walls.' However, the script escaped to journalists (hence my ability to quote it here). The programme was not screened but was intended to be part of a series called 'Without Walls'. Who is playing games with whom here? Does it serve the 'psychoanalytical enterprise' well or does it unwittingly reveal its absurd self-regard? Does psychoanalysis engender caution and humility about the complexities of human frailty or is it just as prone to the egotism and arrogance which is pregnant in any group of well-paid professionals?

A few days after the programme was withdrawn, Evans secured a piece for himself in *The Guardian* (Evans, 1996) in which, like Orbach above, he complained bitterly about a media conspiracy in Britain against psychoanalysis. He also noted that psychologists and psychiatrists, who were not analysts, offered formulations and diagnoses in newspapers but were not criticised. If there is a conspiracy of this sort it would seem that it does not extend to at least one newspaper, which seems content to host innumerable defences of the discipline. As for the fair comment by Evans that other mental health professionals are as guilty of speculations in print, this merely demonstrates that professional arrogance knows no disciplinary boundaries. Far from justifying wild analysis in the public domain, it confirms that it is no better or worse than other forms of professional self-promotion.

Moreover, it is not the case that non-analysts avoid the derision of journalists. For example, when discussing the withdrawn programme, Francis Wheen in *The Guardian* (8 May 1996) singles out the regular space given by the tabloid *Daily Mail* to Raj Persaud, a consultant psychiatrist from the Institute of Psychiatry in London. Wheen notes, sneeringly but accurately, that the latter 'specialises in conducting long-distance diagnoses of people he has never met' (Wheen, 1996: 5).

In another example from 'Shrink Rap' (Orbach, 1996c), the tragic events at Dunblane primary school in March 1996 in Scotland are discussed, in which a man shot dead 16 children and their teacher before turning the gun on himself. The first half of the article is about praising the insights of Winnicott before the aftermath of the shootings is considered. A bridge between the two parts of the article is the statement: 'Winnicott's work still has lots to teach us, both in the ordinary business of day-to-day parenting and in the aftermath of the loss and trauma that is Dunblane.' When Orbach is not idealising Freud she invites her readers to cast their adoring gaze upon Winnicott. But the latter like his predecessor, was an ambiguous hero. In charging mothers with the biological duty to offer 'good-enough' care for their infants, he began a post-war trend in welfare professional surveillance. As White (1996) has pointed out, such a professional preoccupation with mothering skills has often been an oppressive burden upon young women who are already struggling with depression and material disadvantage.

I feel the diverse examples I give above from Orbach (whom I cite more because she has a regular column), Weintrobe, Brenman and Evans are fair and representative of psychoanalytical therapists using the media for their own ends. Taking them as a whole, it is clear that psychoanalytical sermons differ little from Billy Graham selling Christianity or Kellogg's advertising their cornflakes.

It should be noted that the lengthy fee paying therapy associated with the psychoanalytical tradition I criticise here, is not the whole therapy industry. Low fee and free therapy are common in the voluntary sector tradition where eclectic and humanistic models are common (for example in The Samaritans and Relate).

If we are to appraise, rather than merely praise, the work of therapists, what conclusions should we draw? Broadly there are two responses to this question. One is to simply acknowledge that we now live in a postmodern world and, accordingly, focus on deconstructing the 'certainties' of an old modernist project like psychoanalysis, as I have done in part above (see Chapter 2). Such a critical reading or iconoclastic push might then allow in, a rich set of diverse alternatives to exploring subjectivity and distress, which would be unfettered by the rhetorics of knowing 'experts' – the scorn of Derrida.

Paradoxically, I also think that another aspect of the old modernist project can play a role in destabilising older, unwarranted certainties. It is at this point, in this second response, that the democratic relevance of the objectivist discourse I discussed in Chapter 2 reappears. This is not damning of psychotherapy. As I note below and in the next chapter, it provides grounds for a cautious endorsement.

Ironically, apart from professional competitors, who are prone to dismiss prejudicially the utility or effectiveness of verbal psychotherapy (behaviour therapists, organic and some social psychiatrists), there are some trained therapists who find their trade irredeemable, such as Jeffrey Masson in his *Against Therapy* (1988). He seems so concerned to throw the baby out with the bath water, in his nihilistic dismissal of psychotherapy, that he evades the complications surrounding the mixed evidence about its effectiveness (Pilgrim, 1992; Owen, 1995). Because his rejection of therapy is axiomatic, not evidence-based, he condemns but he does not weigh up costs and benefits.

My own view is that the self-promoting and self-policing discourse of therapists is arcane and autocratic and requires democratic checks. Outcome research is one basis for the latter. Another is to take the collective feedback of service users seriously, which is anathema to some therapists – a point I will expand on in the next chapter. Outcome research and user involvement do not solve all the complex questions surrounding the relationship between people with mental health problems and the role of professionals in responding to their distress. However, they do provide us with food for thought in the light of the cautions implied by the neo-Marxian, and particularly the neo-Weberian, perspectives within the sociology of the professions, discussed earlier. They also create the basis for policy debate and guidance about psychotherapy for government.

Because this is not a book on psychotherapy outcome research (see Bergin and Garfield, 1994; Seligman, 1995; Parry, 1997 for reviews of the relevant literature) I will limit myself here only to summarising four main messages from this rich and complex field relating to my argument about democratic accountability.

1   Overall, psychotherapy is effective (compared to no treatment) in ameliorating a variety of types of psychological distress.
2   However, it is not effective in all cases. Some people show no benefit from psychotherapy and some become more distressed.
3   Much of the variance of deterioration effects is attributable to incompetent, inconsistent or abusive therapists. The first two therapist problems reflect poor training or a lack of 'treatment fidelity'. The third reflects unethical behaviour.
4   Differences in outcome in psychotherapy (both positive and negative) are not accounted for by the theoretical orientation of therapists.

Taking these messages one by one, the following implications arise.

1   *Equality of access*   If psychotherapy is effective, a question is raised about equality of access. Are all the people who want it, and could benefit from it, gaining access to competent therapists? We know that there are national, regional, racial and class differences operating here (see Chapters 3–6). Also, some diagnostic groups are favoured. There is some evidence, for instance, that although people with severe mental health problems both desire and can be helped by talking treatments, they are not given the opportunity to access psychotherapy. Once a label of psychosis is acquired, drug treatment tends to predominate and psychotherapists avoid working with psychotic clients (Karen and VanDeBos, 1981; Pilgrim, 1992).
2   *Informed consent to treatment*   If some people are not helped by therapy, or they may deteriorate, this suggests that prospective clients of psychotherapy should be informed about the potential variable outcome at the outset of therapy. To my knowledge, therapists (myself included) do not habitually rehearse these estimates with new clients.
3   *Minimising iatrogenic effects*   Following from the above point, effective ways and means should be sought to reduce the incidence of therapists or interventions which are ineffective or, worse, create iatrogenic damage. In this context, cautiousness about entering or continuing in therapy may be a sign of client wisdom and may not necessarily imply projection or evasion. It *is* resistance (in the everyday rather than technical sense) but it is reasonably warranted. It reflects the subversive glint in Foucault's eye which stares back, defiantly, at Freud's patriarchal scowl.

Professionals may help lay people, but sometimes they can also damage and exploit them. Psychotherapists are particularly vulnerable to this charge because they spend so much time working under conditions of privacy with vulnerable clients. Ineffective or injurious therapists working in private practice are asking their clients literally to pay for the privilege of not being helped.

Because codes of conduct and registers have been closely entwined with social closure and occupational group advancement, these measures need to be assessed sceptically. Do they protect the public or are they simply a professionalisation strategy? Could they be both? Should we be looking at employment and work protocols *other than* registration to make therapists accountable and to protect clients from the vagaries of relationships in which one party is powerful and the other vulnerable?

In a recent critique of the principle of psychotherapy registration, Mowbray (1995) points out that whilst there is no empirical evidence from the USA that registration reduces client abuse, there are grounds for deducing that it reduces the supply of therapists, drives up costs to clients, restricts the entry of educationally disadvantaged ethnic minorities and inhibits innovation. This suggests that whilst there remain strong grounds for the social control of incompetent and abusive therapists, registration may not achieve this end. It may produce the privileges of social closure and upward mobility to practitioners but deliver few demonstrable advantages to their clientele.

4   *There are no special experts in human misery*   Therapists of particular orientations have no privileged insight into human misery and it is fundamentally misleading for them to claim a pre-eminent understanding, supposedly derived from their preferred way of working. The work of Rose, that I discussed earlier, is relevant here. Therapeutic orientations are merely different ways in which narratives about the self can be constructed. Currently, we have no benchmark to judge whether one narrative is better than another, and one may never appear. The arrogance of therapist–journalists is not an answer to this uncertainty. Assertion is not persuasion, unless one wants it to be. Moreover, the journalistic outpourings from psychoanalytical writers, that I discussed above, lack a mandate in empirical evidence. There is a particular irony about the seriousness with which psychoanalytical therapists take themselves, with their 'special' register of practitioners and their self-assured generalisations about inner life, personal relationships and politics. Their tradition currently actually has the *weakest* mandate from outcome research. The psychoanalytical model *may* prove, in time, to be superior to other rationales about problems in living. However, at present, its imperious stance towards these problems is simply not warranted.

I have pointed up two possible responses to the self-promotion evident from some psychotherapists. The postmodern response implies the tolerance of diversity and uncertainty and an irreverent scepticism about professional rhetoric. The old-fashioned empiricist response leads to a similar conclusion. Given these doubts about the professional discourse, I now turn in the next and final chapter to the implications of exploring the views of ordinary people, before re-engaging with the debate about the utility or otherwise of the psychotherapy industry.

9

Ordinary People and Patient Survivors

> Granted all that is wrong with the helping professions . . . most Europeans and Americans may still be suffering more from a lack of what these have to offer than from an overdose.
>
> Abram de Swaan, *The Management of Normality*

INTRODUCTION

This final chapter has four aims. First, I will discuss the views of patients and non-patients about sharing their personal troubles. Second, I will trace some professional responses to consumer feedback about their work. Third, I will summarise the state of play of the mental health service users' movement. Fourth, I will discuss whether or not psychotherapists should be trusted by lay people.

LAY VIEWS ON GETTING PERSONAL

When discussing the post-structuralist account of Rose in the previous chapter, an emphasis was placed on the assumption, imported from the later writings of Foucault, that the confession was pervasive in modern society. Here, for example, Foucault makes the point clearly:

> The confession has spread its effects far and wide. It plays a part in justice, medicine, education, family relationships, in love relations, in the most ordinary affairs of everyday life and in the most solemn rites; one confesses one's crimes, one's sins, one's thoughts and desires, one's illnesses and troubles; one goes about telling with the greatest precision whatever is most difficult to tell. (Foucault, 1981: 59)

Whilst Foucault may be justified in tying the emergence of the obligation to confess to the growth of modernity, his generalisation needs to be tempered by some empirical clarifications. For example, most crimes go undetected and so unconfessed (at least to officers of the law). Church attendance has been on a downward spiral this century. The clinical iceberg shown by community studies of both physical and psychological distress shows that we ail far more than we declare to our doctors. Women often complain that their male partners are hopeless at being personal and construe intimacy differently (Tannen, 1990). And, most importantly in the context of this book, most people do not share their intimate lives with specialised talking therapists in some secularised version of the Catholic ritual of confession.

Having said all this, I still think that the claims of Foucault and Rose about the pervasive impact of the need to 'get personal' are indeed seen all around us: the radio phone-in; psychotherapist pundits in newspapers; TV shows like Oprah Winfrey's; the columns of 'agony aunts' in women's and men's magazines; and the warm personalistic sales pitch of telephone bankers and estate agents, who use their first name immediately and tell you that they 'hear what you say'. But maybe more of us resist this obligation than succumb to its demand. Moreover, some of us who *want* to get personal do not get the opportunity. As the epigraph I use at the start of this chapter from de Swaan indicates, despite the broad cultural influence of the technologies of the self, the empirical evidence suggests widespread unmet expressed need from those who already have mental health problems.

The ambiguities about the nature of intimacy in the everyday life of modern society can thus be understood at two levels. At the conceptual level, social theorists from a variety of theoretical orientations such as Sartre, Elias, de Swaan, Foucault, Sennett and Lasch agree that contemporary intimate relationships are Janus-faced. On the one hand, they offer a haven of personal support, an opportunity for self-understanding and a point of connectedness or solidarity with others. These advantages of intimacy are available in ordinary relationships, as well as with practitioners of the technologies of the self.

On the other hand, these available or secured relationships are a bolt hole we are forced to retreat into, in the face of a complex, fragmented and alienating outer world. Once in that hole, we are obliged, for good or bad, to be with others and to scrutinise and thereby construct and reconstruct our selves unendingly. The obsession with self-scrutiny can then become a form of narcissistic individualism. Moreover, intimate relationships can be abusive as well as supportive and enabling. This ambiguity about the lives of ordinary people is explored in greater depth in Sennett's *The Fall of Public Man* (1977) and in Lasch's *The Culture of Narcissism* (1980) and is overviewed in Giddens's *The Transformation of Intimacy* (1992). Within this current of work, some even go so far as arguing that the class struggle has been superseded by the struggle to harmonise the intimate relationships associated with sex, marriage and parenting (Beck and Beck-Gernsheim, 1995). Such a frame of reference about modernity suggests that the risks and opportunities operating at the micro-level of society shape and dominate the consciousness of individual citizens more than the distal influences of politics and economics.

The second level of contradiction is not conceptual but empirical. That is, the consensus from social theorists about the modern ambiguities surrounding, and the obligation to be, personal, intimate and self-surveying can still provide a wide variability across and within cultures about what could be called the 'practice of intimacy'. For example, it is comparatively easy to argue that the USA is a 'psychiatric society' (Castel et al., 1979), which is highly saturated with the technologies of the self discussed in the previous chapter. Even in the USA we must introduce the caution about social class. The argument holds less strongly in Britain, though this is in flux with the apparently unrelenting Americanisation of our culture. The argument probably cannot be applied at all currently to most of the countries of the African continent. Below I will illustrate a mixed empirical picture about Britain by discussing research on psychiatric patients and other lay people.

People in Service Contact

A national survey of psychiatric patients a few years ago for MIND (Rogers et al., 1993) indicated that they wanted more talking treatment. What they typically got was drugs and ECT. Only 60 per cent of the sample had received some form of counselling or psychotherapy, whereas 98.5 per cent of them had been treated with some form of psychotropic medication. Nearly half had received ECT, even though psychiatrists claim this is a treatment of last resort for a small minority of profoundly depressed patients. Eighty per cent had been given major tranquillisers and 75 per cent anti-depressants.

The demand for alternatives to this dominance of somatic psychiatric treatments is evident from organised users' groups. For example, in Britain a national conference of survivors of the psychiatric system agreed upon a charter of 15 demands (Survivors Speak Out, 1987). Three of these referred to treatment:

> 3 Provision of free counselling for all . . . 12 The phasing out of electro-convulsive therapy and psycho-surgery . . . 13 Independent monitoring of drug use and its consequences . . . (Survivors Speak Out, 1987)

It is important to reinforce the point that these demands are coming from those who have already been in the patient role. Given the disempowering and iatrogenic effects of physical treatments and their unimaginative use by the bulk of the psychiatric profession, it is not at all surprising that recipients want an alternative.

The main appeal of talking treatments for those who have been denied them, to date, is their surface validity: they appear to offer precisely what somatic psychiatry does not – personal respect rather than objectification. In the light of the evidence of outcome research about psychotherapy that I noted at the end of the previous chapter and return to later, such an enthusiasm from potential users of talking treatment may be tempered over time with more first-hand knowledge of the costs, as well as the benefits, of this desired alternative. Indeed, there are already small parts of the users' movement which focus on redress for the damage done to clients by psychotherapists. For example, POPAN (Prevention of Professional Abuse Network) was formed in London in 1990 by a group of survivors of sexual abuse at the hands of therapists.

A final caution to note about the enthusiasm of psychiatric patients for talking treatment is that the endorsement of the latter may be an artefact of siting rather than type of treatment. For example, in a further analysis of the national MIND survey noted above, it was found that satisfaction with treatment was correlated with distance from the inpatient role. For example, anti-depressants prescribed on an outpatient basis received nearly the same level of positive endorsement as that for outpatient psychotherapy (Rogers and Pilgrim, 1993).

People Outside Service Contact

When we turn to those who have not had a mental health problem defined by others or themselves, a slightly different picture emerges about attitudes to getting personal. If a person has given in and confessed to a professional that they have a personal trouble it immediately becomes reframed as a 'presenting problem'. In one way or another, the client is obliged to make their intimate life a public commodity. The minimal version of this is the absolute confidentiality offered by a private psychotherapist. The more typical version is that the person hands over their personal details to a multi-disciplinary bureaucracy. They become a 'case' which is discussed by a number of people privately but in a group and away from the 'client' or 'patient' involved. Letters are written, reports prepared and records are kept about their past and current lives. Given the risks this entails, it is perhaps not surprising that those who have, as yet, evaded the patient role continue to do so for as long as possible. The idea that avoiding personal contact with professionals is merely a 'resistance' to 'the truth' is, in this context, a reductionist and insensitive argument peddled by therapists for their own ends (see my criticism in the discussion of the previous chapter).

So what do non-patients think about getting personal and coping with their troubles? The investigation of non-clinical populations about mental health matters is not common. However, a recent study (Rogers and Pilgrim, 1996b) looked at the views of parents and teenage children from 45 British families. A number of features were evident in the interview material produced by the respondents:

1   Lay people hold a variety of views about the causes of mental health problems. These range from biological to social determinism. However, the latter, social, emphasis dominates the lay discourse on causation.

2   Lay people by and large try to cope alone with their troubles. This is associated with a positive value placed upon privacy and autonomy.

3   The apparent contradiction of points 1 and 2 lies in the assumption that whilst social stressors (e.g. poverty, unemployment, loss, etc.) are considered to be important in causing mental health problems, once distress is experienced, most people have little alternative but to find and emphasise individualistic solutions.

4   The latter solutions include finding time to be alone and working out problem resolution on one's own. The support and help with problem solving from others is positively valued but intimacy is also seen as having risks attached to it.

5   When informal help is sought, some people prefer to seek out those they know to have had problems of their own. This inspires a greater sense of confidence and assured empathy. Thus, those who are construed to be mentally healthy or strong, whether in a lay network or professional services, may not be the first port of call for people seeking help.

PROFESSIONAL PERSPECTIVES ON LAY VIEWS

The above description of lay views represents only a tiny fraction of the total discourse on mental health problems, which is overwhelmingly dominated by the competing perspectives of professionals. To various degrees these objectify the user perspective, ignore it, or frame it as an unrealistic or flawed account. The gaze of professionals constructs both normal and abnormal subjectivity and leaves little space for ordinary people to speak for themselves in ways which are unmediated by the inscriptions and conceptual filters of experts. Moreover, professionals control not just the language associated with the technologies of the self but also the style and even occurrence of these representations. Whether it is the expert pundits in newspapers I discussed in the previous chapter, or the clinical/academic literature of books and journals, professionals control how ordinary experience is depicted and codified.

It is easy and predictable to turn to standard psychiatric texts to find objectification in its most extreme form. There we find patients not people and the role of their communications is reduced to that of evidence for symptoms of particular mental illnesses. For the overwhelming majority of the mental illnesses it diagnoses, biological psychiatry lacks any signs to observe (i.e. bodily markers). As a consequence it is over-reliant on symptoms (what patients say). The patient speaks, the doctor labels and prescribes, and human experience is reduced to pathology, stripped of its existential significance and thus invalidated. Even before the 'treatment' is given by biological therapists, they have diminished the humanity of the patients they encounter.

However, whilst the psychotherapy literature is *ipso facto* more concerned to represent lay subjectivities more thoroughly, these are still used to demonstrate a preferred professional construction. Both traditional psychiatrists and psychoanalysts have 'patients' who are all potential 'cases' to be summarised, in order to demonstrate this or that set of clinical points. If these cases are allowed to speak for themselves in vignettes produced, the professional writer selects and edits this production for their own ends.

Psychotherapists have been just as prone as biological therapists to distrust the accounts of service recipients. In reviewing the status of the client perspective in the mental health research literature, Rogers et al. (1993) found four types of depiction:

1   Researchers tend to ignore client views which fail to coincide with, or confirm, the preferred views of professionals.
2   People with mental health problems are depicted as being continually irrational and so incapable of giving a valid view about their treatment.
3   Patients and their relatives are assumed to share the same perspective and, where they do not, the views of the latter are privileged.
4   Patient views are framed in ways which suit professional interests.

As I note above, this overall trend of patient objectification and invalidation is not limited to biological therapists. Indeed, some of the most elaborate dismissals of the client's experience can be found in the writings of psychotherapists. For example, when reviewing the literature on consumer satisfaction with mental health treatments, Lebow (1982: 254) notes that:

> Distortion is seen as inherent in consumer evaluation because of the client's intensity of involvement in treatment and impaired mental status, and the client is viewed as lacking the requisite experience to assess treatment adequately. Consumer satisfaction is regarded as principally determined by transference projections, cognitive dissonance, unconscious processes, folie à deux, client character and a naivety about treatment, rather than an informed decision process reflecting the adequacy of treatment.

Leaving aside the general vulnerability of the client's view about treatment to be ignored or reframed to the satisfaction of the therapist, there is the specific danger that any abuse or neglect which is reported may not be believed.

Within psychoanalytical therapy the notion of a 'working alliance' concedes that a mutual, rational, adult partnership has to be sustained for treatment to be workable. However, it is the non-rational aspects of the relationship (particularly transference) which psychodynamic therapists get most excited about and concentrate on. If the interpretation of transference comes to dominate the discourse of therapists, clients' views (about anything) will be viewed through this prism. Ironically, the 'distortions' then selectively perceived and reported by therapists will be represented as coming from the client, not the prism. These contradictions were explored by Szasz (1963) in his paper on transference. He points out that this concept was invented by Freud to provide a defence *for the therapist* against difficult-to-handle feelings of hate and desire. Psychodynamic therapists place such great store on transference that it is easy for them to forget that the concept is an invention and to see 'it' as having a non-problematic 'factual' status.

Thus, psychotherapists have a decidedly ambivalent attitude towards subjectivity. On the one hand it is explored credulously, in depth and at great length. Therapists may listen to account after account from their clients for months or even years on end. They construct variants of meta-account (e.g. the various depth psychologies) and use these as hermeneutic templates to construe subsequent accounts in new therapeutic encounters. Moreover, it is common for therapists to assume an expert–defender role about subjectivity in the face of those who, for some reason, are opposed to the personal. Despite all of this endearing concern and intensity about the inner life of humanity from therapists, ultimately clients are deemed by them to be flawed because their presence in therapy is *ipso facto* evidence of their irrationality. As a consequence, client views are generally to be treated as suspect – especially if they are critical of, or incompatible with, the views of therapists.

There is an alternative to this type of professional discourse which subjectifies but pathologises service users via the expert case study approach. However, this creates problems of a different order. The alternative can be found in the literature on 'client variables' within psychotherapy research. The term 'variable' indicates both the strength and the weakness of this alternative to the case law approach common in the psychotherapy (especially psychodynamic) literature. By utilising *aggregate data* the client variable literature provides us with useful information about the relationship between process and outcome in psychotherapy. By the same token, such an aggregate approach silences the voices of individual co-actors in a social process; just as much as the psychoanalytical literature, which recounts the pathology of analysands who are denied rights of authorship. Whereas the latter privileges the therapist's right to provide snippets or summaries of biography and denies the patient's *autobio*graphical voice in print, the aggregate approach to client variables smothers the opportunity of an open-ended account from clients about their *productive* role in therapy. After all, therapy is co-produced by practitioners *and* their clients.

What my analysis points to here is that expert discourse is considered to be non-problematic and is trusted to be comprehensive in its overview, whereas the client perspective is delegitimised by being pathologised or aggregated. These two dominant styles of expertise about patients then render the latter relatively silent. There are some exceptions in this regard (cf. Kadushin, 1969; Rogers et al., 1993), but the extent of this more client-focused literature is minuscule compared to the pincer movement of the pathologising literature, on one side, and the aggregate literature, on the other.

The Rise of the Mental Health Service Users' Movement

Because the roots of psychiatry were in the mass warehousing of madness during the nineteenth century, it was inevitable that the interests of mental health professionals and those of patients would often be incompatible. Concerns about the relationship between psychiatry and oppression can be identified loosely in three phases.

The first emerged at the end of the nineteenth century once the asylum system was properly established. This first concern was *not* about the rights of lunatics but related to the unfair detention of the sane. However, the very fact that unfair detention was a source of public concern implied that the fate of those deemed to be 'properly detained' was unenviable. Such an implicit rather than explicit anxiety about psychiatric treatment and detention reappeared in the 1970s, following reports from the old Soviet Union that sane political dissidents were being coercively treated by psychiatrists (Bloch and Reddaway, 1977). Such critiques implied that it was legitimate for mad people to be locked up and given life-diminishing psychotropic drugs, but that when the sane suffered the same fate then a moral and political outrage was being committed.

The second wave of concern about psychiatry and oppression appeared in the 1960s. Despite denials of the label by its advocates (cf. Cooper, 1968), this international movement came to be known as 'anti-psychiatry'. The form of this movement varied from country to country, but there were common elements throughout. First, there was a libertarian motif to the movement, which contrasted with the authoritarianism of the institutional psychiatry it was criticising. Linked to this, coercive regimes were opposed and voluntary conversational modes of treatment advocated. Second, psychiatry was deemed to have an oppressive socio-political or mystified policing role. This contrasted with the preferred self-ascription in the profession of disinterested scientific medicine guided by a warranted paternalism about suffering. Third, the movement was over-whelmingly a product of *professional dissent*. That is, 'anti-psychiatry' was essentially a minority splinter group within psychiatry. Its leaders, such as Laing and Cooper in Britain, Szasz in the USA and Basaglia in Italy, were all psychiatrists.

The third wave of concern about the oppressive role of psychiatry came from service users themselves in the 1970s and 1980s. When the short history of this patient opposition movement is traced, we find in its early days an overlap with 'anti-psychiatry'. Similar themes are apparent: an opposition to coercion; a preference for talking treatments, rather than drugs, electricity and the scalpel; a critique of the socio-political role of psychiatry; and an opposition to bio-medical regimes inside hospitals.

What marks this third wave off from 'anti-psychiatry' was that it was instigated not by professionals but by patients. Also, the movement has been more action-orientated than its professional predecessor, which was noted more for its intellectual concerns.

The mental health service users' movement is now international but its development has been uneven. For example, it emerged strongly in the USA and the Netherlands during the 1970s (Haafkens et al., 1986; Chamberlin, 1988) but was only strengthened in form and scale in the 1980s in Britain (Rogers and Pilgrim, 1991). Because of the longstanding concern about biological treatments, the users' movement, like its predecessor 'anti-psychiatry', has placed a positive value upon talking treatments. The users' movement has brought with it an important shift in discourse – 'patients' have now become 'survivors'.

DISCUSSION: SHOULD PSYCHOTHERAPISTS BE TRUSTED BY LAY PEOPLE?

In this final discussion of the book, I want to expand on some questions already addressed at the end of the previous chapter. In particular, I will review three positions about the legitimacy of psychotherapy, in order to assess its utility for people who seek help for their mental health problems: idealism; nihilism; critical pragmatism. I will now say a little more about these and review the conclusions apparent when discussing each in turn.

Idealism

In the previous chapter I dealt with the question of psychotherapists idealising psychotherapy. I mentioned then that this has been supported to some extent by the users' movement, which I return to below.

One of the problems facing the lay person in modern society is the credibility of experts. By and large, with the exception of a sub-group within the users' movement noted above, which campaigns about abuse in therapy, psychotherapists have had an easy time from their present and potential consumers. As a consequence, the idealisation of psychotherapy is currently being maintained by the convergent interests of profession-alising suppliers and needy customers. However, a brake is put on this process by the reticence of many ordinary people, currently outside service contact, to embrace psychotherapy as an answer to their everyday troubles.

The promotion of talking treatments is also evident in the expansion of counselling in both medical (especially primary care) and non-medical settings (such as occupational health in industry and student counselling services). In the voluntary sector, diverse groups from the Samaritans to CRUSE (bereavement counselling) and Relate (previously Marriage Guidance) have also established services for people requesting help via talk. The advocates or 'product champions' for these types of services inevitably have to produce rhetorics of justification for talking treatments, both to innovate and to maintain established projects.

These rhetorics emerged before strong empirical evidence existed that the services would offer evidence-based forms of practice. In other words, even in a culture such as Britain's, which has been slow to embrace the secularised confessional, a taken-for-granted assumption has emerged that 'It's good to talk'. The latter slogan has been used recently by British Telecom to encourage people to make more telephone calls. Telephone companies and psychotherapists share an interest in converting slogans about the purported intrinsic therapeutic value of conversation into a need for a professional service. Both BT and psychotherapists have a vested interest in asserting unequivocally that talking enhances mental health. This can be recognised for what it is – an assertion which reflects the needs of those in a communication industry (be it telephonic or psychotherapeutic) rather than those of their 'customers'.

It is a moot empirical point, though, whether it *is* always good to talk. This axiom can obviously be disputed according to context. In the Second World War in Britain, when a fear of German informers was prevalent, a government poster campaign warned the populace that 'careless talk costs lives'. In civil life domestic wars might sometimes imply a similar caution. For example, one survivor of childhood sexual abuse may feel better for disclosing their history to someone but another may simply experience an inconsolable grief. A third might find themselves revictimised by their psychotherapist – they go to a bowl of fruit and bite into an onion. So maybe it is not *always* good to talk.

Nihilism

The nihilistic position about psychotherapy contains interweaving and additive strands of attack, which are derived from different sources or motives. The first strand is scientistic and began in the early 1950s with Eysenck's critique of verbal psychotherapy (Eysenck, 1952). He and colleagues then restated the attack sporadically about the ineffectiveness, and thus worthlessness, of psychotherapy. This was part of a persistent 20-year campaign to capture professional control over behaviour therapy and expel verbal psychotherapy as a pre-existing competitor in the treatment of neurosis (e.g. Eysenck, 1961, 1965, 1966, 1967; Rachman, 1971, 1973).

Thus, the anti-psychotherapy barrage from behaviour therapists was impossible to disentangle from a professionalisation strategy both within, and on behalf of, clinical psychology. This does not invalidate the claims in the critique, but it does illuminate a professionalising motive at work. The attack also had a paradoxical impact. It helped to stimulate the growth, during the 1960s and 1970s, of a large psychotherapy research industry. By contrast, behaviour therapy was studied with less methodological rigour

(Shapiro and Shapiro, 1977). Moreover, the very therapeutic traditions which Eysenck wished to frame as pre-scientific were provoked into using orthodox methodologies, thereby closing the 'scientific' credibility gap he had constructed between behavioural and non-behavioural treatments (e.g. Truax and Carkhuff, 1967; Malan, 1979).

The second strand of attack is moral and is exemplified by Masson's rejection of therapy, which I discussed in the previous chapter. Basically, Masson (1988) argues that the power asymmetry between therapist and client *inevitably* leads to some form of abuse of the latter by the former. This purported pervasive abuse in the therapy industry undermines both its credibility and utility for people with mental health problems. The logical outcome of this form of attack is to entreat potential consumers of psychotherapy to restrain their expressed needs. Because it is a moral attack it culminates in moral exhortation.

The third strand of attack is political and is exemplified by the doubts expressed by Wilden (1972) about therapy as an individualised and mystified solution to oppression and alienation in modern society. The main elements of these doubts are expressed well by Wilden here, even if he takes much for granted about a pre-existing consensus about psycho-logical reductionism and its link to conservative values:

> psychoanalysis is a socioeconomic privilege restricted to people with the money and the leisure to indulge themselves. The question of the 'cure' is in any case entirely debatable, and we well know [sic] that psychology, psychiatry and psychotherapy in general have always been vehicles of the values of the *status quo* . . . And since most of us can learn to live with our hang-ups, whereas it is highly unlikely we can ever learn to live with the alienating effects of our one-dimensional, technological society, why bother with psychoanalysis at all? (1972: 3)

Wilden challenges the second part of the assumption held by Freud that civilisation produces both neurosis (because of the constraints it imposes on the instincts) and the need for therapy. Instead, Wilden queries whether therapy is a necessity in modern society. A similar doubt can be found in the more recent work of Smail, which I discuss below.

Critical Pragmatism

A few years ago I spelled out why psychotherapists were guilty of evading the political context of their work (Pilgrim, 1992). Essentially I focused on two elements to this evasion. The first was about psychological reductionism. Examples were given from both psychodynamic and humanistic versions of psychotherapy about how therapists either engaged in victim blaming or, conversely, opted for good bets for change. That is, fee-paying clients who were already materially comfortable were being confronted with demands to 'take responsibility for their own actions' or were being asked to make cognitive shifts about their existential predica-ments. The second element I discussed related to why professionalisation eroded the capacity of therapists to be self-critical about both their role in society and their iatrogenic impact on their clients. Despite these criticisms, I retained a faint-hearted defence of the utility of psychotherapy. I replay this defence below.

My own doubts about psychotherapy are close to those expressed by Smail (1996). However, his rejection is greater than mine because he finds in the outcome literature few substantial grounds for the redemption of psychotherapy *as it is currently practised*. Smail's work is useful to study because it sprang not from the world of psychoanalytical private practice but from the NHS. It began with a gentle advocacy of a version of psychotherapy within the phenomenological/existential tradition I discussed in Chapter 2 (Smail, 1978). However, over the years, his ideas shifted first towards using the experience of psychotherapy to understand the lives of ordinary people (Smail, 1984). This led to the development of a version of environmentalist psychology (Smail, 1993). The latter has close affinities with the types of social determinism I explored in Chapters 3–6. Although it points strongly towards external determinants and constraints it is *not* a rehash of behaviourism. Smail (1996) remains, as in his early work, committed to the experiential aspects of personhood. However, he thoroughly rejects the emphasis since Freud on victim blaming: placing the responsibility for emotional woes inside individuals rather than their oppressive social context. In his most recent work his rejection of psychotherapy in favour of self-help and socio-political reform is virtually complete. His position is that until psychotherapists can re-evaluate their moral obligation to clients then they will remain a victim-blaming conservative force in society.

If psychotherapy is to be neither idealised nor demonised, there are grounds to be considered about mixing optimism and scepticism about the future of psychotherapy. Any such variable mixture is derived not just from the four main messages from the outcome literature I discussed at the end of the previous chapter but from two other sources. The first of these is the robustness of the current mental health industry. Put simply, any amount of scorn from nihilists will not bring an end to a complex system of professional mental health work. A much grander example of this emerged in the 1970s when some social critics suggested that curative medicine was worthless (Illich, 1975). This anti-medical nihilism provoked a mixture of fury and delighted sympathy in its wide readership but it made little or no difference to the industrial trajectory of medicine. Armchair critics at best can hope that they are blowing a modern equivalent of the trumpets that brought down the walls of Jericho. Eysenck and Masson, provide important food for thought and they may even erode the self-assured posturing of those who idealise psychotherapy. However, it is unlikely that their critiques will *in themselves* substantially reduce either the demand or supply of psychotherapy.

The second source of pragmatism, which lies outside the direct policy implications of the outcome debate, is the users' movement. As I note in the previous chapter, this movement has, as part of its campaigning, demanded more talking treatments and fewer physical treatments. What is interesting about such a demand is that it has been provoked in large part by the very inertia in the mental health industry I have made in the point directly above. It is *because* of services being provider-dominated for the bulk of their history that bio-medical treatments were so widespread and psychological treatments relatively scarce. Moreover, the latter scarcity was uneven. It disadvantaged some social groups more than others. In particular the division of labour in the mental health industry, which left madness to medicine, freeing psychological therapists (of all theoretical styles) to work with richer and less disabled clients, was an important determinant of differential access to talking treatments.

The users' movement has effectively pointed up the need for equality of access to talking treatments. The main source of such a demand appears to have been neither class nor race, which might have been legitimate platforms, but disability. The users' movement is dominated by white ex-psychiatric inpatients who have survived the insults of a hospital-based bio-medical regime. It is hardly surprising that in rejecting the latter they have looked to Eurocentric talking treatments in community settings as an alternative to physical interference.

CONCLUSIONS

Drawing these points together, it looks likely, for the foreseeable future, that psychotherapy will continue to constitute an important component of the mental health industry. Zealous idealists will no doubt still press to enlarge their sphere of influence via journalism and a variety of profes-sionalisation strategies. The nihilists will spread plenty of healthy scepticism around in both the training courses of mental health workers and the minds of those potential consumers who have the rare privilege of genuine informed consent.

In the light of the above discussion, *is* psychotherapy a good bet for people with mental health problems? From my current perspective, the answer is necessarily ambivalent. At the level of the individual client, a reassuring answer can only be given if it can be guaranteed that they manage to access a therapist who is competent and benign and who acts with integrity. The latter refers to both technical consistency and assured personal decency. However, if these guarantees cannot be given, including that of equitable access, then entering therapy is undoubtedly a risky and unfair business. At a population level, therapy can have only a marginal impact in the face of the over-determination of mental distress by the social forces of poverty, warfare, ageism, racism, sexism, violence, trauma and loss. It may be legitimate to argue on both empirical and moral grounds that such a marginal impact is worth supporting and resourcing. However, such a fainthearted defence of psychotherapy could be readily and reasonably challenged by the nihilists I describe above.

My remaining doubt and caution about trusting psychotherapists with human subjectivity is that they are occupationally obliged to limit their interest in the latter to a particular form. As versions of sociology based on phenomenology and, to some extent, post-structuralism demonstrate, personal accounts are a rich and flexible resource. Therapists tend to selectively attend to personal accounts in order to enable individuals to change. Given their job this is quite an understandably limited and narrow goal. However, psychotherapists may not be sensitive to the fact that this *is* a limited goal and, too readily, may conflate their therapeutic interest in conversation with the *total* utility of discourse. The problem is that discourse can be produced and read in so many ways. Psychotherapy is only one amongst many versions of discourse use. Words may be a vehicle for personal change, but they can do much more: wound and comfort; report aspects of external and internal reality; persuade and explain; educate and instruct; amuse and bemuse; illuminate and obscure; anticipate the future and reflect on the past, and so on. The list could go on and on because it reflects a virtually unending capacity of human beings to use language as a resource to explore, and communicate about, the relationship between the symbolic, the imaginary and the real.

This open-textured characteristic of discursivity points to two draw-backs of therapeutic technologies. First, they may ignore the non-therapeutic value of talk. For example, when and if psychotherapists get around to seeing poor non-fee-paying clients they are in a position to bear witness to narratives of oppression. There is a much greater likeli-hood, though, that TV journalists making documentary programmes about, say, poverty or domestic violence will do this job properly. Essentially, my criticism here is that therapists are prone to framing talk as narratives of the problematic, when they are feasibly merely encountering a variety of testimonies to life. Moreover, these reframed testimonies may be records of heroic survival, not evidence of failure or irrationality.

To be clear again, this tendency to pathologise is what is expected of therapists – they are just doing their job. My point, though, is that in doing this job they cannot be relied upon to work with subjectivity in ways which are respectful of its full diverse potential. The latter can be found in the work of dramatists, novelists, poets, painters, song writers, comedians, musicians, dancers, film makers, journalists, anthropologists and sociologists but, in my view, only rarely in the writings of therapists.

The second drawback to trusting therapists with subjectivity and intersubjectivity relates to their zeal to prove the pre-eminence of their particular hermeneutic method or therapeutic technique. In the thrall of their enthusiasm for their preference, psychotherapists will be more, not less, likely to offer a highly limited version of subjectivity. The grand claims of the therapist-cum-journalists I discussed in the previous chapter pointed very strongly to this conclusion. The mere fact that therapists aspire to make generalisations about human life in print is evidence that their desire to colonise the 'truth' about subjectivity and intersubjectivity over-rides the cautious humility we might reasonably expect from those who dabble in the souls of others. This aspiration produces specific versions of reductionist reasoning within an occupational grouping where warring splits, cliques and schisms are unified only by the common hazard of psychological reductionism that I have explored episodically in this book.

My criticisms of the limitations of psychotherapy may seem uncharitable given that versions, particularly in their inception and innovatory phases, have sought and offered genuine insights into mental life and human conduct. However, in line with the arguments I raised in Chapter 2, about the advantages of retaining a respect for objectivism, and at the risk of being accused of scientism, I want to finish on an empirical reflexive turn. The mountain of evidence about psychotherapy outcome and process (e.g. Bergin and Garfield, 1994) confirms the point I make above about unfounded professional zeal and arrogance. These findings include the following.

1   Lay people with no theoretical awareness of psychotherapy asked to take on the role of helper are capable of being effective. Thus, problem resolution and the amelioration of distress can emerge at the hands of untrained helpers.

2   The outcome literature reports few demonstrable differences of effectiveness between therapeutic orientations. Thus, there is no basis for the pre-eminence of one or other therapeutic school.

3   There are no strong differences in effectiveness reported between highly experienced and neophyte therapists. Thus, being 'wiser' within a school of thought does not ensure greater effectiveness.

4   There are wide variations in therapist effectiveness within but not between therapeutic orientations. Thus, effectiveness may reflect common but variable ordinary personal and interpersonal factors operating across orientations.

5   In the absence of therapeutic interventions, for example in untreated and 'placebo' control groups, problem resolution and symptomatic improvement can still occur. The common or 'non-specific' factors across therapeutic orientations (such as warmth, encouragement, empathy, trust, support, etc.) occur, albeit unevenly, in ordinary relationships. This may in part account for the relatively high rate of 'self-remitting' forms of mental distress. What is sometimes described as 'spontaneous remission' rates may actually reflect in part the outcome of unsung informal forms of help. Thus, lay relationships can at times be helpful to those with mental health problems.

The last point needs a caution attached. When I mounted my faint-hearted defence of psychotherapy (Pilgrim, 1992) I pointed out that whilst the therapy industry holds its dangers, so too do ordinary relationships.

Self-help, like therapy, can be abusive because intimacy is a precondition of abuse. Intimate lay relationships are not always benign – witness domestic violence and school bullying. It is for this reason that I do not consider it logical to single out and demonise psychotherapy (as Masson does). Intimacy is potentially dangerous whatever the form it takes. Also, some people have reached the end of their options about help in their lay network. The very people who take the risk of seeking professional help are likely to be the ones who, temporarily or chronically, have found their lay relationships to be either absent or unhelpful.

When the above summary of conclusions is placed alongside the other overlapping one, which I provided from the effectiveness literature at the end of the previous chapter, it becomes clear that a fainthearted defence of psychotherapy as an ameliorative industry can indeed be mounted. What this defence cannot reasonably include, though, is a recommendation that we should rely upon psychotherapists to be trustworthy experts in living or credible secular priests. The presumptuousness of some groups of psychotherapists in becoming self-appointed political consultants (for example, the organisation Antidote I mentioned in the previous chapter) deserves particular critical scrutiny. Whilst the diverse opinions from therapists, as well as anybody else, about politics, are worth considering, there are no particular grounds for *privileging* their insights. The latter are lofty, speculative, internally disputed and corrupted by psychological reductionism and professional self-interest. In such a context, policy-makers and current and prospective patients would be legitimately wary of psychotherapists and their wares. To embellish a point I made earlier for emphasis, and to concur with Masson: there are no experts in human misery, there are only experts at claiming expertise.

Bibliography

Abel, B. (1988) *The British Legal Profession* Oxford: Blackwell.

Abel, G., Becker, J. and Mittleman, M. (1987) Self reported sex crimes of non-incarcerated paraphiliacs. *Journal of Interpersonal Violence* 2, 1, 3–25.

Allport, G. (1961) *Pattern and Growth in Personality* New York: Holt, Rinehart and Winston.

Althusser, L. (1971) *Lenin and Philosophy and Other Essays* London: New Left Books.

Andrews, A. and Jewson, N. (1993) Ethnicity and infant deaths: the implications of recent statistical evidence for materialist explanations. *Sociology of Health and Illness* 15, 2, 137–156.

Antaki, C. (ed.) (1981) *The Psychology of Ordinary Explanations of Social Behaviour* London: Academic Press.

Anthias, F. (1992) Connecting race and ethnic phenomena. *Sociology* 26, 3, 421–438.

Arac, J. (1989) *Critical Genealogies: Historical Situations for Postmodern Literary Studies* New York: Columbia University Press.

Aveline, M. (1996) Training and supervision of individual therapists. In W. Dryden (ed.) *Handbook of Individual Therapy* London: Sage.

Bannister, D. (1968) The logical requirements of research into schizophrenia. *British Journal of Psychiatry* 114, 1088–1097.

Bannister, D. (1983) The internal politics of psychotherapy. In D. Pilgrim (ed.) *Psychology and Psychotherapy* London: Routledge and Kegan Paul.

Barham, P. (1986) Cultural forms and psychoanalysis: some problems. In B. Richards (ed.) *Capitalism and Infancy* London: Free Association Books.

Barnes, M. and Maple, N. (1992) *Women and Mental Health: Challenging the Stereotypes* Birmingham: Venture Press.

Barton, W.R. (1959) *Institutional Neurosis* Bristol: Wright and Sons.

Bassuk, E., Rubin, E. and Lauriat, A. (1984) Is homelessness a mental health problem? *American Journal of Psychiatry* 141, 1546–1550.

Bateson, G. (1942) Regularities and differences in national character. In G. Watson (ed.) *Civilian Morale* Boston, MA: Houghton-Mifflin.

Bateson, G. (1973) *Steps To an Ecology of Mind* New York: Aronson.

Bateson, G., Jackson, D., Haley, J. and Weakland, J. (1956) Toward a theory of schizophrenia. *Behavioral Science* 1, 251–264.

Bean, P., Bingley, W., Bynoe, I., Rasseby, E. and Rogers, A. (1991) *Out of Harm's Way* London: MIND.

Bebbington, P.E., Hurry, J. and Tennant, C. (1981) Psychiatric disorders in selected immigrant groups in Camberwell. *Social Psychiatry* 16, 43–51.

Beck, U. and Beck-Gernsheim, E. (1995) *The Normal Chaos of Love* Oxford: Polity.

Becker, J.V. (1988) The effects of child sexual abuse on adolescent sexual offenders. In G.E. Wyatt and G.J. Powell (eds) *Lasting Effects of Child Sexual Abuse* London: Sage.

Bentall, R.P., Jackson, H. and Pilgrim, D. (1988) Abandoning the concept of schizophrenia: some implications of validity arguments for psychological research into psychotic phenomena. *British Journal of Clinical Psychology* 27, 303–324.

Berger, P. and Luckmann, B. (1966) *The Social Construction of Reality* New York: Doubleday.

Bergin, A. and Garfield, S. (1994) (eds) *Handbook of Psychotherapy and Behavior Change* New York: Wiley.

Berman, E. and Segal, R. (1982) The captive client. *Psychotherapy, Research and Practice* 19, 31–36.

Berry, J. (1969) On cross-cultural comparability. *International Journal of Psychology* 4, 119–128.

Bhaskar, R. (1989) *Reclaiming Reality* London: Verso.

Bifulco, A., Harris, T.O. and Brown, G.W. (1992) Mourning or inadequate care? Re-examining the relationship of maternal loss in childhood with adult depression and anxiety. *Development and Psychopathology* 4, 433–449.

Bion, W.R. (1959) *Experiences in Groups* New York: Basic Books.

Bloch, S. and Reddaway, P. (1977) *Psychiatric Terror: How Soviet Psychiatry is Used to Suppress Dissent* New York: Basic Books.

Bordo, S. (1979) 'Material Girl': the effacements of post-modern culture. In C. Schwichitenberg (ed.) *The Madonna Connection* Boulder, CO: Westview.

Bowlby, J. (1951) *Maternal Care and Mental Health* Geneva: World Health Organisation.

Boyle, J. (1984) *The Pain of Confinement* Edinburgh: Canongate.

Boyle, M. (1990) *Schizophrenia: A Scientific Delusion?* London: Routledge.

Boyne, R. (1990) *Foucault and Derrida: The Other Side of Reason* London: Unwin Hyman.

Breen, R. and Rottman, D. (1995) Class analysis and class theory. *Sociology* 29, 3, 453–473.

Brenman, E. (1996) Understanding yourself. *The Guardian (Society)* 12 June.

Brentano, F. (1874/1973) *Psychology from an Empirical Standpoint* London: Routledge and Kegan Paul.

Briere, J. and Runtz, M. (1987) Post-sexual abuse trauma: implications for clinical practice. *Journal of Interpersonal Violence* 2, 367–379.

Briere, J. and Runtz, M. (1988) Post-sexual abuse trauma. In G.E. Wyatt and G.J. Powell (eds) *Lasting Effects of Child Sexual Abuse* New York: Sage.

Bromley, E. (1983) Social class and psychotherapy. In D. Pilgrim (ed.) *Psychology and Psychotherapy* London: Routledge and Kegan Paul.

Bromley, E. (1994) Social class and psychotherapy revisited. Paper presented at the Annual Conference of the British Psychological Society, Brighton.

Brown, G.W. (1996) Onset and course of depressive disorders: summary of a research programme. In C. Mundt, M. Goldstein, K. Hahlweg and P. Fiedler (eds) *Interpersonal Factors in the Origin and Course of Affective Disorders* London: Gaskell.

Brown, G.W. and Harris, T. (1978) *Social Origins of Depression: A Study of Psychiatric Disorder in Women* London: Tavistock.

Brown, G.W. and Wing, J. (1962) A comparative clinical and social survey of three mental hospitals. *The Sociological Review Monograph* 5, 145–171.

Brown, G.W., Harris, T.O. and Bifulco, A. (1986) Long term effects of early loss of parent. In M. Rutter, C. Izard and P. Read (eds) *Depression in Childhood: Developmental Perspectives* New York: Guilford Press.

Brown, G.W., Harris, T.O. and Hepworth, C. (1995) Loss, humiliation and entrapment among women developing depression: a patient and non-patient comparison. *Psychological Medicine* 25, 7–21.

Browne, D. (1990) *Black People, Mental Health and the Courts* London: NACRO.

Burrell, G. and Morgan, G. (1979) *Sociological Paradigms and Organisational Analysis* London: Gower.

Bury, M. and Gabe, J. (1990) Hooked? Media responses to tranquilliser dependence. In P. Abbott and G. Payne (eds) *New Directions in the Sociology of Health* London: Falmer Press.

Busfield, J. (1982) Gender and mental illness. *International Journal of Mental Health* 11 (1–2), 46–66.

Busfield, J. (1986) *Managing Madness* London: Hutchinson.

Busfield, J. (1994) Is mental illness a female malady? Men, women and madness in nineteenth century England. *Sociology* 28, 259–277.

Busfield, J. (1996) *Men, Women and Madness: Understanding Gender and Mental Disorder* London: Macmillan.

Cahill, C., Llewelyn, S.P. and Pearson, C. (1991) Long term aspects of abuse which occurred in childhood: a review. *British Journal of Clinical Psychology* 30, 117–130.

Carchedi, G. (1975) On the economic identification of the new middle class. *Economy and Society* 4, 1, 1–85.

Carpenter, I. and Brockington, I. (1980) A study of mental illness in Asians, West Indians and Africans living in Manchester. *British Journal of Psychiatry* 137, 201–205.

Casement, P. (1985) *On Learning from the Patient* London: Tavistock.

Castel, F., Castel, R. and Lovell, A. (1979) *The Psychiatric Society* New York: Columbia Free Press.

Chamberlin, J. (1988) *On Our Own* London: Mind Publications.

Chen, E., Harrison, G. and Standen, P. (1991) Management of first episode psychotic illness in Afro-Caribbean patients. *British Journal of Psychiatry* 158, 517–522.

Cicourel, A.V. (1976) *Cognitive Sociology* New York: Free Press.

Clare, A. (1974) Mental illness in the Irish emigrant. *Journal of the Irish Medical Association* 67, 1, 20–23.

Cochrane, R. (1983) *The Social Creation of Mental Illness* London: Longman.

Cochrane, R. and Bal, S. (1989) Mental hospital admission rates of immigrants to England: a comparison of 1971 and 1981. *Social Psychiatry* 24, 2–11.

Cochrane, R. and Stopes-Roe, M. (1981) Social class and psychological disorder in natives and immigrants to Britain. *International Journal of Social Psychiatry* 27, 173–182.

Cooper, D. (1968) *Psychiatry and Anti-Psychiatry* London: Tavistock.

Cooperstock, R. (1978) Sex differences in psychotropic drug use. *Social Science and Medicine* 12, 179–186.

Cope, R. (1989) The compulsory detention of Afro-Caribbeans under the Mental Health Act. *New Community* 15, 3, 343–356.

Cox, M. (1974) The psychotherapist's anxiety. *British Journal of Criminology* 14, 1–17.

Currer, C. (1986) Concepts of mental well- and ill-being: the case of Pathan mothers in Britain. In C. Currer and M. Stacey (eds) *Concepts of Health, Illness and Disease* Leamington Spa: Berg.

D'Andrade, R. (1986) Three scientific world views and the covering law model. In D.W. Fiske and R.A. Shweder (eds) *Metatheory in Social Science* Chicago: Chicago University Press.

Dean, G., Walsh, D., Downing, H. and Shelley, P. (1981) First admissions of native born and immigrants to psychiatric hospitals in South East England 1976. *British Journal of Psychiatry* 139, 506–512.

de Swaan, A. (1990) *The Management of Normality* London: Routledge.

DH (1994) *Health and Personal Social Services Statistics for England* London: HMSO.

Diamont, L. (1987) *Male and Female Homosexuality: Psychological Approaches* New York: Hemisphere.

Dilthey, W. (1976) *Selected Writings* Cambridge: Cambridge University Press.

Dimock, P.T. (1988) Adult males sexually abused as children. *Journal of Interpersonal Violence* 3, 203–221.

Dohrenwend, B. and Dohrenwend, B.S. (1977) Sex differences in mental illness: a reply to Gove and Tudor. *American Journal of Sociology* 82, 1336–1341.

Donnelly, M. (1983) *Managing the Mind* London: Tavistock.

Draguns, J. (1996) Humanly universal and culturally distinctive: charting the course of cultural counseling. In P.B. Pederson, J.G. Draguns, W.J. Lonner and J.E. Trimble (eds) *Counseling Across Cultures* London: Sage.

Dressler, W. (1988) Social consistency and psychological distress. *Journal of Health and Social Behaviour* 29, 79–91.

Dunham, H. (1957) Methodology of sociological investigations of mental disorders. *Journal of Social Psychiatry* 3, 7–17.

Dunham, H.W. (1964) Social class and schizophrenia. *American Journal of Orthopsychiatry* 34, 634–646.

Eco, U. (1990) *Foucault's Pendulum* London: Picador.

Eichenbaum, L. and Orbach, S. (1982) *Outside In, Inside Out. Women's Psychology: A Feminist Psychoanalytic Approach* Harmondsworth: Penguin.

Elias, N. (1978) *The Civilising Process* Oxford: Blackwell.

Eliot, T.S. (1936) *Collected Poems 1909–1962* London: Faber and Faber.

English, H. and English, A. (1958) *A Comprehensive Dictionary of Psychological and Psychoanalytical Terms* London: Longman.

Evans, D. (1996) Pulling power. *The Guardian* 7 May, p. 10.

Evans, G. (1992) Is Britain a class divided society? A reanalysis and extension of Marshall et al.'s study of class consciousness. *Sociology* 26, 2, 233–258.

Eysenck, H.J. (1949) Training in clinical psychology: an English point of view. *American Psychologist* 4, 173–176.

Eysenck, H.J. (1952) The effects of psychotherapy: an evaluation. *Journal of Consulting Psychology* 16, 319–324.

Eysenck, H.J. (1958) The psychiatric treatment of neurosis. Paper presented to the Royal Medico-Psychological Association, London.

Eysenck, H.J. (1961) The effects of psychotherapy. In H.J. Eysenck (ed.) *Handbook of Abnormal Psychology* New York: Basic Books.

Eysenck, H.J. (1965) The effects of psychotherapy. *International Journal of Psychiatry* 1, 97–178.

Eysenck, H.J. (1966) *The Effects of Psychotherapy* New York: International Science Press.

Eysenck, H.J. (1967) The non-professional psychotherapist. *International Journal of Psychiatry* 3, 150–153.

Eysenck, H.J. (1975) *The Future of Psychiatry* London: Methuen.

Fairbairn, W.R.D. (1941) A revised psychopathology of the psychoses and the psychoneuroses. *International Journal of Psycho-Analysis* 22 (whole volume).

Fanon, F. (1970) *Black Skin, White Masks* London: Paladin Books.

Faris, R. and Dunham, H. (1939) *Mental Disorders in Urban Areas* Chicago: University of Chicago Press.

Fenton, S. and Sadiq, A. (1993) *The Sorrow in My Heart: Sixteen Asian Women Speak about Depression* London: Commission for Racial Equality.

Fenton, S. and Sadiq-Sangster, A. (1996) Culture, relativism and mental distress. *Sociology of Health and Illness* 18, 1, 66–85.

Fernando, S. (1988) *Race and Culture in Psychiatry* London: Tavistock/Routledge.

Fernando, S. (1991) *Mental Health, Race & Culture* Basingstoke: Macmillan.

Finkelhor, D. (1979) *Sexually Victimised Children* New York: Free Press.

Foster, J.G. (1971) *Enquiry into the Practice and Effects of Scientology* London: HMSO.

Foucault, M. (1973) *The Order of Things: An Archaeology of the Human Sciences* New York: Vintage Books.

Foucault, M. (1981) *The History of Sexuality* Harmondsworth: Penguin.

Foucault, M. (1988) Technologies of the self. In L. Martin et al. (eds) *Technologies of the Self* London: Tavistock.

Foulkes, S.H. (1965) Group psychotherapy: the group analytic perspective. In M. Pines and G. Spoem (eds) *Proceedings of the 6th Annual Conference of Psychotherapy* New York: Karger.

Frank, J.D. (1973) *Persuasion and Healing: A Comparative Study of Psychotherapy* Baltimore, MD: Johns Hopkins University Press.

Freidson, E. (1970) *Profession of Medicine* New York: Harper and Row.

Freud, S. (1913/1968) On beginning the treatment. In J. Strachey (ed.) *Complete Works of Sigmund Freud* (Vol. 12) London: Hogarth Press.

Freud, S. (1918/1968) Lines of advance in psychoanalytical therapy. In J. Strachey (ed.) *Complete Works of Sigmund Freud* (Vol. 17) London: Hogarth Press.

Freud, S. (1920) Beyond the Pleasure Principle. In the *Standard Edition of the Complete Psychological Works of Sigmund Freud, Vol. 18* London: Hogarth Press.

Freud, S. (1930/1964) Civilisation and its Discontents. In the *Standard Edition of the Complete Psychological Works of Sigmund Freud* London: Hogarth Press.

Fryer, D. (1995) Labour market disadvantage, deprivation and mental health (1994 C.S. Myers Lecture). *The Psychologist* 8, 6, 265–272.

Gabe, J. and Lipshitz-Phillips, S. (1982) Evil necessity? The meaning of benzodiazepine use for women patients from one general practice. *Sociology of Health and Illness* 4, 2, 201–211.

Gabe, J. and Thorogood, N. (1986) Prescribed drug use and the management of everyday life: the experience of black and white working class women. *Sociological Review* 43, 737–772.

Garfinkel, H. (1967) *Studies in Ethnomethodology* New York: Prentice-Hall.

Garrett, T. (1994) Epidemiology in the USA. In D. Jehu (ed.) *Patients as Victims: Sexual Abuse in Psychotherapy and Counselling* London: Wiley.

Garrett, T. and Davis, J. (1994) Epidemiology in the UK. In D. Jehu (ed.) *Patients as Victims: Sexual Abuse in Psychotherapy and Counselling* London: Wiley.

Geertz, C. (1975) *The Interpretation of Cultures* London: Hutchinson.

Gellner, E. (1985) *The Psychoanalytical Movement* London: Paladin.

Gergen, K. (1982) *Towards Transformation in Social Knowledge* New York: Springer-Verlag.

Gergen, K. (1985) The social construction movement in modern psychology. *American Psychologist*, 40, 266–275.

Giddens, A. (1989) *Sociology* Cambridge: Polity.

Giddens, A. (1992) *The Transformation of Intimacy* Cambridge: Polity.

Gilbert, P. (1992) *Depression: The Evolution of Powerlessness* Hove: Lawrence Erlbaum.

Goffman, E. (1967) *The Presentation of Self in Everyday Life* Harmondsworth: Penguin.

Goldberg, D. and Morrison, S.L. (1963) Schizophrenia and social class. *British Journal of Psychiatry* 109, 785–806.

Goldthorpe, J.H. and Marshall, G. (1992) The promising future of class analysis: a response to recent critiques. *Sociology* 26, 3, 381–400.

Gove, W. (1984) Gender differences in mental and physical illness: the effects of fixed roles and nurturant roles. *Social Science and Medicine* 19, 2, 77–91.

Greenslade, L. (1992) White skin, white masks: psychological distress among the Irish in Britain. In P. O'Sullivan (ed.) *The Irish in New Communities* Leicester: Leicester University Press.

Greenwood, J.D. (1994) *Realism, Identity and Emotion: Reclaiming Social Psychology* London: Sage.

Guidano, G.F. (1987) *Complexity of the Self* New York: Guilford Press.

Guntrip, H. (1950) *Schizoid Phenomena, Object Relations and the Self* London: Hogarth Press.

Guy, J.D. (1987) *The Personal Life of the Psychotherapist* New York: Wiley.

Hannay, D. (1979) *The Symptom Iceberg: The Study of Community Health* London: Routledge and Kegan Paul.

Haffkens, J., Nijhof, G. and van de Poel, E. (1986) Mental health care and the opposition movement in the Netherlands. *Social Science and Medicine* 22, 185–192.

Hare, E.H. (1956) Mental illness and social conditions in Bristol. *Journal of Mental Science* 102, 753–760.

Harré, R. and Secord, P.F. (1972) *The Explanation of Social Behaviour* Oxford: Blackwell.

Harvey, D. (1989) *The Condition of Postmodernity* Oxford: Blackwell.

Hawton, K., Salkovskis, P.M., Kirk, J. and Clark, D.M. (1989) *Cognitive-Behaviour Therapy for Psychiatric Problems: A Practical Guide* Oxford: Oxford Medical Publications.

Hayley, J. (1963) *Strategies of Psychotherapy* New York: Grune and Stratton.

Hearnshaw, L.S. (1964) *A Short History of British Psychology 1840–1940* London: Methuen.

Henry, W.E., Sims, J.H. and Spray, S.L. (1971) *The Fifth Profession* New York: Free Press.

Higginbotham, H., West, S. and Forsyth, D. (1988) *Psychotherapy and Behavior Change: Social, Cultural and Methodological Perspectives* New York: Pergamon.

Hildebrand, P. (1982) Psychotherapy with older patients. *British Journal of Medical Psychology* 55, 19–28.

Hildebrand, P. (1983) The contemporary relevance of the psychodynamic tradition. In D. Pilgrim (ed.) *Psychology and Psychotherapy* London: Routledge and Kegan Paul.

Hitch, P. (1981) Immigration and mental health: local research and social explanations. *New Community* 9, 256–262.

Hitch, P. and Clegg, P. (1980) Modes of referral of overseas immigrant and native born first admissions to psychiatric hospital. *Social Science and Medicine* 14a, 369–374.

HMSO (1992) *Report of the Committee of Inquiry into Complaints about Ashworth Hospital* London: HMSO.

Hoffman, L. (1992) A reflexive stance for family therapy. In S. McNamee and K. Gergen (eds) *Therapy as Social Construction* London: Sage.

Holland, R. (1978) *Self and Social Context* London: Macmillan.

Hollingshead, A. and Redlich, R.C. (1958) *Social Class and Mental Illness* New York: Wiley.

Holroyd, J.C. and Brodsky, A.M. (1977) Psychologists' attitudes and practices regarding erotic and non-erotic physical contact with patients. *American Psychologist* 32, 843–849.

Horwitz, A. (1983) *The Social Control of Mental Illness* New York: Academic Press.

Hughes, R. (1980) *The Shock of the New* London: BBC Books.

Illich, I. (1975) *Medical Nemesis* London: Marion Boyars.

Ineichen, B. (1987) The mental health of Asians in Britain: a research note. *New Community* 4, 1–2.

Jacoby, R. (1975) *Social Amnesia: A Critique of Contemporary Psychology from Adler to Laing* Boston, MA: Beacon Press.

James, W. (1892) *Textbook of Psychology* London: Macmillan.

Jeffries, S. (1996) Mixed up mind games *The Guardian* 4 May.

Joffe, J. and Albee, G. (eds) (1981) *Prevention through Political Action and Political Change* London: University Press of New England.

Jones, A. (1997) High psychiatric morbidity amongst Irish immigrants: an epistemological analysis. Unpublished PhD thesis. Milton Keynes: Open University.

Jones, J. (1981) How different are human races? *Nature* 293, 188–190.

Kadushin, C. (1969) *Why People Go to Psychiatrists* New York: Atherton Press.

Karen, B.P. and VanDeBos, G.R. (1981) *Psychotherapy of Schizophrenia: The Treatment of Choice* New York: Jason Aronson.

Keane, J. (1984) *Public Life and Late Capitalism* Cambridge: Cambridge University Press.

Kelly, G. (1955) *The Psychology of Personal Constructs* New York: Norton.

Kenny, V. (1985) The post-colonial personality. *Crane Bag* 9, 70–78.

Kessler, M. and Albee, G. (1977) An overview of the literature on primary prevention. In G. Albee and J. Joffe (eds) *The Issues: An Overview of Primary Prevention* London: University Press of New England.

Klein, M. (1948) *Contributions to Psychoanalysis* London: Hogarth Press.

Klein, M. (1960) *Our Adult World and Its Roots in Infancy* London: Tavistock.

Kohn, M.L. (1973) Social class and schizophrenia. *Schizophrenia Bulletin* 7, 60–79.

Kottler, J. (1986) *On Being a Therapist* San Francisco: Jossey-Bass.

Kovel, J. (1988) *The Radical Spirit: Essays on Psychoanalysis and Society* London: Free Association Books.

Krause, I.B. (1989) Sinking heart: a Punjabi communication of distress. *Social Science and Medicine* 29, 4, 563–567.

Laing, R.D. (1960) *The Divided Self* London: Tavistock.

Laing, R.D. (1961) *Self and Others* London: Tavistock.

Lasch, C. (1980) *The Culture of Narcissism* London: Abacus.

Lazarus, A.A. (1971) *Behavior Therapy and Beyond* New York: McGraw Hill.

Lebow, J. (1982) Consumer satisfaction with mental health treatment. *Psychological Bulletin* 91, 2, 244–259.

Levin, J. (1994) Religion and health: is there an association, is it valid and is the relationship causal? *Social Science and Medicine* 38, 11, 1475–1482.

Lewin, K. (1951) *Field Theory in Social Science* New York: Harper.

Littlewood, R. and Cross, S. (1980) Ethnic minorities and psychiatric services. *Sociology of Health and Illness* 2, 194–201.

Littlewood, R. and Lipsedge, M. (1982) *Aliens and Alienists* Harmondsworth: Penguin.

Lomas, P. (1987) *The Limits of Interpretation: What's Wrong with Psychoanalysis?* Harmondsworth: Penguin.

Lyotard, J.F. (1986) *The Postmodern Condition: A Report on Knowledge* Manchester: Manchester University Press.

McGoldrick, M., Pearce, J. and Giordano, J. (1982) *Ethnicity and Family Therapy* New York: Guilford Press.

McKegany, N. (1984) 'No doubt she's a real little princess': a case study of trouble in the therapeutic community. *The Sociological Review* 321, 328–348.

McNamee, S. and Gergen, K. (eds) (1992) *Therapy as Social Construction* London: Sage.

Malan, D. (1979) *Individual Psychotherapy and the Science of Psychodynamics* London: Butterworth.

Mann, A.H., Graham, N. and Ashby, D. (1984) Psychiatric illness in residential homes for the elderly: a survey in one London borough. *Age and Ageing* 113, 257–265.

Mannheim, K. (1953) *Essays on Sociology and Social Psychology* London: Routledge and Kegan Paul.

Martin, J.P. (1985) *Hospitals in Trouble* Oxford: Blackwell.

Masson, J. (1985) *The Assault on Truth: Freud's Suppression of the Seduction Theory* Harmondsworth: Penguin.

Masson, J. (1988) *Against Therapy* London: HarperCollins.

Masson, J. (1990) *Final Analysis* London: HarperCollins.

Mead, G.W. (1934) *Mind, Self and Society* Chicago: University of Chicago Press.

Mechanic, D. (1972) Social class and schizophrenia. *Social Forces* 50, 305–309.

Merton, R.K. (1949) *Social Theory and Social Structure* Chicago: Free Press.

Miller, P. and Rose, N. (1988) The Tavistock programme: the government of subjectivity and social life. *Sociology* 22, 2, 171–192.

Mills, C.W. (1940) Situated actions and the vocabulary of motives. *American Sociological Review* V, 904–13.

Mitchell, J. (1975) *Psychoanalysis and Feminism* Harmondsworth: Penguin.

Mollon, P. (1989) Narcissus, Oedipus and the psychologist's fraudulent identity. *Clinical Psychology Forum* 23, 7–11.

Mowbray, R. (1995) *The Case Against Psychotherapy Registration: A Conservation Issue for the Human Potential Movement* London: Trans-Marginal Press.

Mullan, B. (ed.) (1996) *Therapists On Therapy* London: Free Association Books.

Murphy, E. (1988) Prevention of depression and suicide. In B. Gearing, M. Johnson and T. Heller (eds) *Mental Health Problems in Old Age* London: Wiley.

Myers, J. (1974) Social class, life events and psychiatric symptoms: a longitudinal study. In B.S. Dohrenwhend and B.P. Dohrenwhend (eds) *Stressful Life Events: Their Nature and Effects* New York: Wiley.

Myers, J. (1975) Life events, social integration and psychiatric symptomatology. *Journal of Health and Social Behaviour* 16, 121–127.

Nathan, T. (1994) *L'Influence qui guérit* Paris: Editions Odile Jacob.

Navarro, V. (1979) *Medicine Under Capitalism* New York: Prodist.

NHSE (1996) *NHS Psychotherapy Services in England* London: Department of Health.

Noll, R. (1996) *The Jung Cult: Origins of a Charismatic Movement* London: Fontana.

Nwachuku, U. and Ivey, A. (1991) Culture specific counseling: an alternative training model. *Journal of Counseling and Development* 70, 106–115.

Oakley, A. (1972) *Sex, Gender and Society* London: Temple Smith.

Offer, D. and Sabshin, M. (1984) *Normality and the Life Cycle: A Critical Introduction* New York: Basic Books.

Oppenheimer, M. (1975) The proletarianisation of the professional. *Sociological Review Monograph* 20.

Orbach, S. (1995) Shrink Rap . . . Remembrance Day. *The Guardian Weekend* 14 October, p. 6.

Orbach, S. (1996a) Shrink Rap . . . Couched in the myth. *The Guardian Weekend*, 10 February.

Orbach, S. (1996b) Psychoanalysis. In B. Mullan (ed.) *Therapists On Therapy* London: Free Association Books.

Orbach, S. (1996c) Shrink Rap . . . Lessons from the past. *The Guardian Weekend* 6 April.

Orwell, G. (1933) *Down and Out in Paris and London* London: Victor Gollancz.

Orwell, G. (1937) *The Road to Wigan Pier* London: Victor Gollancz.

Owen, I.R. (1995) Power, boundaries, intersubjectivity. *British Journal of Medical Psychology* 68, 97–107.

Pahl, R.E. (1993) Does class analysis without class theory have a promising future? A reply to Goldthorpe and Marshall. *Sociology* 27, 2, 253–258.

Parker, I., Georgaca, E., Harper, D., McLaughlin, T. and Stowell-Smith, M. (1995) *Deconstructing Psychopathology* London: Sage.

Parry, G. (1997) Psychotherapy services in the English National Health Service. In N.G. Miller and K. Magmader (eds) *The Cost Effectiveness of Psychotherapy* New York: Wiley.

Parsons, T. (1951) *The Social System* Chicago: Free Press.

Pentony, P. (1981) *Models of Influence in Psychotherapy* London: Collier Macmillan.

Peters, R.S. (1958) *The Concept of Motivation* London: Routledge and Kegan Paul.

Phillips, D. (1968) Social class and psychological disturbance: the influence of positive and negative events. *Social Psychiatry* 3, 41–46.

Pilgrim, D. (1988) Psychotherapy and British special hospitals: a case of failure to thrive. *Free Associations* 11, 58–72.

Pilgrim, D. (1992) Psychotherapy and political evasions. In W. Dryden and C. Feltham (eds) *Psychotherapy and Its Discontents* Milton Keynes: Open University Press.

Pilgrim, D. and Rogers, A. (1993) *A Sociology of Mental Health and Illness* Buckingham: Open University Press.

Pilgrim, D. and Rogers, A. (1994) Something old, something new . . .: sociology and the organisation of psychiatry. *Sociology* 28, 2, 521–538.

Pilgrim, D. and Treacher, A. (1992) *Clinical Psychology Observed* London: Routledge.

Potier, M. (1993) Giving evidence: women's lives in Ashworth maximum security hospital. *Feminism and Psychology* 3, 3, 335–347.

Power, L. and Pilgrim, D. (1990) The fee in psychotherapy: practitioners' accounts. *Counselling Psychology Quarterly* 3, 2, 153–157.

Rachman, S. (1971) *The Effects of Psychotherapy* Oxford: Pergamon Press.

Rachman, S. (1973) The effects of psychological treatment. In H.J. Eysenck (ed.) *Handbook of Abnormal Psychology* New York: Basic Books.

Rapoport, A. (1956) The promise and pitfalls of information theory. *Behavioral Science* 1, 303–315.

Rapoport, A. (1959) Critiques of game theory. *Behavioral Science* 4, 49–66.

Rayner, E. (1993) *The Independent Mind in Psychoanalysis* London: Free Association Books.

Regier, D. Boyd, J. and Burke, J. (1988) Prevalence of mental disorders in the United States. *Archives of General Psychiatry* 45, 977–985.

Rex, J. (1986) *Race and Ethnicity* Milton Keynes: Open University Press.

Richards, B. (1983) Clinical psychology, the individual and the state. Unpublished PhD thesis. Polytechnic of East London.

Richards, B. (ed.) (1984) *Capitalism and Infancy: Essays on Psychoanalysis and Politics* London: Free Association Books.

Richards, B. (1994) *Disciplines of Delight: The Psychoanalysis of Popular Culture* London: Free Association Books.

Roche, R. (1973) *Phenomenology, Language and the Social Sciences* London: Routledge and Kegan Paul.

Rogers, A. and Faulkner, A. (1987) *A Place of Safety* London: MIND.

Rogers, A. and Pilgrim, D. (1991) 'Pulling down churches': accounting for the British mental health users' movement. *Sociology of Mental Health and Illness* 13, 2, 129–148.

Rogers, A. and Pilgrim, D. (1993) Service users' views of psychiatric treatments. *Sociology of Health and Illness* 15, 5, 612–631.

Rogers, A. and Pilgrim, D. (1996a) *Mental Health Policy in Britain: A Critical Introduction* London: Macmillan.

Rogers, A. and Pilgrim, D. (1996b) *Understanding and Promoting Mental Health* London: Health Education Authority.

Rogers, A., Pilgrim, D. and Lacey, R. (1993) *Experiencing Psychiatry: Users' Views of Services* London: Macmillan.

Rogers, C. and Terry, T. (1984) Clinical interventions with boy victims of sexual abuse. In I. Stuart and J. Greer (eds) *Victims of Sexual Aggression* New York: Van Nostrand Reinhold.

Rose, N. (1985) *The Psychological Complex: Psychology, Politics and Society in England 1869–1939* London: Routledge and Kegan Paul.

Rose, N. (1990) *Governing the Soul: The Shaping of the Private Self* London: Routledge.

Rose, S., Lewontin, M. and Kamin, L. (1984) *Not In Our Genes: Biology, Ideology and Human Nature* Harmondsworth: Penguin.

Rosenberg, M. (1992) *The Unread Mind: Unraveling the Mystery of Madness* New York: Lexington Books.

Rosenthal, D. and Franks, J.D. (1957) The fate of psychiatric clinic outpatients assigned to psychotherapy. *Journal of Nervous and Mental Disease* 127, 330–343.

Runciman, W.G. (1990) How many classes are there in contemporary British society? *Sociology* 24, 3, 377–396.

Ryle, A. (1990) *Cognitive-Analytical Therapy: Active Participation in Change* Chichester: Wiley.

Samuels, A. (1995) *The Political Psyche* London: Routledge.

Sartre, J-P. (1963) *Search for a Method* New York: Knopf.

Scheper-Hughes, N. (1979) *Saints, Scholars and Schizophrenics* Berkeley, CA: University of California Press.

Schutz, A. (1962) *Collected Papers Vol. I* The Hague: Martinus Nijhoff.

Schwartz, H. and Jacobs, J. (1979) *Qualitative Sociology* New York: Free Press.

Scott, M.B. and Lyman, S. (1968) Accounts. *American Sociological Review* 33, 46–55.

Scull, A. (1979) *Museums of Madness* Harmondsworth: Penguin.

Seligman, M.E.P. (1995) The effectiveness of psychotherapy: the Consumer Reports study. *American Psychologist* 50, 12, 965–974.

Sennett, R. (1977) *The Fall of Public Man* New York: Knopf.

Shapiro, D. and Shapiro, D. (1977) The 'double standard' in the evaluation of psychotherapies. *Bulletin of the British Psychological Society* 30, 209–210.

Showalter, E. (1987) *The Female Malady: Women, Madness and English Culture 1830–1980* London: Virago.

Smail, D. (1978) *Psychotherapy: a Personal Approach* London: Dent.

Smail, D. (1984) *Illusion and Reality: The Meaning of Anxiety* London: Dent.

Smail, D. (1993) *The Origins of Unhappiness* London: HarperCollins.

Smail, D. (1996) *Getting By Without Psychotherapy* London: HarperCollins.

Smaje, C. (1996) The ethnic patterning of health: new directions for theory and research. *Sociology of Health and Illness* 18, 2, 139–171.

Smart, B. (1976) *Sociology, Phenomenology and Marxian Analysis: A Critical Discussion of the Theory and Practice of a Science of Society* London: Routledge and Kegan Paul.

Smart, B. (1990) On the disorder of things: sociology and the end of the social. *Sociology* 24, 3, 397–416.

Smart, B. (1992) *Modern Conditions, Postmodern Controversies* London: Routledge.

Snow, D., Baker, S., Anderson, L. and Martin, M. (1986) The myth of pervasive mental illness amongst the homeless. *Social Problems* 33, 407–423.

Snowden, J. and Donnelly, M. (1986) A study of depression in nursing homes. *Journal of Psychiatric Research* 20, 327–333.

Spagnoli, A., Foresti, G., MacDonald, A. and Williams, P. (1986) Dementia and depression in Italian geriatric institutions. *International Journal of Geriatric Psychiatry* 1, 15–23.

Spence, D. (1982) *Narrative Truth and Historical Truth* New York: Norton.

Srole, L., Langer, T.S., Michael, S.T. et al. (1962) *Mental Health in the Metropolis: The Midtown Manhattan Study* New York: McGraw Hill.

Stake, J. and Oliver, J. (1991) Sexual contact and touching between therapist and client: a survey of psychologists' attitudes and behaviour. *Professional Psychology: Research and Practice* 22, 297–307.

Steele, R.S. (1982) *Freud and Jung: Conflicts of Interpretation* London: Routledge and Kegan Paul.

Stein, J., Golding, J., Seigel, J. et al. (1988) Long term psychological sequelae of child sexual abuse. In G.E. Wyatt and G.J. Powell (eds) *Lasting Effects of Child Sexual Abuse* London: Sage.

Stein, L. (1957) Social class gradient in schizophrenia. *British Journal of Preventative and Social Medicine* 11, 181–195.

Stoller, R. (1968) *Sex and Gender* New York: Science House.

Stone, M. (1985) Shellshock and the psychologists. In W.F. Bynum, R. Porter and M. Shepherd (eds) *The Anatomy of Madness Vol. 2* London: Tavistock.

Sulloway, F.J. (1980) *Freud, Biologist of the Mind: Beyond the Psychoanalytic Legend* London: Fontana.

Survivors Speak Out (1987) *Charter of Needs* London: Survivors Speak Out.

Sweeting, H. and West, P. (1995) Family life and health in adolescence: a role for culture in the health inequalities debate. *Social Science and Medicine* 40, 2, 163–175.

Szasz, T.S. (1963) The concept of transference. *International Journal of Psychoanalysis* 44, 432–443.

Tannen, D. (1990) *You Just Don't Understand: Men and Women in Conversation* New York: Ballantine.

Taylor, C. (1971) Interpretation and the sciences of man. *The Review of Metaphysics* xxv, 3–51.

Titmuss, R. (1958) *Essays on the Welfare State* London: George Allen and Unwin.

Truax, C.B. and Carkhuff, R.R. (1967) *Toward Effective Counseling and Psychotherapy* Chicago: Aldine Press.

Unger, R. (1984) *Passion: An Essay on Personality* New York: Free Press.

Ussher, J. and Nicolson, P. (1992) *Gender Issues in Clinical Psychology* London: Routledge.

von Bertalanffy, L. (1950a) An outline of general systems theory. *British Journal of the Philosophy of Science* 1, 134–165.

von Bertalanffy, L. (1950b) The theory of open systems in physics and biology. *Science*, Jan 13, 23–29.

von Bertalanffy, L. (1987) General systems theory – a critical review. In Open Systems Group (eds) *Systems Behaviour* London: Paul Chapman.

Waldron, I. (1977) Increased prescribing of Valium, Librium and other drugs: an example of the role of economic and social factors in the practice of medicine. *International Journal of Health Services* 7: 41.

Walsh, D. (1987) Mental health policy developments in Ireland. *International Journal of Social Psychiatry* 33, 2, 111–114.

Watters, C. (1996) Representations of Asians' mental health in psychiatry. In C. Samson and N. South (eds) *The Social Construction of Social Policy* London: Macmillan.

Weintrobe, S. (1996) That old shrinking feeling. *The Guardian (Society)* 1 May.

Westergaard, J. (1992) About and beyond the underclass: some notes on influence of social climate on British sociology today. British Sociological Association Presidential Address 1992. *Sociology* 26, 4, 575–587.

Wheen, F. (1996) More Mail humbuggery. *The Guardian* 8 May, p. 5.

White, S. (1996) Regulating mental health and motherhood in contemporary welfare services. *Critical Social Policy* 16, 67–94.

Wilden, A. (1972) *System and Structure: Essays in Communication and Exchange* London: Tavistock.

Wilden, A. (1987) *The Rules Are No Game: The Strategy of Communication* London: Routledge and Kegan Paul.

Wilensky, H.L. (1964) The professionalisation of everyone? *American Journal of Sociology* 70, 2, 137–158.

Wilkinson, G. (1975) Patient audience, social status and the social construction of psychiatric disorders. *Journal of Health and Social Behaviour* 16, 28–38.

Williams, J., Watson, G., Smith, H., Copperman, J. and Wood, D. (1993) *Purchasing Effective Mental Health Care Services for Women: A Framework for Action* Canterbury: University of Kent.

Wing, J.K. (1978) *Reasoning About Madness* Oxford: Oxford University Press.

Winnicott, D. (1958) Metapsychological and clinical aspects of regression within the psychoanalytical set-up. In *Collected Papers* London: Tavistock.

Wolman, B.B. (1968) *Historical Roots of Contemporary Psychology* New York: Harper and Row.

Wootton, B. (1959) *Social Science and Social Pathology* London: Routledge and Kegan Paul.

Wrong, D. (1961) The over-socialised conception of man in modern sociology. *American Sociological Review* 26, 2, 183–193.

Wyatt, G.E. and Powell, G.J. (eds) (1988) *Lasting Effects of Child Sexual Abuse* London: Sage.

Yamamoto, J., James, Q.C. and Palley, N. (1968) Cultural problems in psychiatric therapy. *Archives of General Psychiatry* 19, 45–49.

Young, R.M. (1988) Biography: the basic discipline for human science. *Free Associations* 11, 108–130.

Index

abnormality, discourses on, 32–5
abuse, of clients, 64, 65, 88, 140, 147
accountability, 22, 23, 134–5
accounts, 150
  lay, 15–16, 18
  as microscopes, 15
  situated and lay, 14–15
addiction, to medication, 61
Afro-Caribbeans, mental health of, in Great
    Britain, 46, 71–2
age, and mental health, 85–93
ageism, 93–6
agency, 18, 81
American Medical Association, 120
American Psychiatric Association, 120
Antidote, 128, 152
anti-psychiatry, 106, 122, 124, 144
arrogance, 11, 127
Asians, mental health of, in Great Britain, 46,
    72–5
assignment bias, 50–1
assumptions, 2
asylum system, 52, 104–5, 105–6, 144
  women in, 59
authoritarianism, 8, 102

Bannister, D., 34, 46, 64, 98
Barlinnie Prison, Glasgow, 108
Bateson, G., 35
Beck, A. 17, 64
behaviour therapy, 62, 146
behaviourism, 13, 15
Berger, P., 33
Berman, E., 108
Bertalanffy, L. von, 36–7
bias
  in diagnosis, 48
  in selection, 49–51, 53–4
bio-determinism, 23, 24, 52, 91, 104, 105
  women and, 56–7
biological psychiatry, 82, 108, 111, 141
Bion, Wilfred, 10, 105

body, commodification of, 57
Bowlby, J., 85
brainwashing, 100
Brearley, Mike, 125, 128
Brenman, Eric, 127
Brentano, F., 13–14
Briere, J., 87
British Confederation of Psychotherapists, 117,
    126, 130
British Psycho-Analytical Society, 52, 104
British Psychological Society, 52, 104
British Telecom (BT), 146
Bromley, E., 49, 50, 51
Brown, G. W., 61, 66, 88–92
Busfield, J., 58, 59–60, 65–6

Carchedi, G., 121
Casement, Patrick, 11
certainty, 30, 31
change maintenance, 101
childbirth, 56–7
childhood, 83, 85–6, 91
  sexual abuse in, 86–8
child-rearing practices, 76–7
children, 94
Church of Scientology, 100
Cicourel, A. V., 16
class, 41–3, 120
  and mental health, 41, 43–9
  and psychotherapy, 49–51, 53–4
class identity, 42–3
client cosmology, 99
client variables, 143
clients, 81–2
  abuse of, 64, 65, 88, 140, 147
  expectations of, 50
  protection of, 65
  see also psychiatric patients; therapeutic
    relationship
clinical iceberg, 47, 138
clinical psychology, 62, 114
closure, 38, 97, 102, 119